Back Burner Press

Praise for
ANDREW WARD'S

OUR BONES ARE SCATTERED
THE KANPUR MASSACRES IN THE GREAT MUTINY OF 1857
"A minor masterpiece." *The Times Literary Supplement* "A great book. Haunting. Unlikely to be surpassed." *The Hindustan Times.*

DARK MIDNIGHT WHEN I RISE
THE STORY OF THE FISK JUBILEE SINGERS
"History as a great journey, following the singers in their odyssey of forging an identity, as voices of justice and memory." *Chicago Tribune* "A wonderful, haunting book." *Jon Butler, Yale University Department of History* • Winner of the Deems Taylor Award

RIVER RUN RED
THE FORT PILLOW MASSACRE IN THE AMERICAN CIVIL WAR
"Ward's story of this notorious 'collision of Southerners—white and black' makes an outstanding addition to Civil War literature." *Publisher's Weekly.* "Judiciously examines all arguments advanced in defense of Fort Pillow as a legitimate, albeit particularly brutal, act of war... He is masterful in setting its context of slavery's unraveling, and in his portraits of perpetrators and victims as well. The conflict in microcosm, Ward's history will capture the Civil War readership." *Booklist*

THE SLAVES' WAR
THE CIVIL WAR IN THE WORDS OF FORMER SLAVES
"Narrated almost entirely in the voices of ex-slaves, this meticulous book dramatizes on a sometimes unbearably intimate scale a war suffered in fields and kitchens, smokehouses and cellars, swamps and forests and demolished cities. ...Every American needs to hear and heed these voices." *St. Petersburg Times.* "Andrew Ward brilliantly captures the complex surface of one neglected aspect of the conflict in his indispensable compilation. ...*The Slaves' War* is as affecting as a novel." Donna Bowman, *AV Club*. A PEN Nonfiction finalist

The Battle of
PLUM RUN
And the Civil War on the Mississippi

by

ANDREW WARD

BACK BURNER PRESS

Published by Back Burner Press
Davis CA 95616 · USA
papajipublishing@gmail.com

First Edition
Copyright © 2010 by Andrew Ward
All rights reserved.

ISBN: 978-0-578-06423-9

American History, Civil War

For the
**WARD
UPCHURCH
& HUNTINGTON**
Families

CONTENTS

LIST OF ILLUSTRATIONS

PREFACE
I

A NOTE ABOUT THIS EDITION
IV

PART ONE
THE CONFEDERATE OCCUPATION

THE GIBRALTAR OF THE WEST
FORT PILLOW
1

SIDEWINDER
THE MISSISSIPPI
14

THE TWIN BASTIONS
HENRY & DONELSON
21

A BEND IN THE RIVER
NEW MADRID & ISLAND NUMBER TEN
29

"MODEST BUT HEROIC"
JOHN BORDENAVE VILLEPIGUE
37

"ALL GOOD MEN"
FOOTE DEPARTS
47

TURTLES & RAMS
DAVIS & MONTGOMERY
56

"A VIOLENT BLOW"
PLUM RUN
65

"A DOUBTFUL CREW"
THE ELLETT BROTHERS
73

PART TWO
THE UNION OCCUPATION

"LOST TO US"
FORT PILLOW & MEMPHIS
87

"FORT PILLOW STATION"
LAUDERDALE COUNTY
101
"LOOK LIKE THE DEVIL"
GUERRILLA WARFARE
108
THE RAILROAD REGIMENT
THE 52ND INDIANA INFANTRY
122

THE CRONY
STEPHEN AUGUSTUS HURLBUT
129
ACTING NEUTRAL
THE LOYALTY OATH
136
THE ABOLITION REGIMENT
THE 32ND IOWA INFANTRY
149
"ILLICIT TRADE"
FORT PILLOW
1162
MISFORTUNE'S PROFITEERS
FORT PILLOW & FULTON
177
CONTRABANDS
FORT PILLOW
193
LAND PIRATES
PARTISANS & SCOUTS
204
THE WIZARD
FORREST'S FEINTS
212
ABANDONED ABSOLUTELY
THE EVACUATION OF FORT PILLOW
219
POSTSCRIPT
224

FOOTNOTES
227
ACKNOWLEDGMENTS
i
SOURCES
iii

Illustrations

Portraits
Listed alphabetically by surname
Pierre G. T. Beauregard CSA • 19
Tyree H. Bell CSA • 212
Braxton Bragg CSA • 26
James R. Chalmers CSA • 147
Chickasaw youth • 15
Patrick Ronayne Cleburne CSA • 4
Samuel Ryan Curtis USA • 161
Thomas Alfred Davies USA • 154
Charles Henry Davis USA • 56
Bill Dawson CSA • 108
James Buchanan Eads USA • 18
Alfred Ellet USA • 73
Camp Ferguson CSA • 115
Andrew Hull Foote • 20 & 54
Nathan Bedford Forrest CSA • 146
Ulysses S. Grant USA • 21
Henry Halleck • 29
Isham Harris TN CSA • 12
Burt Hays CSA • 114
G.N. Hollins CSA • 57
Stephen A. Hurlbut USA • 129 & 131
Fielding Hurst USA • 110
Albert Sydney Johnston CSA • 13
Abraham Lincoln USA • 130
Mansfield Lovell CSA • 59
Gideon J. Pillow CSA • 1
Leonidas Polk • 30
John Pope USA • 30
William Howard Russell • 2
Albert Rust CSA • 40
T.O. Selfridge of the *Cairo* USA • 105
William Tecumseh Sherman USA • 117
Alexander P. Stewart CSA • 28
Mark Twain (Samuel Clemens) • 17
Earl Van Dorn CSA • 133
John Bordenave Villepigue CSA • 37
Henry Walke of the *Carondelet* USA • 34
John Lewis Waller • 157
Gideon Welles USA • 104
Edward H. Wolfe USA • 122 & 222 (statue)

Scenes
Listed in order of appearance
Cannon bursting • 3
CSA Slave labor crew • 6
Slaves digging rebel earthworks • 8
Hound dog • 9
An abatis • 10
Slaves excavating rebel earthworks • 11
River battery emplacement • 13
Map of the Mississippi • 14
Prewar steamboat • 16
Brooklyn Navy Yard • 18
Map of Forts Henry & Donelson • 21
Attack on Fort Henry • 23
Union gunboat *St. Louis* • 24
Map of New Madrid & Island No. Ten • 29
New Madrid • 31
Shipyard at Cairo, Illinois • 36
The Union gunboat Carondelet • 34
Assault on Island Number Ten • 35
Union gunboat *Cairo* • 41
Mortar barge with a gunboat escort • 42
Steamboat passengers disembarking • 44
Wagons crossing a bridge • 45
Riverboat passing along a riverbank • 47
Gunboats on the Mississippi • 49
Mortar boats on the Mississippi • 51
Evening river scene • 52
Reporters on a gunboat crow's nest • 53
Mortar boats firing at night • 58
Columbiad and crew • 63
Union gunboat *Cincinnati* • 65
Union gunboat *Mound City* • 66
Battle of Plum Run • 67
Battle scene on a CSA gunboat deck • 68
Gunboat interior • 74
Queen of the West • 75
Supply train and slaves • 78
Confederates retreating • 79
Union soldiers rowing ashore • 80
Fort Pillow from the river • 81
Fort Pillow battlements • 87

Memphis riverfront • 89
Union river armada • 93
Union fleet steaming to Memphis • 94
Gunboat battery • 95
Union columbiad crew • 95
The Battle of Memphis • 96 & 97
Raising the Union flag at Memphis • 99
Gunboat on the river • 100
Union gunboat *Pittsburg* • 109
Union yawl approaching gunboat • 106
Bird's-eye map of Mississippi • 107
Guerrillas holding up a civilian • 114
Guerrillas raiding a farm • 115
Guerrillas waiting in ambush • 118
Union foragers slaughtering a bull • 120
Union gunboat steaming upriver • 123
Union sutlers • 128
Union encampment 137
Loyalty Oath • 138
Union foragers slaughtering cattle • 139
Union payday at the sutlers' • 143
Map of Fort Pillow • 150
Winter soldiers • 158
Interior of a Union tent • 159
Loading cotton onto a riverboat • 162
Dr. J. Hostetter's Stomach Bitters • 163
Rebel prisoners • 167
Fleeing capture on horseback • 169
Union foragers raiding a farm • 174
Cotton traders • 177
Yankees & Contraband camping out • 180
Soldiers resting on stilt shelter • 185
Buffalo gnat • 186
Mississippi mosquito • 187
Civil War dollar • 191
Contrabands in flight • 193
Contraband laundresses • 194
Camp laundry • 195
Battle flag • 201
Union soldiers waiting in ambush • 207
Union soldiers crouching • 218
Union soldiers warming themselves • 237
Fort Pillow abandoned • 219
Boats moored in the river • 221
Abandoned cannon at Fort Pillow • 225

PREFACE

Though the perils of prolonged occupation have been manifest most recently in Viet Nam and Iraq, Americans long ago experienced both sides of the equation in the western theater of the Civil War. When the Union Army slipped southward to capture control of the Confederacy's waterways, it outraged white Southerners even as it gave hope to millions of their slaves. That outrage and that hope collided in sundry ways, reaching perhaps its most atrocious single culmination at the river bastion of Fort Pillow in West Tennessee.

In *River Run Red: The Fort Pillow Massacre in the American Civil War,* I told the story of the terrible things that transpired on a Tennessee bluff hard by the Mississippi River in the spring of 1864. The new evidence I unearthed and the painstaking examination and analysis I undertook led me to conclude that a massacre did indeed take place. I did not spare much of anybody in *River Run Red,* for Fort Pillow was the squalid vortex of a singularly squalid war, with plenty of blame to go around. Nevertheless my conclusion did not please Nathan Bedford Forrest's admirers. Nor did it give me much comfort, either, for the blood of some of Forrest's men runs in the veins of my own children, whose ancestors joined Forrest's cavalry on one of his recruiting rounds through Henry County, Tennessee and served, God help them, at Fort Pillow.

I do not believe in angels or devils, though I believe they lie latent within all human beings, awaiting their cues from the circumstances in which we may find ourselves. Had I been born into a slave society, whether as slave or slaveholder or poor white, God only knows who or what I might have been. And had I ridden with Forrest or stood

II

with the men of the Fort Pillow garrison, God only knows what I might have done. I try to look at our ancestors not simply as heroes or villains, even if for a moment or an hour or a year or a war they acted with courage or wickedness, or both. I want to know them as human beings who were at least as complicated and flawed and bewildered by their times as we are by our own. So I am always disheartened when people who take pride in their ancestors' accomplishments refuse to take shame in their crimes.

For reasons of space, I could touch only lightly in *River Run Red* on what circumstances could lead good men to commit atrocious deeds. In *Plum Run* I have tried to delve more deeply, and in the process I have encountered a great deal about the scope of the conflict in the western theatre of the Civil War that I had not hitherto ascertained.

Well before Forrest and his cavalry descended like a hammer upon its garrison of blacks and whites, Fort Pillow had already achieved great strategic significance. For years it had blocked the Yankee gunboat fleet's attempts to steam down the Mississippi to take Memphis and, eventually, the entire sidewinding run of the Mississippi River. The capture of this vestige of Confederate grandiosity became the key to the control of the upper Mississippi, and the prize for which both sides vied in the Battle of Plum Run, the largest river engagement of the war.

Though the rebels had withstood a prolonged battering from Yankee mortar boats moored around a bend in the Mississippi, and had narrowly triumphed in their gunboat duel at Plum Run, they were compelled to abandon Fort Pillow to the Yankees, and therein lies a tale as well. The crumbling bastion became a command post for Yankee raids against the hundreds of rebel partisans who roamed West Tennessee. Its initial Union garrison of hard-bitten Hoosiers and abolitionist Iowans embodied the divisions within the Union itself, crippling its efforts to bring the locals to heel and provide a safe refuge for runaway slaves. And long

III

before Forrest's troopers overran Fort Pillow, it had become emblematic of the corruption of Union occupation that extended from the crapulous General Stephen Augustus Hurlbut in Memphis to the squads of mounted soldiers who freely looted the farmers and merchants of West Tennessee.

What it represented to local African Americans ranged from bondage to freedom to military service to death. Some of the African Americans who had excavated its miles of trenches and artillery emplacements under the Confederate lash were the same men who, after the rebels abandoned their bulwark, ran away from their masters and sought refuge with their families in its Contraband Camp. And some of those, in turn, were the same men who would join the Union Army, only to be killed or re-enslaved at Fort Pillow by their former masters.

In *Plum Run* I have tried to assemble not just a companion volume to *River Run Red*, but an autonomous account of Union occupation, rebel resistance, and the dangerous dilemma of the runaway slave that is little understood. Though what follows may help to explain the particularly charged atmosphere in which the notorious massacre transpired, I believe that even if Nathan Bedford Forrest had galloped past Fort Pillow, the post already had a compelling story to tell, filled with heroes and villains, exploits and misadventures that shed new light on the passions, vices, outrages, and divisions within divisions of our bloodiest and most transformative war.

A NOTE ABOUT THIS EDITION

This book represents my first and perhaps only experiment in self publishing. After decades of selling my books through the good offices of various distinguished houses, I wanted to find out how one of my books might fare entirely on its -- that is to say, *my* -- own terms. The reward has been to assemble a volume that reflects some of my own sometimes-frustrated opinions regarding a book's design and distribution.

I have always wanted, for instance, to directly integrate caption-less illustrations with the text, and not merely pack them together in an insert. To accomplish this, I have set in grey type the names of the men pictured on a particular page and allowed the text to provide the context. I have also listed their portraits on the illustration page not in order of appearance but alphabetically, so that readers can look them up at any point in their reading.

Though the upside of self publishing is that this book has gone through fewer filters, that may also prove to be the downside. If the doctor who treats himself has a fool for a patient, the writer who proofreads his own prose may well have a fool for an editor. I have tried to address the pitfalls by submitting my proofs to friends and family, but no doubt errors have survived their scrutiny, and mine.

On the other hand, such are the logistics of self publishing that readers themselves can participate in the editorial process, for should you find a typo or a factual error and would be kind enough to e-mail Back Burner Press about it, it can be corrected immediately, and thus you can help me to spare the next reader that particular hitch in the proceedings.

As for distribution, the larger houses, for reasons of scale, often employ scattershot methods that may miss a particular book's constituency, whereas by taking on the role of publicist and distributor, I can at least test out some theories I've developed about how to target my audience. All of this may eventually prove unavailing, but at the urging of my children, who understand the emerging landscape better than I, I thought I would give it a try. In any case, I thank you for your consideration.

The Battle of
PLUM RUN

And the Civil War on the Mississippi

PART ONE

THE CONFEDERATE
OCCUPATION

"THE GIBRALTAR OF THE WEST"
FORT PILLOW
1861-1862

Unrolling a map of America in 1861, any Yankee cadet could have told you that the key to winning the war in the West was controlling the Mississippi. But he might have added that before the Union could wrest the mighty river from the Confederacy it must first conquer the convergence of four state boundaries and three great rivers. It is here, in an area only thirty miles wide and fifty miles long, that the Tennessee rises out of its namesake state; and, just to its east, the Cumberland meanders northward out of Tennessee and into Kentucky to join the Ohio as it curves westward to Cairo, Illinois, where their waters hitch a long ride to the Gulf of Mexico in the Mississippi's inexorable flow.

In April 1861, only a week after Sumter's fall, Union troops got off to a good start by occupying Cairo. But to block any further progress down the Mississippi, Confederate General Gideon J. Pillow proposed the construction of a string of river bastions. Chief among them were Fort Henry on the Tennessee, Fort Donelson on the nearby Cumberland; and, 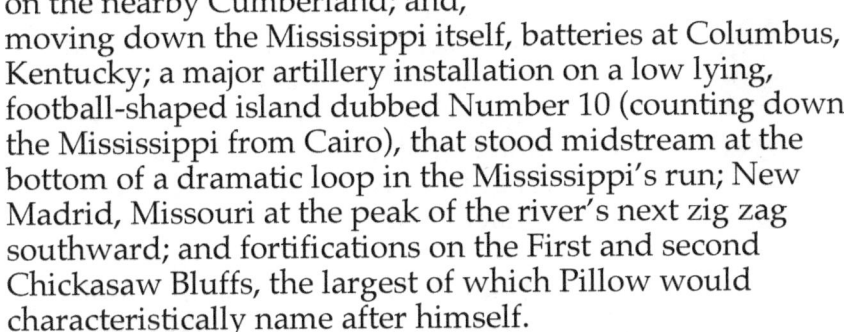 moving down the Mississippi itself, batteries at Columbus, Kentucky; a major artillery installation on a low lying, football-shaped island dubbed Number 10 (counting down the Mississippi from Cairo), that stood midstream at the bottom of a dramatic loop in the Mississippi's run; New Madrid, Missouri at the peak of the river's next zig zag southward; and fortifications on the First and second Chickasaw Bluffs, the largest of which Pillow would characteristically name after himself.

Pillow was not a man for details so much as *le geste grand*. Rich, cunning, vain, voluble, inept, politically well connected, almost comically self-aggrandizing, Pillow was the kind of general to set professional soldiers' teeth to gnashing. But, fortunately for the Confederacy, his vanity, negligence, and at least intermittent cowardice would keep his heyday brief.[1] An astute politician, gifted lawyer, and crony of President James Knox Polk, he had been given a brigadier generalship in the war with Mexico. Serving first under Zachary Taylor and then Winfield Scott, Pillow was said to have erected a battery facing the wrong direction.[2] After he was severely wounded at Chapultepec, he did his best to see to it, as he declared to his wife, that all eyes in Tennessee would be "fixed upon my movements." Campaigning unsuccessfully for the U.S. Senate, Pillow had denigrated Scott and huffed away at himself, drawing the scorn of a fellow veteran named Simon Buckner whom he would one day leave holding the bag at Fort Donelson.[3] "Pillow is a blustering, blundering, red faced, self conceited, good natured sort of fellow," sneered the New York *Herald*: "quite popular among his soldiers," but "a laughing stock among educated military men."[4]

Fresh from his tour of the Great Mutiny in India, the pioneering Irish war correspondent, William Howard Russell, found much to ridicule as he accompanied Pillow on an inspection of his Mississippi bastions. At Fort Randolph, a desultory outpost some fifteen miles downriver from Fort Pillow, the General had his artillery demonstrate the efficacy of a new friction tube he had introduced to replace the

linstock: the three-foot pole with a match at one end with which gunners lit their charges. Pillow's new friction tube consisted of a small length of pipe packed with gunpowder and containing a second tube filled with flammable material, all of which his gunners were to insert in the cannon's vent and ignite by yanking on a lanyard. What followed would have been worthy of Mack Sennett.

> An old forty-two pound carronade [a short cannon employed on the upper decks of gunboats] was loaded with some difficulty, and pointed at a tree about 1700 yards -- which I was told, however, was not less than 2500 yards -- distant. The General and his staff took their posts on the parapet to leeward,

and I ventured to say, "I think, General, the smoke will prevent your seeing the shot."

To which the General replied, "No sir," in a tone which indicated, "I beg you to understand I have been wounded in Mexico, and know all about this kind of thing."

"Fire!"

The string was pulled, and out of the touch-hole popped a piece of metal with a little chirrup.

"Darn these friction tubes! I prefer the linstock and match," quoth one of the staff, sotto voce, "but General Pillow will have us use friction tubes made at Memphis that aren't worth a cuss."

Tube No. 2, however, did explode, but where the ball went no one could say, as the smoke drifted right into our eyes. The General then moved to the other side of the gun, which was fired a third time, the shot falling short in good line, but without any ricochet.

Gun No. 3 was next fired. Off went the ball down the river but off went the gun, too, and with a frantic leap it jumped, carriage and all, clean off the platform. Nor was it at all wonderful, for the poor old-fashioned chamber carronade had been loaded with a charge and a solid shot heavy enough to make it burst with indignation. Most of us felt relieved when the firing was over, and, for my own part, I would much rather have been close to the target than to the battery.

General Pillow addressed the garrison "in a harangue in which he expatiated on their patriotism, on their courage, and the atrocity of the enemy, in an odd farrago of military and political subjects." But the only matter that appeared to interest them much was the announcement that slaves were on their way to take over the job of digging entrenchments. Pillow wound up his "florid peroration" by assuring them that "when the hour of danger comes I will be with you." But according to Russell the response "was by no means equal to his expectations. The men did not seem to care much whether General Pillow was with them or not at that eventful moment." When one of the officers called out, "Boys, three cheers for General Pillow," they could only muster a single, feeble rebel yell. Russell concluded that "the General would not be very popular," at least not until they could hand over their picks and shovels to slaves.

Later that day, Pillow all but repeated this performance upriver at Fort Pillow.[5] The little General ordered another artillery demonstration, but it was "fully six minutes between the giving of the orders and the first gun being ready," Russell reported.

> On the word "fire" being given, the gunner pulled the lanyard, but the tube did not explode. A second tube was inserted, but a strong jerk pulled it out without exploding. A third time one of the General's fuses was applied, which gave way to the pull, and was broken in two. A fourth time was more successful -- the gun exploded, and the shot fell short and under the mark.

"Altogether," Russell concluded, "though Randolph's Point and Fort Pillow afford strong positions, in the present state of the service and equipment of guns and works, gunboats could run past them without serious loss, and, as the river falls, the fire of the batteries will be even less effective."

In truth, Pillow had little to do with his namesake fort's design. The real work had been initiated in April 1861 by an Irishman from across the river named Patrick Ronayne Cleburne. Colonel Cleburne had set his Arkansans to digging entrenchments and embrasures, but as Russell observed, the crew was poorly equipped and flagged in the heat. Though many of them were experienced sappers and miners, the

Memphis quartermaster refused to provide them with uniforms and held up their pay. As winter approached, they grew restive.

"These men are demanding and crying for money for their starving wives and children," an officer declared. "General! If you think this place of any importance for the defense of our country, I have to say, that these men are necessary for the completion of our work – which negroes never can finish – and for this reason they ought to be paid what is due to them."[6]

In November they mutinied, refusing to serve another day until they received their wages. When their colonel scornfully asked whether they had signed up to fight for $11 a month or the defense of their country, one man answered that officers like the colonel could afford to be patriotic, "as they drew their pay regularly every month." In the end, the colonel relented, and two days later distributed their pay.

Pay was by no means the only issue. After toiling on the works at Fort Wright, the 1st Arkansan Infantry arrived at Fort Pillow on July 1st and "drew up petitions, requesting that the planters, who were at home doing nothing, should send their slaves to work on the fortifications."[7] It was not as though the farm boys who made up the workforce at Fort Pillow were strangers to hard labor. Even most of those whose families' owned slaves had worked in their fathers' fields.[8] But plowing a field for the good of one's family was one thing, digging a ditch at an officer's whim was another. They had come to fight, they told their commanders, not to do the negro's work. They were willing to die to defend their families, their property, their homeland. But they would not debase themselves. Slaves had brought on this war, so let slaves do the heavy lifting. Northern soldiers would make the same argument, but generally with less vehemence, for to a Southern boy there was something intolerable about digging in the dirt while their officers' slaves looked on, betraying, perhaps, the special contempt they reserved for poor white trash.

Besides, it was an Antebellum article of faith that blacks could better withstand the heat than whites could. Slaves, after all, were a great Confederate resource. In November 1861, the Montgomery *Advertiser* reckoned that slavery would put the South at a considerable advantage over the North by providing laborers to take the place of white men in the rebel army, which could be thereby "much larger in proportion" to her white population. "The institution," the *Advertiser* insisted, "is a tower of strength to the South."[9]

Pillow himself, at the urging of his junior officers, had ordered that "a large force" of slaves from Alabama, "with troops to protect them," be sent to buttress Forts Henry and Donelson on the Tennessee, where "efforts were made to push it to completion as fast as the means at command would allow."[10]

So Cleburne began to cast around the vast riverside plantations of Northern Mississippi for laborers. He instructed his agents to assure planters that the government would provide their slaves with "safe and comfortable transportation to and from the fort, comfortable quarters at the fort, and ample provisions." In addition, "medical attendance and attention will be paid to the comfort and health of their slaves."

The white class that stood to lose the most if the Confederates were defeated was the least cooperative, however, at least when it came to loaning their slaves to the cause.[11] "I find there is some backwardness in planters sending the second time," complained a rebel officer, "but I shall endeavor to overcome that objection."[12] Later, in the course of fortifying Vicksburg, Colonel Thomas Jordan felt called upon to declare that he expected "the large slave-owners of the vicinity to come forward with their slaves, with the same alacrity and liberality that has characterized all *other* classes of our people during this war."[13] An agent warned a recruiter that the planters of Issaquina and Washington Counties, Mississippi were "rather contrary" and would require a lot of talking-to.[14]

As a former Giles County slave named Richard Martin recalled, some planters feared their slaves would be mistreated. As he remembered the case: "Old Jeff Davis come to Marse and say: 'Give me them negroes, and I will carry them down to Fort Pillow and hide them in the cave until this is over,'" by which the recruiting agent probably meant the warrens which the Confederates were constructing as shelters against a Union cannonade. "Then Marse run them off," Martin continued, "and said, 'Better not put any of *my* people in a cave. They worked for me and made all my money. I gwine to do right by these people.'"[15]

Those planters who did contribute slaves only signed them away for brief stints. In December, Frederick A. Metcalfe, a planter in Washington County, Mississippi sent his slaves Henry Pickle, William Wallace, Isaac Stark and Harry Taylor up the Mississippi "to work on the fort Pillow in Tennessee;" they returned three weeks later.[16] By harvest time, a rebel officer complained, the planters' patriotism had "subsided into their cotton bales."[17] Among the least seemly holdouts was General Gideon Pillow himself who, upon learning that half of his slaves had been requisitioned at Helena for duty on his own fort's works, wired his overseer to return them immediately to his plantation.[18]

Laboring on Confederate fortifications slaves were either brutally treated or grievously neglected; and in the absence of their wives, mothers, and masters, some gambled and fought. They assembled in large numbers to discuss the ways of the world, and, if they did not escape to the nearby Union lines, returned to their masters sullen and restless.

Some planters chose to hire free blacks to serve in their slaves' stead, afraid their impressed slaves would return from their labors on Confederate fortifications with "dangerous ideas and information" and sow "dissatisfaction and unrest."[19]

Many slaves were themselves loath to work for the rebels. After most of Nashville's white labor force had gone into the army, local Confederates struggled to procure enough slaves to construct the city's defenses. "As yet there have been but 7 reported for duty on Cockrill's Hill," reported an officer, "and we need at least 300..." Officers ordered rebel detachments to go out and bring in more slaves with their "bed-clothing, eating and cooking utensils." Masters who expected their slaves to return home every night were directed to bring them their dinners instead. But many masters protested that since their slaves had been hired out until the end of the war, they could not sign them away to the Confederate Army.[20]

The former slave Tines Kendricks recalled how the Confederates "required all slave owners to send so many negroes to the army to work digging the trenches and throwing up the breastworks and repairing the railroads what the Yankees done destroyed.

Every master was required to send one negro for every ten he had. If you had a hundred negroes, you had to send ten of them to the army. I was one of them that Marse was required to send. That was the worst times that this here negro ever seen, and the way them white men drove the negroes, it was something awful. The strap, it was going from before day till way after night. The negroes — heaps of them — just fall in they tracks — give out — and them white men laying the strap on their backs without ceasing.[21]

"Just before dark," reported a Union lieutenant after steaming up the Cumberland in December 1861, "a negro ran down to the river bank, near the boat, chased by blood hounds in full cry after him." After the lieutenant sent a boat to rescue him, the slave told his deliverers that his master was a secessionist and that he was being chased "by rebel cavalry (he had run 18 miles), with the intent of seizing him" and putting him to work on rebel works. The Lieutenant and the exhausted slave watched together as the bloodhounds barked and bayed along the riverbank until summoned back into the woods by the whistling of their unseen masters.[22]

Nevertheless, Cleburne managed to ship as many as 2,000 slaves to Fort Pillow, where they disembarked in chains from transports under rebel guard. Fearing it might turn Lauderdale County's most prominent citizens against him, Cleburne was reluctant to press the local tobacco growers for their slaves.[23] So most of the first batch had come from Marshall County, Mississippi. Subsequent teams were recruited from the concentrated and accessible slave populations who worked the vast plantations of Mississippi's river counties. Cleburne asked planters to send half of their work force for fifteen days, equipped with axes, shovels, spades and two days' rations, plus an overseer for every 45 to 50 slaves they contributed. Better yet, he urged planters to escort their slaves themselves, as their presence might tend to make them work more strenuously.[24]

Their arrival had a quieting effect on his white troops. "The employment of slaves to do the hard work was of great advantage in several respects," one of them wrote. "It allowed the men to drill and take care of their health, as the planters sent overseers who superintended the negroes. It kept the men in better spirits, and made them more cheerful to endure whatever legitimately belongs to a soldier's life, when they had slaves to do the toilsome work."[25] But there was some labor – "finish & dress-up work" – that the command would not entrust to slaves, and some 200 Irish sappers remained on the job as foremen and stonemasons.[26]

The first order of business was to clear the site, which meant felling a vast stand of hickory, oak and poplar; dragging the trees down to the base of the rise; and arranging and sharpening the fallen trunks and branches to form an obstacle – an *abatis* -- against a cavalry attack.[27] Then, just within the *abatis*, they began to excavate a vast trench as the garrison's first line of defense. In time the bluff was almost entirely denuded of trees, and the air resounded with the slaves' chants and hollers as they pick-axed and shoveled, heaping an earthen parapet along the outer edge of a trench dug so wide as to prevent an attacker from leaping across in a single bound.

In time, other commanders along the Mississippi would cast an envious eye on Cleburne's sable workforce. His pharaonic army of slaves with their shovels and hoes and bullwhip-wielding overseers may account in part for the grandiose extent of Fort Pillow's rearmost entrenchments, which would eventually extend several indefensible miles.[28] But slaves continued to rotate in and out of the fort while Cleburne's recruiting agents circulated among the river plantations of Northern Mississippi to round up more.[29]

As slaves took their places in the ditches and *abatis*, Cleburne's grateful men proposed naming the fort after him. But in July 1861 the honor inevitably fell to the eternally self-promoting Pillow, whose slaves he had forbidden Cleburne to employ.[30] Though it must have seemed unjust at the time, it was perhaps better after all that the fort that would come to symbolize rebel barbarity was not named after Cleburne, who, though no particular friend of black people, would sign a petition shortly before he was killed in battle urging Jefferson Davis to lure slaves into the rebel army with the promise of emancipation.[31]

❖   ❖   ❖   ❖

Though Fort Pillow had been designed to accommodate many more, by the middle of September only twelve 32-pounders had been mounted.[32] The ever expanding fort was grossly undermanned: in late September it could muster only 945 officers and men: by the end of October, a mere 787.[33] Conditions at the fort were giving West Tennesseeans the jitters. A panic-stricken Lauderdale County man barged into Confederate headquarters in Memphis one day to report that there were "only sixty-five small arms there for a regiment of men." The garrison "greatly feared the enemy might seek the river at or below New Madrid and seize one of our boats and run down to Fort Pillow and take it in this defenseless position."³⁴ In addition, the fort's gunpowder was wet from the fall rains, and needed to be either replaced or "reworked to be useful"³⁵ lest it render the fort's batteries so impotent as to "bring ruin and disgrace upon us all."³⁶

The work continued into the New Year. "In the rear," wrote General Superintendent Lewis Williamson on October 24, "the ditching and breast-works lack only about a half mile of joining the two wings together," and almost every wall had been reinforced with stone and brick. "I shall be able to finish the entire rear line of breast-works in the course of next week," and with more slave laborers from Tunica and Coahoma Counties in Mississippi and Phillips County in Arkansas, he promised to complete the fort within a matter of weeks. In the meantime, a captain at Fort Pillow asked Polk to permit him to construct a saw and grist mill close by to enable him to reinforce his works.³⁷

The Confederate navy contrived to run a heavy iron chain across the river at Fort Pillow, held in place by a series of barges.³⁸ Mocked by the soldiers as "Pillow's Trot Line," it held until the river began to rise, whereupon the buoyant barges hauled up their anchors and broke the chains, and the whole clinking mess floated away, coming to rest on Flour Island a few miles downriver.³⁹ On November 17, Governor Isham Harris reported from Columbus that a large Union force was "gathering on my front" and anticipated "being entirely surrounded and cut off from supplies as fairly within the range of probabilities." Now that the works at Fort Pillow were practically complete, he urged General Albert Sydney Johnston to "call out the militia of West Tennessee" and place "10,000 men in Fort Pillow, and the balance at Union City or that vicinity."⁴⁰ Writing from

Nashville on November 17, Pillow seconded the Governor's call to protect his namesake post from the "large bodies of troops" that were gathering at Cairo.[41]

Johnston sent fifty barrels of gunpowder, and Polk ordered Louisiana to send to Fort Pillow "every artillerist that could be spared," plus two regiments of infantrymen with one hundred rounds of ammunition each. Johnston believed the fort was so important that it needed to be commanded by no less than an "able and experienced" brigadier general.[42] "I look upon this place as one of great importance," opined an observer who toured the fort on behalf of the Tennessee legislature. "Should boats be able to get past Columbus, they could be very effectually stopped here. It is not so much exposed, or at least the main batteries are not, to a mortar fire; and it would form an excellent rallying point to any troops that might meet with a reverse in front."[43]

After "Pillow's Trot Line" tore loose, chief engineer Captain Montgomery Lynch began to sink a line of pilings extending out into the river in an attempt to restrict its navigable width to 600 yards, but since no such obstruction is mentioned in any subsequent ship's log, they too must have been swept away that winter in the swollen current.

By December 1, 1861, the fort's batteries had reached their peak strength: 58 32-pound guns, four of them rifled and all but one of them "mounted and ready for use." The rearmost parapet was not quite finished, and the northern entrenchment that was supposed to extend down to Coal Creek was barely begun because all but 45 of the garrison's slave laborers had been transferred to other posts.[44] Nevertheless, within two weeks, Superintendent Williamson reported that his work was nearly done. The garrison's strength was now almost 4,000 well armed men from Alabama, Mississippi, and Tennessee and "the rear fortifications are closed, well executed, & in a state of readiness to resist any attack from our invading foe."[45]

SIDEWINDER
THE MISSISSIPPI

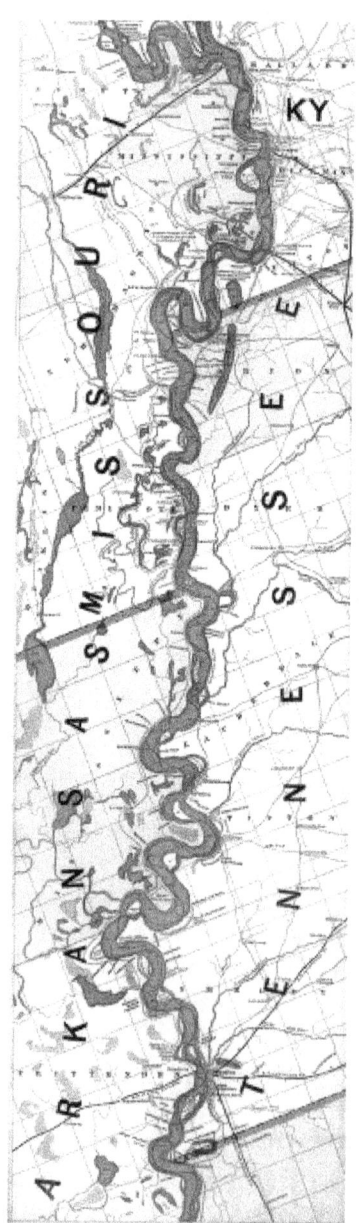

Measured from its true source in the Rocky Mountains of Southwestern Montana, the Mississippi is the third longest river in the world, and by every measure carries more water than any other. Millions of gallons rush and tumble and glide some four thousand miles from the mountains and lakes of the North to the Gulf of Mexico. Restive, deceptive, turbulent, the river seems sometimes to defy the laws of physics. Here and there along its labyrinthine course, foaming whirlpools appear to race upstream. Some portions of the current rise two feet higher than their own swirling vicinity. As it reaches present-day Tennessee, the river raises sand bars and mud humps that bulge like aquatic volcanoes, spewing gases and mud.

This serpentine river is a sidewinder. It shifts its course with regal caprice, mocking the white man's boundaries and property lines. It writhes westward, breaking through its own curves, sometimes as much as thirty miles in a single burst, stranding river towns in the middle of its current. Instead of widening as it flows southward, it pleases the Mississippi to narrow, forcing its aggregate mammoth flow to dig channels hundreds of feet deep along the outward banks of its wriggling curves. Its last 450 miles actually sink below sea level — over 170 feet at New Orleans — and so the Mississippi must tumble over itself, roaring like a freight train to the Gulf.

On May 12, 1542, what was left of the first European expedition into America's heartland dumped the remains of Hernando de Soto into the Mississippi in an attempt to hide his inconvenient death from a hostile Indian tribe known as the Pahacas. In 1673, after sundry Iberian diseases had decimated the Pahaca, Father Jacques Marquette and French Canadian explorer Louis Joliet set out from Lake Michigan to find the fabled river that the Indians told them ran to the southern sea. Shooting out onto the broad stream from the mouth of the Wisconsin River, they bickered over what to name it: Marquette proposed "Conception;" Joliet, "Colbert" in honor of the French finance minister. They compromised by dubbing it the Mississippi, one of the many names by which it was known to the tribes that lived along its banks. They turned back at the mouth of the Arkansas River for fear of encountering Spanish explorers further downriver, but they needn't have worried. Nine years later, the fur trader René Robert Cavelier La Salle was glad to safely complete his exploratory run down this colossal river to the Gulf, and lay claim to the entire Mississippi watershed in honor of his liege and patron, Louis XIV.

Over the next century and a half, the lower Mississippi Valley ostensibly passed from the French to the Spanish, back to the French, and at last to the fledgling American Republic as part of the Louisiana Purchase. During this period of shifting alliances, shuffling treaties and secret deeds, the Chickasaw nation had managed to hold sway along the Mississippi's bluffs, camping in dwellings of wattle and daub, fishing in the great river and its tributaries, and hunting elk and bear, deer and beaver in poplar forests carpeted by lilies, orchids and rye, and entangled in a twisting

calligraphy of hickory.⁴⁶ "Proverbially polite, friendly, and wholly inoffensive," the Chickasaws had shared their venison with the first American settlers, only to fall into step with the Cherokees and their slaves on the Trail of Tears, forced into exile in Oklahoma Territory.

In their wake came well connected Easterners with their own gangs of slaves, who laid claim to vast areas of Mississippi bottom land which the great river yearly enriched with its sediment. They tried to harness the Father of Rivers with levees: long mounds of earth built to fill the gaps along the Mississippi's crumbling banks. Usually they worked, but by raising the level of the water, they made the river's inevitable floods more dangerous, for where rising water once merely seeped out the river's natural spillways and spread across its bottom lands, now it rose and rose into a vast wall that roared down in torrents wherever a levee gave way. Some men advocated relieving the pressure by digging canals and dredging outlets. But others argued that this would raise the river bed and clog its already treacherous shipping lanes with sediment. The contest between levees and outlets persisted for decades, but the levees always won. By the time of the Civil War, gangs of slaves had constructed over a thousand miles of levees along the Mississippi's course.⁴⁷

Despite its lethal crotchets, the Mississippi became the primary trade route between the American Northwest and the Deep South, and soon bustled with flatboats and steamboats. The perils of navigating the Mississippi are best described by a former steamboat pilot who took his pen name from the cries of the leadsman who measured the river's depths, dropping his weighted line and shouting up to his captain, "M-a-r-k three! ....Quarter-less three! ...Half twain! ...Quarter twain! ...M-a-r-k twain!"

Fully to realize the marvelous precision required in laying the great steamer in her marks in that murky waste of water, one should know that not only must she pick her intricate way through snags and blind reefs, and then shave the head of the island so closely as to brush the overhanging foliage with her stern, but at one place she must pass almost within arm's reach of a sunken and invisible wreck that would snatch the hull timbers from under her if she should strike it. ... I went to work now to learn the shape of the river; and of all the eluding and ungraspable objects that ever I tried to get mind or hands on, that was the chief. I would fasten my eyes upon a sharp, wooded point that projected far into the river some miles ahead of me, and go to laboriously photographing its shape upon my brain; and just as I was beginning to succeed to my satisfaction, we would draw up toward it and the exasperating thing would begin to melt away and fold back into the bank! ...No prominent hill would stick to its shape long enough for me to make up my mind what its form really was, but it was as dissolving and changeful as if it had been a mountain of butter in the hottest corner of the tropics. Nothing ever had the same shape when I was coming downstream that it had borne when I went up.

But after young Sam Clemens's apprenticeship, the river captains of the Northern and Southern navies would face all of these hazards and more, steering their fleets of cumbersome, overloaded converted steamboats and experimental rams not on the peaceable and profitable zigzag of Clemens's day, but in battle: firing and under fire, dodging and groping their way through storms of shrapnel and sulfurous banks of gun smoke.

❖ ❖ ❖ ❖

By the beginning of the Civil War, forty-one year-old James Buchanan Eads had made a fortune off the Mississippi's sunken wrecks. Long before he went into the salvage business, he had gained firsthand knowledge of riverboat disasters. When he was thirteen, the steamboat that was transporting his family west caught fire and sank, so impoverishing his father that James was compelled to quit school and sell apples on the street. Soon afterward, he found a job as a "mud clerk" – a kind of Johnny-on-the-spot -- on the steamboat *Knickerbocker,* but a tangle of driftwood promptly pierced its hull and sent it to the bottom of the river.

Jinxed, impoverished, haunted by the thought of these great boats and their cargoes lying at the bottom of the river, Eads began to piece together a design for a diving bell in which to descend to the bottom of the river and retrieve sunken cargoes. In 1842, he found a couple of business partners and began to walk the Mississippi's riverbed, salvaging chunks of lead and pig iron. Eventually he would devise systems of hoists and pumps with which to raise entire vessels from the deep, and within twelve years Eads had amassed a fortune of some half a million dollars. By the time of his death in 1887 he would construct the first bridge to span the Mississippi, and establish himself as one of history's half dozen greatest engineers.

As the dogs of war strained at their leashes, Eads applied his ingenuity to the Union cause. He approached the U.S. Navy with a plan to construct ironclads to ply the nation's waterways. At first the War Department was skeptical, but as the government began to realize the full dimension of what it faced along its coasts and waterways, Eads was given the go-ahead.

Characteristically, Eads came through, building four ironclads in his first one hundred days. By 1862 he had launched an entire fleet of rams and gunboats.

❖   ❖   ❖   ❖

In early 1862, the resourceful Pierre Gustave Toutant Beauregard, the Confederacy's "Hero of Sumter," came west to oversee the rebel defenses along the Mississippi, a river for which he had gained the greatest respect, having tried to tame her as Chief Engineer at New Orleans. In addition to capturing Sumter, the commander  his soldiers fondly called the "little black Frenchman" had held the rebel line in the First Battle of Bull Run, despite a raging recurrence of the vestigial ague he had picked up in the Mexican War. Compounded by jaundice, the fever had persisted, and his progress west had to be interrupted by recuperative stops along the way. Too weak to proceed to his final destination at Columbus, he ground to a halt east of Fort Pillow in Jackson, Tennessee, and there held court in bed, feverishly studying his maps and interrogating his engineers.[48]

Beauregard concluded that though the rebels might be compelled to abandon the mammoth fortification they had constructed on the chalk bluffs known as Iron Bank, a little north of Columbus, Kentucky, the Confederacy's "naturally and artificially strong position" at Fort Pillow should be "defended to the last extremity, aided also by Hollins' gunboats, which will then retire to the vicinity of Memphis, where another bold stand will be made."[49]

❖   ❖   ❖   ❖

Back in August 1861, Navy Secretary Gideon Welles had placed his old friend, Commodore Andrew Hull Foote, in command of naval forces on the Mississippi, with orders to support Ulysses S. Grant in his Western Campaign. The pious son of a Connecticut governor, Commodore Andrew Hull Foote had studied at West Point for a mere two months before deciding to join the navy. He had chastened pirates in the West Indies, chased slavers from the coast of Africa, returned  hostile Chinese fire on a journey up the Canton River. The commencement of the war had found the Commodore in command of the Brooklyn Navy Yard, where he subjected his crews to Calvinist instruction, preaching temperance and conducting nightly prayer meetings on the deck of his flagship *Benton*.

One of the perks of naval service was the so-called "rum ration," which in the American navy usually took the form of a twice-daily serving of a pint of whiskey mixed with a quart of water. Liquor was regarded as a boost to morale, and a means of turning the slimy, stagnant water that was stored aboard ships on extended voyages into a somewhat more palatable and wholesome beverage. The result, however, was that most sailors went about their duties perpetually soused, and New Lights like Foote ascribed all floggings, mutinies, and below-decks mischief to its influence. In 1844, then Lieutenant Foote, speaking in his "usual happy way," induced some 290 sailors to sign a temperance pledge, which they then forwarded to Congress. "Everything requisite to render a man-of-war creditable to a nation, at home or abroad," wrote Foote, "are only to be secured by the discontinuance of intoxicating drinks."[50] But it would not be until September 1862 that the navy officially discontinued doling out whiskey to its crews.

THE TWIN BASTIONS
HENRY & DONELSON

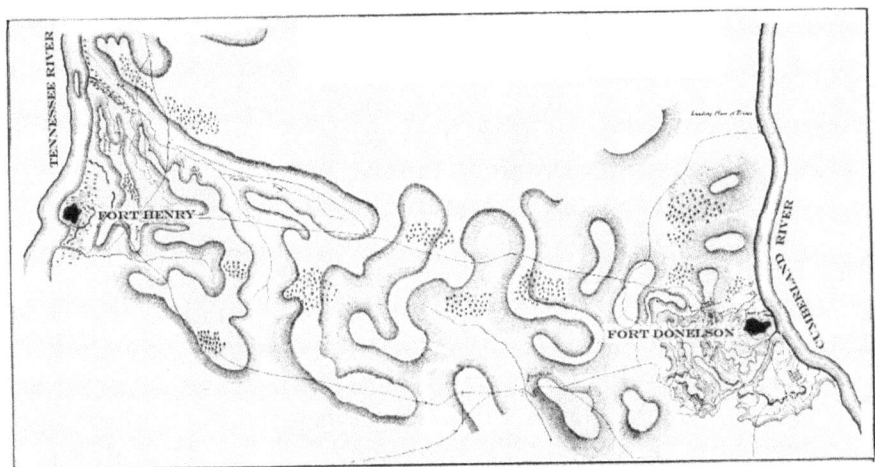

On a bluff on the western bank of the Cumberland, and in the marshlands that sopped the eastern bank of the Tennessee, the Confederates had erected a pair of back-to-back bastions: Fort Donelson on the Cumberland, Fort Henry on the Tennessee. On a course along which these rivers run almost parallel, the two forts were separated by a mere twelve miles. Determined to attack the rear of Albert Sidney Johnston's western army, U.S. Grant regarded their conquest as a prerequisite to securing the Mississippi for the Union, ensuring Kentucky's continuing neutrality, freeing up trade for the wavering states of the Northwest, and effectively breaking the Confederacy in two.

The campaign would require that both army and navy work together, which few held out much hope they could manage. But even though the abolitionist, teetotalling New Englander was the opposite of the equable, occasionally inebriated Midwesterner, Foote and Grant got along famously, cooperating in a manner almost unprecedented in American military history.

On the Confederate side, however, Johnston had turned Donelson's command over to a bickering triumvirate of generals, two of whom -- Pillow and Simon Bolivar Buckner -- had despised each other ever since the Mexican War. The third was John B. Floyd, whom the North suspected of sending materiel South as Buchanan's Secretary of Defense, and a Federal grand jury had indicted *in absentia* for bribery. Fearing he would be hanged if captured, Floyd had to be cajoled into obeying Johnston's order to go to Donelson, and yet the caprice of seniority put the inexperienced Floyd in command, Pillow second-in-command, and the comparatively professional Buckner a distant third.

On February 6, 1862, Fort Donelson's sentinels could hear cannon-fire from Fort Henry's direction. Having expected a Yankee attack on his twin forts, Johnston had sent the better half of his army to Donelson: 28 crack regiments, including thirteen from the state of Tennessee alone. No-one walking among Donelson's eighteen thousand troops and along its batteries of six light and seventeen heavy guns could have imagined that despite this generous deployment Johnston had grossly underestimated his foe.

Fort Henry was another matter. Laid out on three acres of marshland, commanded by some half-dozen promontories that its commander, General Lloyd Tilghman, had neglected to secure, Fort Henry boasted only 2,610 men armed with a miscellany of obsolete weapons, including flintlocks dating back to the War of 1812. Along its battlements jutted seventeen heavy guns (six old 12-pounders had to be discarded after two of them blew up), only nine of which were supplied with ammunition. As winter rains flooded his works, Tilghman deemed Fort Henry "a wretched military position."

Thus it was that despite Foote's river fleet's own deficiencies – untrained crews, three out of his seven gunboats out of commission – he would make quick work of Fort Henry before Grant's troops could even reach it. Seeing that a Union victory was inevitable, Tilghman evacuated all but one hundred invalids and artillerists to Fort Donelson, returning to Fort Henry in time to witness Foote's siege.

Trying to give as good as it got, the vestigial garrison proved skilled artillerymen, striking Foote's fleet fifty-nine times. But the Rebels got the worst of it, losing gun after gun to Foote's shells, until at last, wringing his hands in despair, Tilghman lowered his flag and surrendered.

As Grant settled his men into the ruins of what one of his generals now dubbed "Fort Foote," the man himself restlessly steamed southward on the Tennessee, destroying bridges and clearing the river of Confederate gunboats as far south as Florence, Alabama. He then chugged back up the Tennessee, hooked down the Ohio and into the Cumberland to join forces with an army of 15,000 men under Grant's command.

On the night of February 11, Grant ordered his men to advance on Fort Donelson. Reinforcements arrived on the 13th, boosting his force to about 27,000 men, and the fort was soon invested. The next day, Foote's gunboats arrived in the midst of a blizzard and, like knights' squires, prepared their armored craft for battle by heaping their decks with chain, coal, sandbags: whatever might impede a rebel shell. Foote boarded the *St. Louis*, one of four gunboats in the lead, with two timberclads puttering a thousand yards astern. At three o'clock in the afternoon of February 14, Foote's armada steamed to within about a mile of the fort. The rebels fired two rounds that fell short, whereupon Foote's gunboats, varying their speed to confound the rebel gunners, approached within some three hundred yards of Donelson's battery and opened fire.

Though their barrage did some damage to Donelson's battlements, it was nothing compared to the rebel batteries' reciprocal fire. The Confederates found that from their height they could lob their shells at Foote's boats and penetrate their iron-plated slopes. In a duel that lasted over an hour, the four Yankee gunboats were struck 160 times, and Foote himself was wounded by a chunk of shrapnel from a shell that killed the pilot of the *St. Louis*. Carried into the hold, Foote had just begun to cheer on his gunners when a second shell burst below decks, knocking down six gunners and wounding their limping commander in the left arm. By the time Foote's battered fleet withdrew, their gunners were slipping in puddles of blood.

The Confederates cheered as the boats withdrew, and the next day an emboldened Confederate left pushed southward, opening an escape route to Nashville. But the three generals could not agree on what to do. Floyd at first approved Buckner's refusal to obey Pillow's idiot command to withdraw his men to the trenches, but then he changed his mind, and ended up ordering his outraged troops back into the shadow of the fort.

After conferring with Foote, Grant advanced, reclaiming the ground the Confederates had won and more, until the fort was entirely and hopelessly invested. Its generals again fell out among themselves. They grudgingly allowed a hitherto untested Nathan Bedford Forrest to attempt to lead his troopers and whoever else might follow him to Nashville, which he managed to do without drawing a single round of fire. Floyd decided he would turn his command over to Pillow and escape while he could, whereupon Pillow deemed himself so vital to the cause that he in turn passed command to Buckner before escaping in a stolen scow.

Thus, on February 16, 1862, it fell to the ablest of the three to accede to Grant's famous demand for Donelson's unconditional surrender, and march into captivity with what remained of half of Albert Sidney Johnston's army. For many Americans North and South, Donelson's fall seemed to assure the Confederacy's ultimate doom.

❖   ❖   ❖   ❖

The brilliant Gustave Beauregard had thus taken command of the Confederate Army of the Mississippi just as the Mississippi itself was slipping out of rebel control. He ordered the force at Fort Pillow to shrink to a mere guard detail while the rest, including its labor force of slaves, proceeded up to New Madrid "with utmost celerity."[51]

Not everyone was sorry to see the slaves go. "I am truly glad that we got no more negros," one officer declared. Ever since the weather had turned brutally cold, "many of the negros as well as whites have been very sick here. One negro died, and I fear several more will die from diseases contracted here."[52] More than half of Fort Pillow's guns were dismounted and shipped to other posts upriver. When Union troops began to mass around Columbus, one of a succession of river forts the Confederates had dubbed the "Gibraltar of the West," General Leonidas Polk ordered the vast post evacuated and its garrison shipped off to reinforce the rebels' downstream bastions.[53]

The consolidation was necessary, but it delivered into Yankee hands almost the entire Jackson Purchase portion of Kentucky without a fight. Columbus would now combine with the bastion at Paducah and Forts Henry and Donelson to form an archipelago of Union strongholds. Once again deeming Fort Pillow his last-ditch defense against the Federal occupation of Memphis, Beauregard second-guessed Polk's decision to all but abandon Fort Pillow and sent in three Alabama regiments and a company of sappers and miners, to be joined, should Island No. 10 and New Madrid fall to the enemy, by their evacuees. He intended to supplement Fort Pillow's depleted battery of 20 guns with fifteen of the guns the rebels had evacuated from Columbus and ten shell guns on their way from Pensacola, Florida, for a total of 47 pieces: ten shy of its previous maximum.[54]

For all that, Captain Lynch saw disaster looming ahead. "There are here two small artillery companies, perfectly green;" he wrote from Fort Pillow on March 4th, "no laborers or tools. All sent to Island No. 10." He had "no one to mount guns except these two companies." Besides, no other guns had yet turned up, and of the guns he had on hand, only four defended the rear and most of the rest were in danger of being submerged by the rising Mississippi.[55] Polk promised more heavy guns and a thousand impressed slaves to build levees out of "stakes, sand bags, and earth."[56] But a few days later, an engineer at Fort Pillow deemed the rear defense's three-mile-long entrenchment "injudiciously established," and asked for still more slaves to begin digging "a shorter and better line" nearer the river.[57]

❖ ❖ ❖ ❖

Beset by migraines and flatulence, the upright, disciplined and almost universally disliked General Braxton Bragg arrived from Florida to ruffle the hedgerow of his brow over the Confederacy's western field of operations. "The whole country seems paralyzed," he wrote from Corinth, where he had been transferred, at his own insistence, to help his grey-backs brace for attack. The locals refused to sell anything to the Confederates: the result, Bragg declared, of the rebel troops "unrestrained habits of pillage and plunder" which had effectively "reconciled the people of the country to the approach of the enemy, who certainly do them less harm than our own troops."

The railroad system, upon which the Confederacy would increasingly have to rely now that its great rivers were being cut off by Yankee forces, was "utterly deranged and confused. Wood and water stations are abandoned; employees there and elsewhere, for want of pay, refuse to work; engineers and conductors are either worn down, or, being Northern men, abandon their positions, or manage to retard and obstruct our operations." Unless something was done "speedily for the defense of Fort Pillow," whose garrison he urged to "glean the country for provisions," and "husband ammunition," Bragg feared "we shall lose the Mississippi," which was "of more importance to us than all the country together."[58]

Polk ordered General John Porter McCown to send all the slaves at New Madrid to Fort Pillow "by the shortest route and with the greatest dispatch," and "furnish them with three days' rations."[59] As the Confederacy's remaining river bastions braced themselves for the Yankee onslaught, Richmond looked to Fort Pillow to keep the Yankees off the lower Mississippi. "Fort Pillow will be our main defense above," and if only "we can have a few weeks more for preparation, New Orleans will be secure from assaults from above or below."[60]

Accompanying the guns from Pensacola was a disabused young Floridian lieutenant named Mark Lyons. "I would like very much to get home," he wrote a friend, "as the life of a soldier does not suit me, merely from the fact that I have always controlled my own actions, but, in my present circumstances, I am only a piece of a mechanism, moved by the will of others."[61]

In early December, 1861, The New York *Herald* described the situation in Memphis as a Secessionist "reign of terror." No-one could criticize "any act of the rebel government, however arbitrary," nor utter "a word in favor of the people of the North. The most bitter curses and denunciations, and foulmouthed epithets are heaped upon the whole Northern people, and the charitable wish to be able to poison all of them is ever in their hearts and constantly on their lips." The *Herald* liked to think that there was "a large class of the community that is heartily sick of this reign of terror, and who would gladly see an end put to it." But they were "powerless and terrified in the universal madness," and "discouraged by the powerlessness of the national arms in Missouri, and the abandonment of Union men in Eastern Tennessee and elsewhere."[62]

Contrary to the *Herald*'s portrayal of the town, after the fall of Fort Donelson and the subsequent abandonment of

Columbus, Lyons had found Memphis "much disaffected" with Secessionism. All through Mississippi, Lyons and his men had been cheered by throngs of white women, but their Memphis sisters were merely civil, and now that the Yankees' progress down the Mississippi seemed inexorable, contrary to the *Herald*'s report, their men folk betrayed "a great deal of Union sentiment." Lyons was therefore glad to board the steamboat *Lackland* and push off for Fort Pillow.[63]

After disembarking at Fort Pillow's riverfront and exploring its mud-slicked slopes,[64] Lyons and his men concluded that the place was so impregnable that the "Blacks," as he called the Union gunboats, "will not venture to attack us."[65] "At present there is no danger here," wrote Charles Stewart of the 22nd Alabama Infantry. "We live very well, get good Butter, Eggs, &c. &c."[66]

Their new commander at Fort Pillow, however, the former West Point mathematics instructor and now Brigadier General Alexander Peter Stewart, was not so confident. On March 21, he was still awaiting the arrival of the ten Columbiads the post had been promised weeks before and without which he doubted he could "defy the gunboats." His riverside battery of eight 32-pound guns were awash with floodwater, and the three-mile rearmost entrenchment was going to require some 20,000 men to man it; with only 3,000 soldiers at his disposal, he would have to continue digging an intermediate entrenchment in case of a Union attack from the east, employing such slaves as he could spare from the river defenses.[67] But he could not spare many, for he was under orders to "put all river batteries in immediate serviceable condition."[68]

Then, on March 13, the garrison began to make out the ominous thump and rumble of naval guns upriver as Yankee gunboats commenced their bombardment of Island No. 10.

A BEND IN THE RIVER
NEW MADRID & ISLAND NUMBER TEN

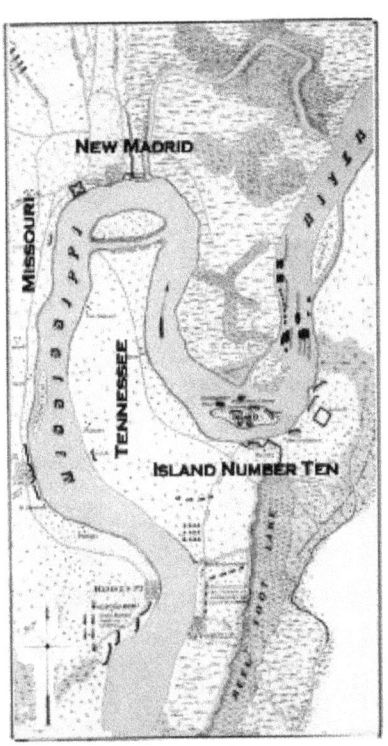

After the fall of Forts Henry and Donelson, Beauregard pinned his waning hopes of retaining control of the Mississippi on New Madrid, Missouri and nearby Island Number Ten, where substantial defenses had been established at a precipitous bend in the river. The island lay some sixty steamboat miles south of Columbus, and boasted land batteries, gunboats, and a floating battery anchored in the Mississippi's veering flow.

On February 28, Beauregard's Union counterpart, Brigadier General John Pope, set forth from Commerce, Missouri with 12,000 men. Pope was a professional soldier, a Kentuckian émigré to Illinois who had served in the Mexican War with distinction. A crony of Lincoln's, he had ridden in the President's escort on inauguration day. Promoted to Brigadier of Volunteers, he ran successful recruitment drives in Illinois before serving under the troublous Major General John Charles Fremont in the West.

In February 1862, Fremont's replacement, Major General Henry "Old Brains" Halleck, had decided to cease interminably chasing Sterling Price around western Missouri and fixed his protuberant gaze on New Madrid, where the ostensibly neutral state's Confederate legislature was scheduled to meet on March 3rd. Disrupting such an assembly provided Halleck with a convenient short-term goal that served much larger purposes: weakening the rebels' hold on the Mississippi and breaking the Confederacy's left flank.

Ambitious and bombastic, Pope drove his men relentlessly, and in only three days they accomplished the remarkable feat of slogging fifty miles, much of it through swamps, and brushing aside a contingent of the Missouri State Guard. Its commander, Meriwether Jeff Thompson, had a vested interest in the neighboring bastions of New Madrid and Island Number Ten. They had been long neglected by his commander, Gideon Pillow, whose decision to concentrate his defenses upriver at Columbus in neutral Kentucky was proving as militarily precarious as it was politically disastrous. Pillow had left Thompson, a former civil engineer, holding the bag at Island Number Ten, with vague instructions to complete its fortifications but without any reasonable means of doing so.

When the reverend General Leonidas Polk moved his headquarters to Columbus, he recognized that he would require a fallback position, and ordered that the two river bastions be completed forthwith. Polk sent a couple of Arkansas regiments down to finish the earthworks at New Madrid, while his engineers rounded up hundreds of local slaves to complete the works on Island Number Ten. Overall command fell to a rather rickety forty-seven year-old officer from Tennessee named John Porter McCown, who set off in late February with a division from Columbus and arrived in considerable disarray. A West Point graduate with some artillery experience in the regular army fighting Seminoles, Mexicans and Mormons, he was nonetheless generally regarded as a dithering nonentity.

McCown's men went to work mounting more heavy guns, but the conditions bordered on the anarchic. Polk expected an already overtaxed McCown to not only accommodate the hordes of soldiers and heaps of supplies he sent his way, but at the same time prevent any disruption of Missouri's Confederate legislature. Nevertheless, by the time General Pope closed in on New Madrid, there were over sixty heavy rebel guns in place, few smaller than 32-pounders, manned by a full artillery regiment under Brigadier General James Trudeau and backed up by a floating battery, nine infantry regiments, and squads of cavalry.

The late winter rains had raised the level of the river almost to its brim. But unlike the rising waters that had weakened Fort Henry's defenses, here the rebels hoped the flood would work to their advantage by raising McCown's floating batteries to a level from which they could sweep the thousands of intervening yards between Pope's army and New Madrid.

Missouri's Confederate legislators apparently did not share such optimism, for they abandoned their meeting and fled westward under the escort of the ever restless M. Jeff Thompson and his Swamp Rats. Infected perhaps by the contagion of these gentlemens' anxiety, McCown decided to abandon New Madrid after a Union sortie on March 7 and a 24-hour artillery duel with Pope six days later. Under a pouring rain, he shifted some of his forces across the river to Island Number Ten and the rest to Tiptonville, Tennessee. Though McCown had billed the evacuation as a tactical maneuver, the better to concentrate his forces against Pope's advance, his men took it as a wholesale rout. As lightning flashed overhead, they fled the town without spiking their guns or even burying their dead. Crowding onto a paucity of vessels, they threw their caissons and limbers overboard, nearly capsizing their transports in the rain-pocked Mississippi.

Peering through the downpour, the Yankees could

not tell whether what they were observing was the garrison in flight or rebel reinforcements come to the rescue. But Pope had been prescient, and almost as soon as McCown disembarked on Island Number Ten, he found himself cut off from his supply line by the Yankee batteries Pope had meanwhile positioned along the Missouri bank of the Mississippi, both above and below the rebel bastion.

The day after Pope occupied New Madrid, Union Flag Officer Andrew Hull Foote arrived upstream of Island Number Ten with Eads's extraordinary armada of armed and armored river boats. That winter, in the ice-littered waters off Cairo, Illinois, the fifty-five year-old commander of the Union's western flotilla had raised his flag over the largest American fleet ever assembled: for an expedition, raved the New York *Herald*, "that, in point of military strength, throws completely into the shade that which, under Com. Dupont and Gen. Sherman, has given us possession of Port Royal and the control of the Southern coast."[69]

Admiral Foote had been badly burned and wounded in the foot at Fort Donelson when the rebels staggered his fleet with a terrific cannonade. Evacuated to Cairo, Foote thumped around the shipyard with his scorched appendage bound in gauze, overseeing his damaged fleet's repair and adding more boats to its number. He mounted over a hundred guns on twelve gunboats; prepared a flotilla of floating batteries, each armed with a 64-pound Columbiad; equipped almost thirty steamboats; and accumulated "immense numbers of heavy guns and ordnance stores."

Foote's innovation was to organize a fleet of light draft boats that could navigate the shoals and shallow backwaters of the Mississippi. But one reason they rode so high in the water was that their engines were undersized and underpowered. Because many of them barely had strength enough to defy the Mississippi's current, it was fortunate that they were now headed downriver toward Island Number Ten. On the other hand, they ran the risk that should any of Foote's vessels be damaged in battle they would drift helplessly in the stream, and pass within easy range of the rebel batteries. On the 17th, Foote lashed his flagship *Benton* between two of his gunboats and led his Western Gunboat Flotilla within some 2,000 yards of the island, where he opened fire with ten-gun salvos from their bows. The rebels answered promptly, and before long some hundred guns were firing back and forth across the bend. The water around Foote's fleet became a forest of spouts as the rebel gunners sought their range.

Though a shot found the *Benton,* it did not do much harm. Far worse was the damage aboard the gunboat *St. Louis* when a rifled gun exploded, maiming its crew. Realizing that the island could not be reduced by gunboats alone, Foote led his flotilla back upriver to its anchorage, beyond the reach of the island's batteries, and turned the siege over to his mortar boats, whose relentless rounds arced high above the Mississippi and plunged in and around the island some two miles off.

His ranks swollen to some 20,000 men, Pope meanwhile endeavored to cross to the Tennessee side of the Mississippi and block the rebels' sole remaining avenue of escape. But how to get his transports to New Madrid without passing McCown's island batteries? A subordinate proposed an audacious solution, which was to dig a canal from the Missouri bank above Island Number Ten to a marshy stream called Wilson's Bayou that emptied into the Mississippi at New Madrid, thus enabling Pope's own motley fleet of light-draft vessels to circumvent Island Number Ten completely.

With Halleck's eventual approval, Pope's crews and engineers dug a fifty-foot-wide canal some two and a half miles long, cutting down trees with submersible saws to a depth of four and a half feet. The rebels deemed the project a desperation measure that was doomed to failure. But they underestimated Yankee ingenuity, for Pope's men accomplished this singular feat in a mere eight days without suffering a single casualty. Pope's little fleet crept up the canal and down the bayou, splaying out along the town's waterfront. Pope knew it would be no match, however, for an errant rebel gunboat or the Confederates' batteries scattered downstream along the Mississippi's banks: not unless it were joined by at least one of Foote's ironclads. But none of his gunboats boasted a light enough draft to navigate the canal.

❖   ❖   ❖   ❖

How, then, could the Yankees get a gunboat past the island? Captain Henry Walke of the leviathan *Carondelet* proposed steering his turtle along the Tennessee bank at night with its boilers encased in cords of firewood, its guns tucked away and its portholes shut, its decks heaped with anchor chains and timbers, its port side protected by a coal barge lashed to its hull, and its crew supplied with a pirate's armory of pikes, cutlasses, pistols, muskets, and grenades. They in turn were to be joined by sharpshooters from the 42nd Illinois, whose colonel had led a commando raid on April Fools night amid flashes of lightning, overwhelming the defenders of the rebels' Tennessee battery and spiking their guns.

By April 6, the *Carondelet* was ready. The heavens seemed at first to bless its progress by hauling in great banks of clouds, deepening the gunboat's cover of darkness. But the clouds merely precursed a furious storm that roiled the river into violent chop and foam almost as soon as the Union gunboat cast off. Initially, neither the lightning nor a fiery belch of soot from the *Carondelet's* stacks caught the damp and drowsy rebels' attention, but a second hapless blast of sparks roused a sharp-eyed rebel picket, and soon the sky was streaked with rockets alerting the rebel garrison to the gunboat's approach.

Walke ordered full steam ahead as the *Carondelet* pitched and rolled, and a ferrous precipitation of rebel round shot plunged around it, raising great geysers of river water. After a round shot struck the coal barge, Walke knew that if he stuck to the Tennessee bank he would be a sitting duck for the island's relentless 34-pound lobs. But instead of turning back, he boldly steered the *Carondelet* up along the island's own bank, gambling that at such close quarters the rebels would be unable to depress the barrels of their cannon sufficiently to hit their target. It worked, and the Union gunboat steamed out of the rebels' range and around the bend to New Madrid, where it was greeted by throngs of cheering soldiers. Two nights later, the *Pittsburg* made the same successful run, and over the following weeks joined the *Carondelet* in hectoring rebel positions almost as far downstream as Fort Pillow.

❖ ❖ ❖ ❖

Secure downriver as well as up', Pope transported his troops across the Mississippi to Tennessee and marched them along the rebels' sole avenue of escape. Though probably doomed from the moment Fort Donelson fell, the island had been bravely if haplessly defended. But now the jig was up, and the rebels surrendered their precipitous bend in the Mississippi River.

Seven thousand men and as many muskets fell into Pope's hands, plus enormous stores of ammunition, over 150 guns, some 700 horses, and enough tents to shelter 12,000 men. Handing over command to his subordinates, McCown escaped capture but not the calumny of his own superiors.

Pope, however, could boast of capturing three Confederate brigadiers. Nor was that all, for as Pope's men poked among the ruins of McCown's island bastion, Foote's gunboats made quick work of the rebels' motley vessels, turning the surface of the Mississippi into a groaning, hissing Hades of burning, careening, and sinking gunboats, steamboats, and assorted small craft.

Now it was on to Fort Pillow.

"MODEST BUT HEROIC"
JOHN BORDENAVE VILLEPIGUE

As the siege wore on upriver, more rebel regiments jammed their way into Fort Pillow. On March 25, Beauregard assigned John Bordenave Villepigue, the "most energetic young officer at my command" to oversee the garrison.[70] Though not given to fawning upon his officers, Braxton Bragg described the South Carolina Creole as "an educated soldier, possessing in an eminent degree the love and confidence of his officers and men," and blending "in perfect harmony, the modest but heroic soldier with the humble but confiding Christian."[71] When the Confederate armies of Kentucky and the Mississippi were consolidated under Albert Sydney Johnston, with Beauregard second-in-command, Villepigue was on the long roster of promotions to Brigadier General.[72]

Formerly Bragg's chief of artillery, thirty-two year-old Villepigue was a West Point graduate and a veteran of the Indian wars on the American frontier, where he had contracted malaria that intermittently wracked him with fever. He arrived with his arm still smarting from a splinter he had received in battle, but he never allowed his wound or his bouts of ague to interrupt his rounds, even as his subordinates chased after him through Fort Pillow's mud, trying to shield him from the rain. April arrived with a severe windstorm that drew him to the riverbank in his oilcloth slicker to oversee the salvaging of a capsized steamer whose crew, clutching at the wreckage, had been blown downriver.[73] "Fort Pillow was the muddiest fort, or any other place, that I ever saw," recalled a rebel soldier, "and the meanest water on the continent."[74]

Villepigue gave his post a mixed review. "It possesses the advantage of being quite elevated and of commanding the river for 2 or 3 miles above and below, thus bringing vessels for a long time under the fire of heavy guns mounted in proper position." And it lay "not more than 29 miles from Mason's Depot, on the Memphis and Ohio Railroad," to which a "a good military road has been constructed," crossing the redundantly named Hatchie River (*hatchie* meaning "river" to the tribes who once hunted along its banks) some eleven miles away, across which troops could be ferried by flat boat. But the topography of the country was "such that I fear it will be impossible to construct any line of intrenchments that will enable a small force to hold the position securely against a large one." Not only were the rearmost works too long to man, they were "badly located," commanded by "several hills" that were "entirely protected from fire." Slaves were still at work "on a shorter line nearer the river, and in twelve or fifteen days more will probably have it finished; after which a brave garrison of 5,000 men ought to make a protracted and obstinate resistance," providing he could requisition and obtain twenty guns from Pensacola or Mobile and mount them on the new work. Since "circumstances might justify the enemy in advancing" even with the rebel garrison at "Island No. 10 in his rear," Villepigue intended "to be prepared for the worst."

His force consisted of the 1st Confederate Battalion, the 12th and 21st Louisiana, the 31st Tennessee Regiment, plus a loosely disciplined heavy artillery battalion, an ill-equipped company of irregulars, and a light battery "in splendid order:" enough, he thought, to defend the new line of defenses that intervened between the outer works and the river. But he badly needed at least two companies of cavalry to keep on the lookout for a landward assault. His artillery consisted of twenty-two smooth-bore 32-pounders, five of them mounted to the rear; six rifled "old-pattern light 32-pounders" that were "certain to explode after a few rounds;" and four 10-inch and three 8-inch Columbiads. Villepigue was right to fret about his guns. One of his artillerists recalled working for three days mounting a mortar. "Just let them Federal gun boats stay still till we get this pointed," bragged his comrades, "and we'll give them *Hail Columbia.*" And so "they got her ready, charged her well with fifteen-inch shell, turned her loose, and she split open just like a rail cut."[75]

Ordered to contribute 12,000 pounds of powder to the defense of Island Number Ten, Villepigue asked for 15,000 pounds more "to raise my supply on hand to what prudence would require me to keep." His small-arms ammunition was "quite limited, the only reserve ammunition being 149,000 cartridges, of which 16,000 are for the Enfield rifle, 118,000 for the musket, 5,000 for the rifle-musket, 1,000 for Hall's rifle, and 1,500 for the Mississippi rifle."

He intended to double the sixty days' ration he had on hand with the "considerable quantities of forage and provisions within reach." There was good hunting to be had in the surrounding woods, and outstanding fishing in the Mississippi and Coal Creek. His purchasing agents, however, were meeting resistance. "The different departments are greatly in arrears with the contractors and employees," he explained, and "consequently there is great dissatisfaction and distrust." Nevertheless, he was certain that "a just and systematic administration of affairs will soon restore confidence."[76]

After the Confederate retreat from Shiloh and the evacuation of Union City on March 31, Yankee scouts began to nose around Fort Pillow's neighborhood. Peering through the freezing rain that bespattered the lens of his telescope, one scout slightly underestimated the number and size of the fort's guns and the length of the rearmost entrenchment, and his estimate of 1,200 slave laborers at work on the intermediate entrenchment was probably high. But he gave his commanders a fairly accurate description of Villepigue's position, just as Pope was winding up his operations upriver.[77]

With the fall of the upriver rebel fortifications of New Madrid and Island No. 10, rebel reinforcements continued to pass through Fort Pillow. An Alabama Gray arriving at Fort Pillow deemed it "underequipped, undersupplied, and undermanned by a garrison half submerged in mud and

rainwater and beset with disease."[78] Just before dark on April 9, the 3rd and 14th Arkansas arrived by steamer under the command of former Congressman and now Brigadier General Albert Rust.[79] Their arrival did not go unnoticed by the Yankee gunboats that lurked around the bend. Standing on his transport's hurricane deck, one of Rust's Arkansans saw something in the darkening sky "that looked like a gigantic lightning bug flying with incredible speed through the heavy timber of the river bottom.

> I could not tell how far away the thing was, neither did I know what it was, but you may bet that before the ten days were out that we remained there I knew what it was. Just as the thing got opposite our boat, it flashed, then was gone, but about that time we heard a report that told us that it was one of Uncle Sam's 'baby wakers,' which was the first bomb shell I had ever seen.[80]

It would not be the last. On April 13, "the gunboats of the Feds made their appearance opposite our batteries," wrote Lieutenant Lyons. "Several of our gun boats fired at them, but they did not reply, as they were merely on a reconnoitering expedition."[81] After seven Union gunboats chased the rebel gunboat *Macrae* around Craighead Point to within the protective range of Fort Pillow's guns, her captain sent an urgent message downriver to the South's flotilla. "The ball will open in the morning," he said. "Come up at once."[82] But "at once" would prove not soon enough, for the "ball" would commence that very afternoon.

Grant had meanwhile managed to get his army pinned back against the Tennessee River by Albert Sydney Johnston. Though the Yankees eventually held their line, and mortally wounded Johnston himself, they suffered terrible casualties, as did the rebel army after Union Major General Don Carlos

Buell came to Grant's aid. While unprecedented numbers of the dead and dying of both armies still littered the field at Shiloh, Foote's squadron steamed down the Mississippi, his flagship *Benton* in the lead, followed by his gunboats with the *Cairo*, the fastest ironclad in his fleet, trailing an armada of mortar boats.[83]

By April 13, Foote had moored his fleet just five miles above Fort Pillow, on a treacherous stretch of the Mississippi known as Plum Run. Plum Run lay in the shape of an S. Its upper bend formed a kind of peninsula on the Tennessee side of the river known as Plum Point, and its lower bend

turned a sharp curve around Craighead Point. Foote kept most of his fleet, including gunboats, mortar boats, repair boats, and steamboats, moored along both sides of the river. Fort Pillow lay downstream, where the Mississippi straightened out somewhat, bending less dramatically westward and then eastward on its side-wind south.

❖   ❖   ❖   ❖

Foote kept picket boats near the tip of Craighead Point to watch for the enemy flotilla he expected to come steaming upriver at any moment. In the meantime, he positioned a mortar boat with a gunboat escort behind Craighead Point where, obscured by a stand of timber, its crew could lob its shells in virtual safety, pausing occasionally to peek through a gap in the popple and watch their shells explode among the rebels' tents.[84]

The first few rounds sent the garrison into an uproar. They had rehearsed for this eventuality, but the real thing was terrifying. The noise alone was enough to drive men mad. Soldiers ducked for cover; slaves ignored their guards' warning shots, tossing aside their shovels to pick up their chains and stagger down into the woods; officers mounted their rearing horses and sent confused alarms by bugle and wigwag.

"A piece of one of the exploded missiles fell in our encampment, doing no damage but tearing a hole in a tent," wrote Lieutenant Lyons, who was tending to a comrade deathly ill with pneumonia. "Amidst the roaring of cannon and explosion of shells," his comrade expired, and "to add to our distress, we were ordered to prepare three days' rations by sundown and prepare ourselves for a forced march." Lyons asked his superior what would become of his friend's remains and was told that invalid soldiers would remain behind to bury his corpse.

As his men scrambled to pack their gear, however, Villepigue began to take the measure of the Yankee shells. Their mortar crews were literally shooting in the dark, and most of their shells exploded too far above the rebels' works to do much damage. In fact, their contents dispersed like pea gravel tossed in some boyish rock fight. No doubt the Yankees would one day find their range and cut their fuses to sufficient length, but for now Villepigue ordered his men to return to their stations, and the garrison hunkered down under roofs and boxes and wagons that clattered under a shrapnel hail.

That evening, as the mortar fire receded, Villepigue ordered Lyons and his battalion to strike their tents and move about half a mile back from the river, "out of reach of shell." There Lyons ordered his carpenters to construct a coffin for his comrade -- "or rather a box," he said, "as it was merely four rough planks nailed together" -- and helped his men dig a grave in the rebel cemetery that lay on the upper slope of the defile dividing the bluff, where they buried him "at midnight by the pale light of the moon." Lyons imagined that his fiancée might wonder why he had not allowed his men to carry his kit for him. Because, he told her, "I never forget that they are men, and I hold my position through them. Too much sympathy cannot be expressed for the poor soldier. Their fare is hard. Everything connected with the life of a soldier is severe."

It looked to Lyons as though their lives were about to become a great deal worse. "The health of our company is very bad," Lyons wrote. Seventeen men from his company alone were on the sick list. "Taking men from the delightful pure air of the Gulf," he wrote home to Florida, "to a rich, muddy and damp locality is very bad in its effects."[85] But more threatening still was the Yankee host they expected to descend upon them at any moment. On April 14, Major General John Pope rounded Plum Point with some twenty Union transports "laden down to their guards with soldiers, wagons, ambulances, horses and commissary stores," plus forty bales of black market cotton he had seized along the way.[86] Fort Pillow's sentinels guessed that Pope's infantry,

noisily disembarking some five miles up the Arkansas bank, numbered about 30,000.

In fact, there were less than 20,000, but even with this correction Lyons would not have changed his opinion of his garrison's chances. "Now, to meet this force we have six thousand effective men," he wrote, " -- merely a handful." They might hold the Yankees "at bay for a day or two, but no longer. Well, consequently we will have to surrender; those who are not killed will be made prisoners, lodged in some northern penitentiary. We are expecting reinforcements but fear they will be too late. Ere this reaches you," he told his truelove, "you will be informed by the telegraph of the evacuation of this point and one of the most desperate battles will be fought on record, not even second to Fort Donelson. I do not pray;" he concluded. "I leave that to the ladies." But he did hope "to contribute with the aid of providence my share in deeds."[87]

The garrison's effective strength was actually less than half the six thousand Lyons reported. But "six thousand" is repeated in so many rebel letters and dispatches that it appears that Villepigue instructed his men to overstate their strength in case the Yankees intercepted their mail. If so, the ruse worked. Though Fort Pillow's garrison actually contained only 2,766 soldiers fit for duty, and the reinforcements Lyons expected would add less than a thousand men to that number by the end of April, Commodore Foote continued to believe throughout the spring that he faced a rebel force of from six to as many as eight thousand.[88]

By April 15, the largely ineffective fire from both sides had acquired a certain alarming beauty. "I frequently saw as many as a dozen shells in the air at one time," recalled George Yost of the U.S.S. *Cairo*, "crossing each other's fiery tracks. Some of them burst in mid air, some landing in the water, others in the heavy woods on the Arkansas shore. One shell, a very large one, passed directly over our upper deck when I was sitting, missing our wheelhouse about twenty feet, and dropping into the water twenty yards away, where it burst, making a tremendous splashing of the water." Yost came to enjoy "the commingling of clear starlit southern skies; bombs flying through the air from our mortars; shells crashing through the woods and over the water," and the "black masses of the gunboats floating quietly upon the river's bosom, lined on either bank with a heavy growth of forest trees."[89]

Villepigue reasonably feared that the incessant Yankee mortar fire was intended to soften up the garrison for a land assault, but, lacking the cavalry companies he had requested weeks before, he would be unable to check on any enemy movement to his rear.[90] Answering Villepigue's call for more arms with a pithy, "No arms here, or available at present," Beauregard rather wishfully assured Villepigue that "ample additional forces" had been "ordered to your assistance." He urged the ailing brigadier to send out his slave laborers and any unarmed whites he could spare to prepare an escape route by building bridges across the Hatchie on the roads to Covington and Randolph.[91] But he could not spare many, for already men rattled by the regular booming of Yankee mortars had begun to slip away to their homes, to the swamps, to the Yankees.[92]

The most powerful mortar at Villepigue's command lacked the range to strike the Yankee mortar boats. But Foote's powerful shells, their fuses properly calibrated by now, were able to spit and burrow at will among Fort Pillow's

works. To many West Tennesseeans, escape seemed the garrison's only hope. Far downriver, a Mrs. Marianne Webster could hear the Yankee mortars' incessant boom. "Fort Pillow can hardly hold out under the daily bombardment that we hear from the gunboats;" she wrote, "and if it falls, Memphis, on taking leave of the Confederate officers, will usher in the Federals to quarters in the Gayoso,"[93] Memphis's premier hotel.

"ALL GOOD MEN"
FOOTE DEPARTS

The Yankee flotilla at Plum Run was becoming a refuge for Unionist refugees from Memphis. Six of them turned up in late April, having rowed and squattered through Arkansas's swamps and bayous, to insist that the majority of Memphians were Unionists compelled by rebel soldiers and secessionist ruffians to hold their tongues. "There are several Union societies," they told Foote, "which assist their members who emigrate, and are pledged to aid in the reestablishment of the Federal authority."

For Foote and his staff, disposing of all these purported turncoats was proving to be a fulltime job. Some Northern men who had been pressed into rebel service signed up to serve the Union, others were sent home. Their holding pen was the steamer *Swallow,* a blacksmith and machine shop that Foote kept moored upriver to make his flotilla's repairs. Only deserters whose allegiance to the Union could be vouched for by Union sailors were ever allowed to set foot on the gunboats or the mortar boats, and then only after Foote had debriefed them.

They told so many "plausible yarns," wrote a reporter, "we hardly know whether to believe them or not." Many of them insisted they had been kidnapped and forced to join the Confederate army at gunpoint. The Pennsylvanian bar-keep of the steamboat *Silver Wave* told a reporter that while enjoying "a little tear" in New Orleans, he had been "jerked up and calaboosed" and forced by the police into rebel service.[94] Other deserters from the Confederate Army said they had simply concluded that, for good or ill, the rebel cause was lost.

Having arrived after his triumph upriver at New Madrid and Island No. 10, Pope expected the reduction of Fort Pillow to take his men a maximum of two weeks.[95] He had been surprised at first that the rebels had not done more to strengthen their river defenses. But after his brilliant and arduous campaign upriver, he had come to realize that the rebels could rely in part on the Mississippi herself to obstruct the Union infantry's advance. "Every position occupied on the river," he wrote, "required for its reduction one of the most hazardous operations of war." Crossing "a wide, deep, and swift river" with "frail transports in the face of an active and vigilant enemy" was a task of "exceeding peril."[96]

Though such an enterprise was especially hazardous against a position like Fort Pillow, Pope was sufficiently buoyed by his recent successes that he urged Foote to support a proposed land assault with a naval bombardment. But the limping Commodore insisted that he could not and would not attack Fort Pillow's batteries for fear of "incurring the risk of losing most of his boats," for as the detrimental Union General Stephen Augustus Hurlbut would later characterize the situation,

> the steamboat channel at Fort Pillow runs right under the bluff and brings every boat as it passes within musket shot of the shore, and a couple of guns mounted up above them would stop most effectually the navigation of the river and drive away any of the tin-clad gunboats we have, for a plunging fire would go right through them and they could not get elevation enough to strike.[97]

Thus, Pope forlornly concluded as his men encamped in tents and abandoned slave cabins on the Arkansas shore, "the whole labor of reduction would again fall upon the land forces."[98] But how to approach Fort Pillow? For forty miles above the fort the Tennessee side of the river was impassably swamped from heavy spring rains. Pope's only choice was to sneak his troops down the Arkansas side of the river and then ferry them across to some point south of the fort.[99]

The Arkansas side was not much dryer, but before Pope could lead his men into a quagmire, Halleck came to his rescue by summoning him east to fry bigger fish on the Tennessee River.[100] After having accomplished nothing but "some very effective fighting against the mosquitoes," on the morning of April 17, only three days after his arrival, Pope and his men set off for Pittsburg Landing.[101] The reporter for the Brooklyn *Daily Eagle* bemoaned Pope's departure, and deemed the two Hoosier regiments he left behind too weak even to protect Foote's mortar crews. But he recognized that their first duty was at Corinth, where a Union victory would "insure a bloodless triumph at Fort Pillow, and one engagement fulfill the purpose of two."[102]

In the meantime, however, this left Foote holding the bag. "I think you had best continue the bombardment of Fort Pillow," Halleck suggested, "and if the enemy should abandon it, take possession or go down the river, as you may deem best."[103] But the mortar siege of Fort Pillow would be Foote's last engagement. Feverish with sepsis from his wounded foot, the pious Commodore stoically limped and hopped about the decks of the *Benton*. "By unusual strength of will he bears up bravely against his infirmities," wrote a reporter, "and still pays his personal attention even to the minutiae of transportation."[104] Thus far he and his men had been doing -- "although not very successfully thus far," Foote allowed -- "all in our power to accomplish good results with our feeble means." The Union had predicated the fall of Fort Pillow upon "our having a large land force to co-operate with us." But Pope's departure had left Foote without "troops enough to occupy, even if we take, this place," and without the necessary

"implements for mounting guns and opening bayous to blockade the river below." He was "at a great loss whether I risk all and dash by the Forts and attack the rebel vans and Gun Boats," he wrote his brothers on May 2. "If we escape the Forts," he said, "we might then attack the Forts from below with a better chance of success, but still our land force is inadequate to our wants, and were we to proceed to Memphis we would find perhaps 6,000 rebels in arms."[105]

"Secession feeling" was so strong among the men and women who lived along the Tennessee bank, that the few who deigned or dared to board the iron turtle that passed for the Yankees' flag ship told Foote only that the Confederates would prove "very determined."[106] So it seemed to Foote that there was nothing for it but to lie low and harass the garrison with round after round of mortar fire. According to the Confederate partisan M. Jeff Thompson, Foote kept his Union gunboats "on each side of the river in a position to command a long stretch where we cannot reach them without being under a cross-fire for from forty to fifty minutes." These lay some five miles upriver while two of Foote's twelve mortar boats took turns commuting with a single gunboat escort to within a couple of miles of the Fort and firing "at irregular periods during the day," every day of the week, for the Commodore's piety did not extend to the Sabbath. As one wag put it, the old man apparently kept up his fire on the rebels "to influence them religiously through the agency of iron and gunpowder."

They made a tremendous racket. Foote's mortar boats were like walled-in floating paddocks with a single mortar mounted in their open center. The crew would load it up, light its fuse, and then duck out to the exterior deck and brace themselves for the explosion, their hands clapped over ears tightly stuffed with tow. "The mortars, especially when the atmosphere is humid, roar tremendously," wrote an observer, but though they shook "the surrounding boats violently with their explosion," the mortar crews felt less of the concussion themselves, "as the water receives the recoil, and acts as a cushion."[107] But familiarity with mortar duty sometimes bred a perilous contempt. The fleet deplored the loss of a crew killed and maimed when one of their number detonated a charge he was carrying by accidentally igniting its fuse with his lit cigar.

❖   ❖   ❖   ❖

By the first week of May, Foote was barely able to swing himself about the *Benton* on a pair of crutches. For weeks he had been nagging his men about a possible rebel attack. Every boat was to keep her bow pointed downriver and her engines running for any maneuver such an encounter might entail. But as the week uneventfully dragged on, it was difficult to keep his crews on the alert. There was simply not enough to do in the drag of spring, especially as runaway slaves and rebel deserters took on more and more of the heavy lifting. Their make-work completed, crews dozed, boxed, smoked, fished, sneaked whisky, played cards, prayed; while their officers generally pursued more scientific and aesthetic avocations. The gunship *Carondelet's* skipper, Henry A. Walke, passed his off time seated on deck in a folding chair, painting watercolors of the fleet and the river and the plantation houses that sparsely punctuated the Arkansas shore. "Here is the finest farms I have ever seen," wrote a Hoosier infantryman. "They are however overflown with the high water. We do not see so many poor people here as in other slave states I have been in."[108]

The Brooklyn *Daily Eagle*'s man found the days oppressively "hot, dry and enervating" on the "Hotel de Dickey," where his fellow scribes jostled for places on the steamboat's shady side. But the nights were magical. "Sitting out on the guards of the boat," he described the "round, fair moon shedding its glad reflection in a broad sheen upon the turbid bosom of the river, and in front the green forests of Arkansas, illuminated here and there by a glimmering light from some plantation house, and occasionally a white steamer nestling beneath the shore from which float strains of martial music in the rear, the deep morasses and lagoons of Western Tennessee, inhabited by numerous sweet-voiced songsters of the wood," then "south of us the flotilla, with the smoke of an enemy's gunboat floating gracefully over the point beyond," and finally, "at the north, the unbroken, silent but swift flowing stream."[109]

J.H. Browne of the New York *Tribune* was too busy swatting mosquitoes to delight in the scenery at Plum Run. He not only elaborated on his disdain for the pests but even accused them of having "strong secession sympathies." They were certainly "bitter enemies of the Nationalists and phlebotomized them without mercy." The mosquitoes "had the honor of extracting the earliest sanguinary fluid" of the bombardment. "They seemed as anxious to die as the Rebels pretend to be." Browne pitied his fellow correspondents who "often arose in the morning with their visuals so swelled, from the bites of the winged pests," that they looked like pugilists.[110]

Foote himself was forced to keep to his starboard cabin on the *Benton,* soaking his wound in mineral salts. Though weak from the infection in his foot, he received reports of puffs of smoke ranging back and forth behind Craighead Point as if the rebel boats were preparing for something. The intelligence he received began to fit a pattern. Deserters brought him news that Confederate General M. Jeff Thompson had sent scouts along both banks of the Mississippi to spy on the Yankee flotilla, and that an armada was assembling downriver from Fort Pillow and preparing to attack. Word reached him that Villepigue had commanded all the planters in the area to report to him at Fort Pillow. "We cannot conjecture what this proceeding indicates," wrote the Brooklyn *Daily Eagle*'s man, "unless the enemy are afraid of their own people." In any case, several planters had reported this to Foote, pleading with him for "probation."[111]

On April 28, Foote again put all his gunboats on alert, mooring them within firing range of the tip of Craighead Point, where they hoped to give the rebels a "warm reception," as one reporter put it. "The rest of the afternoon was spent in momentary expectation of the coming of the enemy," but the night came and went, and, much to the Yankees' disappointment, the rebel fleet again failed to materialize.[112] The next day Foote received the same report and took the same precautions, but still there was no sign of the rebels off Craighead Point.

Over the next week, Foote's crews grew weary of such false alarms, and hopped to his commands with diminishing alacrity. Had these rebel deserters fed Foote all this bunk just to stir things up? Or, worse, to give Thompson's spies the opportunity to see just how he might prepare for an attack? Either way, his men did their best to accustom themselves to the enfeebled Commodore's alarms as they had to the mosquitoes, the sultry heat, and the rhythmic downriver boom of mortar fire. It was obvious to some of them that Villepigue was more afraid of Foote attacking him than the Commodore should have been of the rebels attacking him; witness the rainy night of May 4th, when Villepigue sent a squad to Craighead point to build huge bonfires on the bank, "illuminating the entire region, that they might discern the first approach of the dreaded Yankees and their horrible boats."[113]

The fact was, however, that Foote was no longer well enough even to contemplate such an attack. "The effects of my wound have quite a dispiriting effect upon me," he confided to his friend, Navy Secretary Welles. "The increased inflammation, and swelling of my foot and leg" had made him feverish, "depriving me of a good deal of sleep and energy."[114] Too weak to stand, Foote at last gave in to his surgeons' pleas that he at least temporarily relinquish command and return home to recuperate.

At seven in the morning of May 9, he greeted his replacement, Charles Henry Davis, as he arrived aboard the dispatch steamer *Desoto*. After a brief meeting, Foote ordered "all hands to muster" so that he might bid them goodbye. Though some of his men had grown weary of the old man's reproaches, his prayer services, his temperance lectures, and his caution, few could control their tears as his orderly helped the old man to his feet to deliver his farewell.

Introducing Davis as the very man he had urged the navy to send for his "temporary relief," Foote choked up. Apologizing to his successor that he could not introduce him individually to all his officers, he burst into tears. "But I am so weak," he sobbed. His men cheered warmly as the Commodore's orderly helped him make his way down the *Benton*'s gangway to the deck of the *Desoto*, all the while hiding his tears behind a fan. "Farewell!" Foote croaked back to his crew as he hobbled onto the *Desoto*'s deck. "You've got good officers, and you're all good men."

As the *Desoto* chugged upstream, Foote was eased into a chair from which he feebly saluted the sailors assembled on the deck of each of the gunboats he passed, cheering him now "three times three." "From the most gallant and worthy officer to the most humble seaman," wrote an observer, "there was scarcely a dry eye visible."[115] Those eyes would never see him again. Within one year Foote would receive the thanks of Congress and a promotion to Rear Admiral, and then, en route to command of the South Atlantic blockade, die at last of his infected wound.[116]

TURTLES & RAMS
DAVIS & MONTGOMERY

It now fell to fifty-five year-old Charles Henry Davis of Massachusetts to take Foote's place as Flag Officer *pro tempore* of the Mississippi flotilla.[117] His luxuriant mustache and trim, jaw-line whiskers, aided by his tonsure's shoulder-length locks, made his balding Boston Brahmin pate as prominent and defiant as a gunship's prow. But he was cautious, cerebral, scientific. Davis had surveyed coasts the world over, and at one point proposed the patriotic but impractical idea that America establish its own prime meridian from which its mariners would calculate their longitude.[118] A man of the sea, Davis now found himself cast as a river warrior. Within a mere twenty-four hours of taking the helm of Foote's flagship, he would come to know the difference.

Davis knew enough about river navigation to see that Plum Run was one of the Mississippi's most treacherous stretches. The channel changed constantly, raising sandbars in the unlikeliest places. The most detectable bars broke the surface or lay shallow enough to snag vast tangles of driftwood. But others lurked, rolling and shifting, far enough under the river's opacity to be undetectable to all but the best trained eyes, yet still shallow enough to crush a wayward hull. Nor did Davis find Foote's sailors in the best of spirits. Three Hoosier infantrymen had deserted and joined the rebel garrison, and twenty-five men on the gunboat *St. Louis* had fallen ill – half of them desperately -- after supper one evening in late April. At first they suspected that they had been poisoned by rebel spies, but the real culprit turned out to be a copper vat in which their food had been stored too long.[119]

❖   ❖   ❖   ❖

Young Brigadier Villepigue would have gladly traded his problems for Davis's. As frequent bouts of frontier fever soaked and shook the young general down to hide and bone, a concerned Beauregard offered to replace him with Major General Samuel Jones, an only slightly healthier veteran of the Indian Wars. Convinced, however, that he alone could defend Fort Pillow, the conscientious Creole respectfully refused to step aside.[120] He held out no hope, nor did his superiors encourage him to hope, that any infantry or cavalry reinforcements were forthcoming. All had been sent to Corinth. "If the fort falls," Villepigue groused to his officers, "it will be the fault of the authorities at Richmond, who have constantly interfered with my plans." But if it fell, Villepigue intended to fall with it.

His only hope was the fresh if curious looking rebel armada that was now gathering just below Fort Pillow, crowding the "six or seven apologies for gunboats" Confederate Navy Admiral G.N. Hollins had stationed in hopes of blockading the Yankee fleet. (One Yankee journalist took pity on Hollins, whose beat encompassed the entire Mississippi from Fort Pillow to the Gulf. "One day he receives news of a threatening nature from New Orleans, and he hastens in that direction with half a dozen vessels. Scarcely does he reach Memphis on his downward trip when he is called back to look after the burnt-footed Commodore and his Yankee fleet. So poor Hollins is kept running up and down, his weary soul finding no rest in any place.")

The gunboats Hollins had stationed off Fort Pillow had barely given the Yankees any pause. "It is hardly probable that these boats will make a stand," wrote Foote, who had expected them to "run as we approach them till they reach the cover of their heavy batteries." The exception was the rebel *Macrae*, a former Spanish slaver with "a great deal of power, and a sharp, concealed prow," reported the Brooklyn *Daily Eagle*'s man on the scene. "Being very swift," she might "do our boats a good deal of damage by running into them."[121] But the rest, in Confederate Brigadier General William Whann Mackall's own opinion, were "worthless for offense or defense:"[122] less than worthless after an April Fools Day storm came hurtling down the Mississippi, capsizing a steamer and sending her crew into the river's roil, clinging to her wreckage.[123]

❖ ❖ ❖ ❖

The Confederacy's chief advantage in the struggle for the Mississippi was the hard-won expertise with which Dixie pilots could navigate the Southland's waterways while many of their Northern counterparts blundered into snags and bars. But these same skilled boatmen-turned-navy-captains were unaccustomed to taking orders, deeply resented any interference in the running of their ships, and seemed almost incapable of cooperating with each other in battle.

If no American, as Mark Twain observed, was as autonomous as the Mississippi boatman, no Mississippi boatman was more of a power unto himself than Twain's pilot-tutor, James Edward Montgomery. "He was always a cool man;" recalled Twain, "nothing could disturb his serenity."[124] A Kentuckian of tireless ingenuity and irrepressible audacity, he had astonished the Confederacy by transforming a steamship into the ironclad steam ram *Manassas*. Montgomery had intended to skipper his vessel as a privateer. But Hollins appropriated her for duty on the lower Mississippi, where she would terrorize Union boats. In the end the *Manassas* ran into Farragut's fleet off Fort Jackson, and, after a valiant struggle, sank in flames. But she had proved her worth, and Montgomery was able to convince a cabal of New Orleans investors to bankroll a million-dollar conversion of fourteen speedy steamers into lightly armed iron-clad rams.

Not one but two million dollars later, Montgomery had clad each boat's machinery with an inner bulkhead of bolted twelve-inch-square timbers and an outer bulkhead of six-by-twelves plated with inch-thick railroad iron. Between them he had jammed cotton bales jack-screwed and compressed and topped by iron bolts. He plated the outer bulkheads with railroad iron an inch thick and two and a half inches wide, and reinforced the bows with timbers twelve inches square, sheathing them first in oak and then in two-and-a-half-inch iron plate.

In the doomed hope of preventing the Yankees from capturing New Orleans, Major-General Mansfield Lovell had requisitioned six of Montgomery's rams at the Mississippi's mouth. But the Kentuckian wrested five others from the rebel fleet for what he dubbed his River Defense Expedition and led them up to Fort Pillow to prove their mettle.[125] But Montgomery's little fleet was fit only for deep water navigation and armed with only two guns among them, forcing Villepigue to donate three of his river battery's smooth-bore 32-pounders to Montgomery's experimental fleet.[126]

"It is a vulgar fiction among the rebels," sniffed a Yankee reporter, "that these crafts will sail boldly up to our boats and transports, fasten to them by means of grappling irons, and tow them down to New Orleans, the exact point," the correspondent pointed out, "our boats *wish* to reach. The favor will doubtless be appreciated by the Flag Officer," he continued with his little joke, "and will be a matter of economy to the Federal administration."

Apparently some of Montgomery's sailors were already fed up with their privateering commodore and his stifling rams, one of whose chief deficiencies was an entire lack of creature comforts. Or perhaps they were unimpressed by the fort they had come to defend, or they simply despaired of the cause they had sworn to uphold. But according to Lyons, three of them immediately went over to the Yankees and gave them "full information in regard to this place which is at present very weak as we have not more than one-third the troops required to defend it." They were not alone. Another rebel sailor escaped from one of Hollins's gunboats to report that he and his mates had spent the past week cruising up and down between Fort Pillow and Memphis, burning thousands of bales of cotton.[127] It was beginning to look as though the garrison's only hope was that the Yankees might decide simply to abandon their siege and "make their way to Memphis, leaving us in their rear."[128]

However routine the Union mortar bombardment may have become, it was getting on the garrison's nerves. The mortars could be heard as far upstream as Columbus, Kentucky. Deserters were going over to the Union at the rate of about nine a day, and that did not include the men who bypassed the Yankees and shinned it home.[129]

Though the fort was still well stocked with ammunition, in the muggy heat of May rations and morale ran low. "Our meat gave out today," wrote a Louisianan named Jarrette Law on April 28, "so we had none to fry to get lard to put in the biscuit." When their rations gave out, men had to buy their own flour from sutlers who charged exponentially higher prices as Confederate scrip lost its value. Typhoid had crept into camp, forcing Villepigue to invalid some of his men down to the rebel hospitals in Corinth. "Mr. Lewis and Anderson" and "two others of the recruits died and were buried here," wrote Law. "Since then the sick have been sent to the hospittle, about eighty of our regiment was sent." Law tried to find some solace in his regiment's Wednesday and Sunday night prayer meetings, but within two weeks, typhoid had claimed Law himself, and he was buried with the others on the bluff.[130]

By May 1, Yankee mortars had lobbed some 700 shells into Fort Pillow, "causing a general stampede and making vast holes in the ground that prove their terrible power of destruction. Men burrowed into a warren of magazines, shot furnaces, bomb-proof casements and "ratholes." One shell nearly killed Villepigue himself, sending a piece of shrapnel buzzing inches from his head and knocking him out with its concussion.

"We thought you was dead," one of his men said when he finally came to.

"I was of the same opinion," the General replied, with perhaps a touch of disappointment, for he later told his officers that he had hoped there for a moment that he had been bound for "a country where we could hear something else than the damned negro question discussed, and where a gentleman wouldn't be bored by a war that had become very annoying."

This, of course, was an understatement. According to deserters, the ailing young brigadier had been compelled to clap an entire company of artillerists in irons "for refusing to serve after the term of service had expired." At another point, Villepigue had to station infantry along the bank to prevent his own artillerists from fleeing the shells that occasionally burst above their batteries. The squads of slaves he kept at work gouging out trenches in the rear also tried to flee from the Yankee's descending shrapnel, and they too required a guard to keep them in position. "The Infantry were instructed to shoot down the first negro that attempted to shirk from labor," reported a Yankee paper, "owing to the fire of our mortars."[131] This unhappy duty apparently fell to the 1st Confederate Battalion, for, as Villepigue told Lieutenant Lyons "more than once," he could not "depend on any troops here but our battalion."[132]

An Alabama soldier wrote home that though most of the Yankee shelling had been ineffective, it was nevertheless terrifying. A single shell could "blow a hole into the ground large as half your room," and one day he said a shell hit a man "and literally tore him into fragments. You could find pieces of him scattered all around."[133] It is a matter of debate whether Villepigue lost many men to Foote's mortars. The rebel annals say he did not, but several deserters claimed that he buried some 180 men before the siege was over, most of them killed by Yankee shells. Another reported that after Villepigue forced his artillerists at gunpoint to return to their posts, thirteen were killed by mortar fire, while others insisted that though none were killed by the Yankee shells, many were wounded. Yet another deserter contended that when Fort Pillow's new Memphian mortar exploded, another 26 were killed.[134] Lieutenant Lyons wrote home that after three barrages, his battalion had lost one killed and three wounded, and after one engagement wrote that "as usual, 'many hurt.'"[135] Villepigue would have been as eager to keep such casualties to himself as the Yankees were eager to believe them. There is no debate, however, about the fate of the garrison's exposed mules. Scores of them were killed by mortar fire, their obstinacy extinguished in sulphurous mists of blood and bone.

❖   ❖   ❖   ❖

During the first week of May, three more of Montgomery's vessels arrived at Fort Pillow, bringing the number of rebel rams to eight. Montgomery sent a boat under a flag of truce for the ostensible purpose of exchanging two Union doctors whom the Confederates had captured in the Battle of Belmont. But its true purpose was reconnaissance, and the crew returned from its parlay with the Yankees to report that the Federal gunboats, God bless them, had gone back to sleep and lay at their moorings, vulnerable to attack. This was especially true of the gunboat *Cincinnati* which had caused the Confederacy such grief at Donelson and now guarded the rotation of mortar boats that continued to lob their shells over Craighead Point. Buoyed perhaps by news of Foote's departure, Montgomery decided it was time to attack.

Though the partisan rebel chieftain M. Jeff Thompson doubted that Montgomery's vessels would prove "fast enough to catch a retreating boat," he admired the bold privateer's determination to test his rams against the Yankee fleet. On the morning of May 10, Thompson, the ferocious, lanky former mayor of St. Joseph, Missouri, deployed his "Swamp Rats" – some five hundred of them, by one count -- among Montgomery's vessels and climbed aboard the *General Bragg*.[136] At dawn the next morning, with the ragged and much depleted garrison cheering from the bluff,

Montgomery's flag ship *Little Rebel* led his small, ferrous fleet away from the landing.[137] Chugging up through a thick fog, the flotilla slowly rounded Craighead Point, from which they could dimly make out the Yankees' eight gunboats and twelve mortar boats.

❖   ❖   ❖   ❖

Despite their departed Commodore's warnings that an attack was imminent, the jaded Yankees were about to be caught flat-footed. Convinced the rebels would only attack at night, they had turned their engines down to a low sputter. Their crews were eating breakfast or scrubbing decks, and their new commander was still trying to acquaint himself with the names of his officers, the mood of the river, and the disposition of the fleet he had inherited only the morning before.

Apparently the fleet's officers had marked Foote's departure by letting down their guard. To Montgomery's astonishment and relief, there were no picket boats at Craighead Point to alert the Yankees to a rebel advance. Three of the Union gunboats were anchored off Plum Point on the Tennessee side of the river, three others off the Arkansas shore, three miles upriver from the point. Of these, only one, the *Carondelet*, was ready for action. In the calm of a backwater a mile down the upriver edge of Craighead Point, the *Cincinnati* lay tied to a tangle of driftwood, sighing complacently as her crew rubbed her down with holystones and the mortar boat resumed her rote and intermittent fire.[138]

Roused by sentinels aboard his flagship *Benton*, Captain Davis emerged from his compartment with his telescope raised, peering downriver at the eight ominous curls of black smoke staining the thick morning haze. The *Benton* itself – a former catamaran snag boat weighing in at an enormous 1033 tons -- was not prepared to scramble, so Davis ordered the *Carondelet* and its neighbor the *Pittsburg* to meet the rebels while he vainly signaled through the morning scrim to the three gunboats anchored along the Arkansas bank.

As Lieutenant Walke dropped his paint brushes and raced his ever-ready *Carondelet* downriver with the *Pittsburg* lagging in her wake, the rebel *Bragg,* with General M. Jeff Thompson aboard, immediately made for the isolated *Cincinnati*, whose sailors by now had abandoned the burnished deck and scurried down below. During the eight minutes it took the *Bragg* to reach her, the *Cincinnati*'s crew frantically tossed oil into her burners to raise a head of steam. Firing her heavy guns at the speeding ram, she heaved sluggishly against the current with her mortar boat in tow, yearning toward the shoals off Plum Point.[139]

"A VIOLENT BLOW"
PLUM RUN

Watching from the *Benton*, Davis trembled for his newfound fleet. It was he who had observed that his secondhand gunboats' engines were so disproportionate to their weight that when the Mississippi was in full flood they could hardly make their way upstream. Now, sure enough, the *Cincinnati* was loath and straining against the current as the *Bragg* charged after her, racing so fast her iron bow cut a ten-foot wake.

Though the cotton-clad *Bragg* was now within range of the advancing *Carondelet*'s guns, she "continued boldly on," Montgomery reported, and struck the *Cincinnati* "a violent blow that stopped her further flight." The *Bragg*'s iron and cotton armor survived a broadside from the *Cincinnati*'s nine-inch Dahlgrens, and before her Yankee gunners could swab their barrels, Thompson's rebels emerged with pistols and grappling hooks. Firing into the *Cincinnati,* they tried to set their hooks in her, but their grapnels merely slid off her iron flanks. One of the rebel marines managed to knock a Yankee fourth mate back with a pistol shot to his stomach, but the *Cincinnati* answered them with a scalding burst of steam that sent Thompson's men reeling.[140]

As the *Bragg* veered off, rounding downriver, a hail of shrapnel from the Union mortar boat bobbing in the *Cincinnati*'s wake apparently severed her tiller rope, and the gallant ram began to drift. Seeing her distress, the 633-ton

Sterling Price, looking every inch the tow boat she had been before donning her skirts of iron, jabbed the *Cincinnati* from behind, "carrying away her rudder, stern-post, and a large piece of her stern." As the proud *Cincinnati* staggered from this blow, the rebel *Sumter* now sped into her as well, jamming her iron bow underwater and thereby dousing her fires and swamping her magazines.

The *Mound City* was the first of the Union gunboats from the Arkansas side to join the fray. As her sister ship, the *Cairo*, strained to keep up, the *Mound City* hurtled down with the current, towing a mortar boat and pelting the *Sumter* and the *Price* with shells. The *Van Dorn* made quick work of her mortar boat and struck the *Mound City* a glancing blow, plowing up a ten-foot-long furrow in her hull and littering her own iron prow with splinters.[141] Groaning and shuddering past the wounded vessel, its paddle wheel grinding up against the *Mound City*'s iron stern, the *Van Dorn*'s momentum carried the Union gunboat helplessly ashore, where, as her crew desperately reversed engines, she sustained "a terrific cannonade."[142]

❖   ❖   ❖   ❖

While the *Bragg*'s crew repaired her steering and the *Van Dorn* came about, the rebels' three rear rams chuffed into the fray under a tremendous barrage from the Union flotilla. Alarmed by their rebels' advance, the captain of the steamboat *John H. Dickey,* which had ventured into the current to give the reporters on board a better look, finally got his paddle wheel turning and retreated upstream, to the relief of the gentlemen of the Fourth Estate who now stood cheering along her decks in their pajamas and breakfast bibs.[143]

Jeff Thompson watched approvingly from the crippled *Bragg* as his sharpshooters fired at the *Carondelet,* gravely wounding its skipper as he stood on a deck swept clean by rebel shrapnel. Montgomery's flagship, a screw steamer he had dubbed the *Little Rebel* "ran about amid the storm as heedlessly as if charmed," Thompson reported; but unfortunately Montgomery's skippers were equally heedless of their commander's signals and lunged around the river in uncoordinated sorties, squandering their opportunity to gang up on the Union boats and pick them off one by one.

Nevertheless, Montgomery could see amid the smoke and bursting shells that his rams had done the Union fleet some serious damage: submerging the *Cincinnati* up to its pilot house, running the *Mound City* onto a sandbar. But now the element of surprise was gone and the Yankee ships could be neither grappled nor boarded. Montgomery's 32-pounders were having "no more effect than an Indian rubber ball,"[144] but a Yankee shell had burst the *Price*'s boilers, sending it careening downriver in a great gust of steam that combined with sluggish clouds of gun smoke to turn every boat on Plum Run into a ghostly adumbration.

Outgunned, outnumbered, approaching water too shallow for his iron-laden steamboats' draft, Montgomery decided to quit while he was ahead and signaled his fleet to fall back. This time his skippers were not so heedless, and executed their withdrawal "with a coolness that deserves the highest commendation."[145] "The enemy's boats were enough injured to repay our attempt and damage fourfold," exulted Thompson, and as Montgomery's fleet returned to Fort Pillow, the rebel crews, their faces black with soot, danced upon their decks, "cheering and shouting."[146]

Despite thirty minutes of "most terrific fire," Jeff Thompson claimed that Montgomery's swift and sturdy fleet had lost only two men killed and one wounded, a figure denounced as a lie by rebel deserters, who claimed he buried a score of men, many of them scalded by the *Price*'s exploding boiler.[147] Nevertheless, watching from atop Fort Pillow's bluff, Lieutenant Lyons thought it "strange to say that our boats escaped unhurt amidst such a shower of shot and shell."[148] Though the Union fleet's position above Fort Pillow had offered "more obstacles to our mode of attack than any other between Cairo and New Orleans,"

Montgomery trumpeted proudly to Beauregard, "of this you may rest assured: if we can get fuel" and "unless the enemy greatly increase their force, they will never penetrate farther down the Mississippi."[149]

On the face of it, Montgomery had indeed prevailed at Plum Run in one of the largest naval engagements of the war. Though he had not destroyed Davis's fleet, he had badly dinged it up. Emboldened by Montgomery's success, Villepigue ordered two of his brand-new Memphis mortars out to Craighead Point to blow away the Yankee mortar and her gunboat escort. These new mortars and shells apparently equaled "in weight of metal and efficiency those used by this fleet," wrote a worried Yankee, and their crews showed signs of "rapidly gaining in their gunnery." Though Jeff Thompson had better luck with a sortie to Plum Point, where his sharpshooters drove off a Yankee picket. it was all for naught, for Davis had gotten wind of the rebels' plan and withdrawn his vessels out of range.

The damage Montgomery had inflicted proved exceedingly temporary. Within five days, Davis had managed to raise the *Cincinnati* and the *Mound City* out of the sand and mud and return them to service, and as Yankee rams steamed downriver from Cairo to reinforce his fleet, his mortar boats resumed their daily fire. Having lost only one man killed and three wounded, Davis depicted the battle as a Union victory, and he was perhaps half right. After all, had he not driven the rebels back into their lair? "The Republic is safe," exulted the Brooklyn *Eagle*'s man, who testified to the confusion of the day by reporting a tad hastily that he had watched from the deck of the reporters' "Hotel de Dickey" as Davis sunk two rebel gunboats and disabled the remainder of the enemy's fleet. At least his collision with Montgomery's rams had slapped his jaded crews awake and notified the Union Navy of the efficacy of the Confederacy's quick and armored rams. It had slapped him awake as well, and from that day forward he positioned picket boats a mere mile from Craighead Point with their guns trained on the approach to Fort Pillow.

❖ ❖ ❖ ❖

As Union mortar boats, "eliciting very few replies," resumed their commute to Craighead Point to belch shell after shell over Fort Pillow, rumors filtered up to the Yankee command that Villepigue's garrison was packing up to leave. Now it was the Yankees' turn to venture forth under a flag of truce and try to scout out the enemy's position under the ruse of a prisoner exchange. On May 21, the captain of the steamer *Kennett* returned to report no signs of life along the bluff, but two hours later a rebel steamer muddied the waters a little by rounding Craighead Point under a white flag and effecting an exchange.[150]

"We have reliable information that nearly all the rebel troops have been withdrawn from Fort Pillow and Memphis, very small garrisons only being left at each place," Halleck wired Foote on May 13 (apparently as yet unaware that Davis now commanded *pro tempore* in his stead). "Is it not possible to prepare the gunboats with cotton or hay bulwarks and run past the enemy's works to Memphis? He has a large fleet of river boats there, but no formidable gunboats. By doing this you would cut off the enemy's supplies from Arkansas and open a direct communication with the army of General Curtis."[151]

As Davis's gunboats and Montgomery's rams played a coy and remote game of cat and mouse, Fort Pillow seemed to keep a "constant supply" of exchangeable Yankee surgeons on hand "for occasions when a reconnaissance may prove desirable." Union Brigadier General Isaac Ferdinand Quinby led some 2500 infantry, cavalry and artillery from his District of the Mississippi to the vicinity of Fort Pillow in anticipation of its imminent abandonment.[152] Colonel G.N. Fitch, the commander of the small force that Pope had left behind, had searched for a land approach to Fort Pillow up the Forked Deer River, but found its waters treacherous and the woods infested with rebel guerrillas.[153] Now Quinby's "personal reconnaissance" likewise demonstrated that despite the weeks of bombardment, the rebel position was too strong for "a land approach with my small command:" this despite the solid evidence he had obtained from "spies, deserters, and refugees," that there were not six thousand rebels "in and about the fort" but only "three old and well-filled regiments, averaging at least 1,000 effective men."

Despite Halleck's urging that he steam past Fort Pillow and attack Memphis, Davis was unwilling to risk his fleet unless Quinby could promise to provide covering fire from artillery emplacements across the river.[154] This required Quinby to repair three miles of rain-gashed levees and transport his guns and ammunition across them before the rebels caught on. But heavy rains ruined his men's hasty, furtive repairs and a Yankee picket firing on and killing one of its own men alerted the rebels to their presence, forcing Quinby's men back to the safety of the Union flotilla. Fed up with Davis and concluding that "the easy, and perhaps bloodless" landward capture of Fort Pillow would require twice his force, Quinby returned his men to their various district posts.[155]

Davis's mortars continued to fire on the half-hour like the ticking of some monstrous clock. Though Lieutenant Mark Lyons and his 1st Confederate Battalion were now encamped some distance from the fort, "with a very good parade ground and our tents shaded with majestic trees" that were now "clad in their spring drapery," he and his battalion nonetheless hoped to be evacuated to Mobile any day now.[156] Morale among the other regiments was dismal. A runaway slave of one of Villepigue's officers had overheard his master say "it was all nonsense to attempt to hold Fort Pillow against the flotilla," that the Yankees "were only playing with its defenders, and that the first thing they knew, they would be cut off from retreat." And that was not the worst of it. Others deemed the recent fall of New Orleans the Confederacy's death knell unless it "obtained some great and overwhelming success within the next few weeks." And a few officers were openly declaring that the rebel cause was lost anyway, and Lincoln "would soon have things all his own way."[157]

"A number of men belonging to a Tennessee artillery battalion mutinied for pay," Lyons wrote. "They were taken to the guard house, tied by the thumbs and fed on bread and water for three days, when they begged most piteously to be allowed to return to duty."[158] By May 26, Jeff Thompson's "Swamp Rats" were deserting the western Confederacy's apparently sinking ship at the rate of three a day.[159]

On May 20, Halleck added to Villepigue's woes by transporting, under a flag of truce, 202 Confederates captured at Pea Ridge from their prison at Alton, Illinois downriver to Fort Pillow for exchange. In Villepigue's absence, a subordinate accepted the prisoners before realizing that the reason they had been evacuated from Alton was because of an infestation of smallpox, in the advanced stages of which at least three of Halleck's prisoners were already suffering. Fearing they would spread "the loathsome and infectious disease" throughout his garrison, Villepigue tried to return the prisoners to Captain Davis. But Davis, pleading ignorance, refused to take them back, offering instead to establish a neutral hospital for any Confederate or Yankee who contracted the disease.[160] Denouncing Halleck for his "bad faith and inhumanity," the Southern press was convinced that like some Rennaissance Tuscan prince he had purposely set out to infest Fort Pillow with pestilence.[161]

Alarmed by the news of Corinth's imminent fall and the continuing threat to Villepigue's weary garrison, Jeff Thompson hoped "that another daring exploit will raise the spirits of our desponding countrymen."[162] But the river was quickly falling, and though this opened the country along its banks to rebel guerrillas, it not only made navigation more difficult for Montgomery's deep-draft rams, but returned a Union land assault to the realm of possibility.[163] Now General Villepigue expected an attack at any minute. Lieutenant Lyons looked forward to it, or that is what he told his sweetheart. "Should we be gratified so much," he wrote, "I hope I shall be able to render a good account of the Spartan band that are entrusted with the safety of this *point*."

"A DOUBTFUL CREW"
THE ELLET BROTHERS

On May 25, Colonel Charles Rivers Ellet, Jr. arrived at Plum Run. An elderly civil engineer, in February Ellet had sent the Federal War Department a pamphlet in which he maintained that a fast ram would inevitably sink a gunship. In March, the Confederate ram *Virginia* had proved his point by sinking the *Cumberland* at Hampton Roads, whereupon Stanton had signed  off on Ellet's proposal to construct a fleet of rams. Inspired by Montgomery's armada, Ellet and his brother, Lieutenant-Colonel Alfred Ellet, constructed a flotilla of formidable wooden rams that was attached not to the navy but to the army.

Though instructed by Stanton to gain "the 'concurrence' of the senior naval officer present,"[164] the Ellets were a power unto themselves. With characteristic zeal, Colonel Ellet urged Captain Davis to undertake "a combined movement with a view to surprise and destroy the enemy's gunboats, rams and transports, now lying before the guns of Fort Pillow." Unless such a movement were made promptly, Ellet warned Davis, "the opportunity for it may possibly be lost altogether." He therefore proposed "to join the whole, or a portion of the rams under my command, to the whole, or even a single one of your gun boats, and placing them all under the shelter of the barges which I have prepared for the purpose, and hope will soon arrive, run below Fort Pillow by daylight, and attack the rebel fleet where ever it can be found."[165]

Unlike Ellet, however, Davis had seen how cumbersome his own vessels were in battle, and "was unwilling to assume any risk at this time." The New York *Herald's* man-on-the-scene explained that the Commodore would have been "much more vigorous and active" if Foote had left him with boats "that could be easily handled." But every vessel – except Ellet's rams, of course – "had only one wheel, and that, with a fastidious regard to its safety, is placed somewhere near the middle of the boat. The gun-deck also is level with the surface of the water, and all the machinery that can possibly be put there is below it. This," concluded the *Herald*'s man with a sneer, "is an excellent arrangement."[166]

However eager he was to test his rams against the fleet he had emulated, Ellet had no more luck budging Davis than Pope had had budging Foote. But there was a difference this time. Though Foote had also been loath to risk his fleet, there was something more troubling about Davis's caution. In Foote it had been a virtue, or could at least be seen as such when weighed against his bold service upriver. Observers had praised Foote's "matchless caution and sagacity and perseverance," had "full confidence in his prudence," and it did not hurt his case that he had suffered his wound so manfully.[167] He deserved, and received, the benefit of a doubt.

Though Davis had seen action at Hilton Head, South Carolina, as far as the Mississippi fleet was concerned he was an unknown and untested quantity. It had been unfair of the fates, let alone the navy, to expect him to perform at his best a mere twenty-four hours after taking command, but such are the injustices of warfare. His defense had been a shambles and the survival of his fleet had depended more on his boats' light draft than their nimbleness, speed, or accuracy; or, for that matter, on their Commodore's tactics and precautions.

Davis had convinced himself that he had won a victory at Plum Run, but Montgomery's attack had compounded his

Brahminical caution. Even as reports mounted that the rebel garrison was about to evacuate, he refused to risk such a scrape again, at least until he had all his ducks in a row: his gunboats rearmed and re-armored, his engines boosted, his crews better trained and disciplined. He was beginning to betray that instinct for the capillaries, the McClellan-like fastidiousness and reluctance to act, that would ultimately cost him his command.

Not soon enough, however, in the view of the ever restive Ellet, who insisted that Davis was running a greater risk mooring in Plum Run "with my small guard, and within an hour's march of a strong encampment of the enemy," than racing past the battery, guns blazing, while he could still "take advantage of the high water."[168]

If it was Fort Pillow's batteries that Davis was worried about, Captain Bernard Schermerhorn of the 46th Indiana proposed doing something about them. After scouting along Coal creek, and observing that the rebels' picket battery at the northernmost edge of the bluff withdrew every morning, he convinced Fitch to allow him and a work-detail to build cypress bridges across the bayous that lay above the creek, with the intention of attacking from the north with a few companies of infantry, spiking the guns one by one, and withdrawing before they drew fire. By June 1, they had reached within a few hundred yards of Fort Pillow and were building a pontoon raft to cross the creek when shells suddenly buzzed and crashed through the surrounding woods. Believing the rebels had found them out, Schermerhorn and his Hoosiers scuttled back to Plum Run.[169]

In fact they were firing not at Schermerhorn but at Ellet who, in ignorance of the captain's plan, and without consulting Davis, had taken it upon himself to send a few of his rams downriver to feel out the rebel batteries.[170] Contending that "a demoralization, proceeding wholly from cowardice," had begun to "agitate the fleet," he had decided to "take the temper of a doubtful crew" by steaming downriver on the *Queen of the West* and attacking a rebel steamer lying just around Craighead Point.

No doubt citing their commodore's respect for Fort Pillow's batteries, "the captain, two out of the three pilots, the first mate, and all the engineers, and nearly all the crew declined the service and were allowed to go off with their baggage to a barge," whereupon Ellet assembled a crew of volunteers and proceeded on. He should have followed the captain's example, however, for by the time he rounded the bend, the rebel vessel had withdrawn, and the cannoneers along the bluff had lit their fuses. "The firing of the fort was at short range and quite brisk," Ellet reported, "but I think only revealed about seven or eight guns." Ellet retreated before the rebels could find their range, and thus their shells crashed and smoldered in the woods of Craighead Point, sending the enterprising Captain Schermerhorn and his detail scrambling back to their lines.

Not in the least humbled by this fiasco, Ellet deemed the strength of the rebel batteries "greatly overrated." Though their fleet of rams and gunboats was "much larger than mine" -- eight gunboats just below the fort and four more downstream at Randolph – Ellet continued to try to shame Davis into taking some action. "Commodore Davis will not join me in a movement against them," he complained to Stanton, "nor contribute a gunboat to my expedition, nor allow any of his men to volunteer, so as to stimulate the pride and emulation of my own. I shall therefore first weed out some bad material, and then go without him." But according to Ellet, after his return to Plum Run, the "bad material" who had deserted the *Queen of the West* came to him "and expressed their humiliation and begged me to give them another chance, promising never to fail me again."[171]

❖   ❖   ❖   ❖

Like a man hanging on by a branch from the edge of a cliff, the Confederacy was losing its hold on the Mississippi and its tributaries as the Yankees pried away its fingers one by one. After Beauregard's ingeniously stealthy but nonetheless dispiriting withdrawal from Corinth, he finally ordered Villepigue to abandon the fort he had "so long and gallantly defended," in hopes at least of luring "the enemy further into the interior, where I hope to be able to strike him a severe blow."[172] Villepigue was ordered to withdraw to Grenada, Mississippi by the best and shortest route.

As soon as Villepigue evacuated the garrison, he was to "telegraph the commanding officer at Memphis to burn all the cotton, sugar, &c., in the vicinity of that city," and "destroy all Government property--arms, guns, that you will not be able to carry off with you." As soon as he reached Grenada, Villepigue was to "assume immediate command of all troops there assembled, to organize and discipline them. Arms will be furnished you from the depot at Columbus, Miss.," Beauregard promised, but he was compelled to add: "should there be any there. You might also throw up some light works (batteries and rifle pits)," he gratuitously suggested, "for the defense of that important position against a small force of the enemy."[173]

Like the "important position" he was now compelled to abandon, Villepigue was on his last legs. With what energy remained in his frail body, he began to oversee the evacuation of his post. Montgomery assisted him, mounting eight of the bastion's guns on his rams, and loading powder, shells, cannon balls and commissary stores in their holds.[174] To fool Davis into thinking reinforcements had arrived, Villepigue apparently ordered his supply of Silby tents erected behind the bluff, visible from the river, while Montgomery lined up his boats to form a kind of blockade off Craighead Point in case Davis or Ellet assumed that his fleet had departed.[175] Once his men were lined up for the march to Randolph, carrying with them what they could, Villepigue ordered a volatile young artillery Captain named Thomas Blount to remain behind with twenty men and a steamboat "to destroy all the guns, burn all the quarters, and then to embark on the boat for Memphis."[176]

Sunday night, Lieutenant Lyons and his Floridians returned from guard duty to find their battalion "under arms, each having his knapsack and other equipment on." He and his men had expected the evacuation, "but not so near at hand." Around 10 o'clock at night, the garrison received the order to march, and as Lyon's company made its way out of the fort, "many were the speculations as to our destination or what we were going to do."

What they were going to do was slog their way through a steady downpour to the river town of Randolph, Tennessee and climb aboard a hastily assembled fleet of transports bound for Memphis. Lyons was "an active participator in the retreat," he wrote, "which was of a most fatiguing nature." Though "all the wagons in the county had been pressed into service to transport our camp equipment -- that is, tents and cooking utensils," the garrison had nearly run out of live mules to haul them. Each company was therefore allotted only one wagon, compelling Lyons and his men "to leave everything but what was actually necessary."[177]

As they shuffled down the Fulton Road, the fort was put to the torch. "First we set fire to the quartermaster's stores," wrote a member of the demolition detail, "next, the commissary, and then every 'shanty' on the 'hill.' We blew up all the guns, except two which would not burst. It was a terrific sight: the rain pouring down, the thunder rolling midst the lightning flashes," making the night "sublime, though terrible."[178] Lieutenant Lyons and his men had not marched more than a mile before they felt the ground shake as the abandoned magazines exploded in the heat, sending gigantic fizzgigs and whizzbangs hissing into the rain.[179]

Though the Union encampment at Plum Run was not so desperate as the rebel garrison at Fort Pillow, the receding of the Mississippi had introduced a new hardship that was making the Yankees' extended stay intolerable. The camp had become "the filthyest place" that one infantryman ever saw, for the spring floods had drowned "hogs and cattle by the hundred," and now their carcasses dotted the exposed banks, giving off "the most disgusting smell that I ever smelt."[180]

On June 1, after Schermerhorn's Hoosier skirmishers had returned to Plum Run, a deserter from Fort Pillow informed Davis that the bastion's upper battery was being dismantled and its field pieces hauled away. Though Foote had advised Davis to be wary of such intelligence, it seemed to confirm all the rumors that had been floating around, and the

Commodore "prepared to fall upon the rear of the retreating rebels and take immediate possession of the works."

That night, however, Davis began to second-guess what the ragged rebel deserters had been telling him with such unanimity. Suppose this so-called "evacuation" was a ruse? he wondered. Or what if the rebels had left behind a vestigial artillery company of sufficient skill and number to sink his boats? Ignoring Ellet's posturing and pestering, the Commodore refused to risk his fleet the next morning, at least not until he could send a tugboat downriver to assess the situation. But even after the tug returned to report no sign of activity except for a number of smoldering cotton bales on the landing, Davis would only permit his boats to proceed as far as the Arkansas shore across from Craighead Point, from which his sailors and marines spent the afternoon slapping at mosquitoes and "gazing at the grim cliffs and wondering when they could set foot upon the promised land."[181]

Around 6:30 in the evening, "dense volumes of smoke were seen rising in the direction of the Fort," reported the *Cincinnati Gazette*.

> They were succeeded by fierce flames which shot up from a hundred different points, above the tops of the highest trees, brilliantly illuminating the scene in the immediate vicinity, and leaving no doubt in the minds of those on the flotilla that the immense barracks of the enemy had been fired and abandoned. During the conflagration, some twelve or fifteen heavy discharges of artillery were heard, and before the evening was too far advanced, some of the shot and shell from these could be seen plunging into the river a short distance below the gunboats, and sending their huge columns of spray high in the air.[182]

An exasperated Colonel Fitch loaded his men onto transports, intending to launch a dawn attack on the vulnerable picket battery that Captain Schermerhorn had scouted some days before. But by morning Fitch was so convinced that the rebels had withdrawn that he and Ellet decided to take a small party downriver, first by transport and then by rowboat, to see for themselves.[183] Their oarsmen straining across the Mississippi current, they gazed up at the gloomy bluff, fringed now with smoke and flame. No one fired, no-one called, no-one stirred among the exploded magazines and batteries. "The bluff was as tenantless as when Ferdinand De Soto discovered that great river."[184] The fort was empty. The rebels were gone.[185]

A party of soldiers rowed ashore in a yawl and escorted Ellet's brother Alfred to the top of the bluff, where he introduced Fort Pillow to the Union flag. As it climbed up a vestigial staff, a cheer arose from the soldiers and sailors massed on Davis's gunboats rounding Craighead Point, "and in a short time the rebel fortifications were alive with Union soldiers."[186]

They were astonished by the immensity of their prize. "On the summit of the bluff there were breast-works running in a zigzag course for five or six miles," exclaimed a Union soldier, "and inclosing a large area. The works along the river were very strong, and could easily hold a powerful fleet at bay."[187] But if the Yankees expected rich spoils, they were to be disappointed. Villepigue's demolition detail had done their work well. "A place more barren of trophies than Fort Pillow," reported the Cincinnati *Gazette*, "it would be difficult to find."[188] "Camp equipage, supplies, cotton, spades, wagons, &c., had been burned," reported the New York *Herald*, "together with a new and apparently well built house, which had been the headquarters of the commanding officers.

> Several casks of molasses had been spilled, and the mixture of clay and treacle formed a by-no-means pleasant compound in its adhesion to each pedestrian's boots. A single tent had been left standing, on one side of which was the figure of a huge pelican, and on the other the words "New Orleans boys don run for Yankees."

Davis was embarrassed to find "but few marks of our cannonade," only "several trees on the high ground cut off by shot and two huge cavities in the ground where shell had exploded."

On works designed for fifty guns, "only ten remained, three of them exploded" and the rest "carefully spiked and their muzzles wedged with ball or stands of grape. The gun carriages were more or less burned, some of them still smoking. One huge 120-pound rifled gun had been burst, the entire breech being projected more than thirty feet."[189]

The Yankees pored over the abandoned fort, salvaging what little they could from the flames. In one tent they found a table with a defiant note pinned to it by a rebel lieutenant. "To the first Yankee who reads this," it said, "I present this table not as a manifestation of friendship -- yet I entertain no personal animosity -- but because I can't transport it.

> After six weeks' bombardment, without doing us any harm whatever, I know you will exult over the occupation of this place, but our evacuation will hurt you from another point with disastrous effect. Five millions white men fighting to be relieved from oppression will never be conquered by twenty millions actuated by malice and pecuniary gain, mark that. We have the science, energy and vigor, with the help of God, to extricate ourselves from this horrible

and unnatural difficulty pressed upon us by the North; the day of retribution is approaching and will fall upon you, deadly as a bolt from heaven; may your sojourn at this place be of few days and full of trouble.[190]

The Yankee occupation of Fort Pillow would last for years, not days. But he was right about the trouble.

PART TWO

THE UNION OCCUPATION

86 · **PLUM RUN** *BY* ANDREW WARD

LOST TO US
FORT PILLOW & MEMPHIS

But what, exactly, had the Yankees conquered? A correspondent for the New York *Herald* called Fort Pillow "by far the strongest position yet selected on the river for Confederate batteries." The bluff rose "abruptly from  the stream about a hundred feet and at all points is very difficult of ascent except where artificial means are used. Along its base, for nearly three fourths of a mile, strong works have been constructed about twenty feet above the level of the river. The glacis is at the highest possible angle for earth to be placed, and can now only be ascended in places where the men have dug small steps or foot holes." A road from the river to the top of the elevation had been cut in the side of the 50° cliff, "with a steady though not steep ascent throughout."

On a narrow terrace about halfway up the bluff was "a work mounting two guns, which swept the river in their front." A few batteries had been constructed on the summit of the bluff, "one overlooking the river and mounting six guns, one of them a hundred and seventy-pounder of recent manufacture." At regular intervals the work was "properly" bastioned with "sand bags, planking and rammed clay." Some of these positions were designed for mounting one or sometimes two guns, each "protected by embrasures, though none of them were casemated." The embrasures had been constructed "in the strongest manner possible: one of them, and in fact the entire bastion, being of granite, chiseled and built up with great care and nicety," probably by Cleburne's Irish sappers.

"On the summit of the bluff," the *Herald* continued, "commenced a series of extensive field works" laid out in a zig-zag course that stretched over a series of ridges and hills for about six miles, "all provided with a ditch in front" and extending "from Coal Creek, on the northern point of the bluff, to a point below the lowest of the water batteries." Beyond the works, a swath a half a mile wide had been cut out of the woods, and its felled trees, their branches pruned and sharpened, left lying where they fell to obstruct cavalry.[191] "One cannot pass over these works," remarked a visitor, "without wondering how the rebels ever did so much labor in so short a time."[192] It was not the rebels, however, but their slaves.

❖   ❖   ❖   ❖

Like the popinjay general for whom it was named, even after Fort Pillow had demonstrated its worthlessness, it would refuse to sink into insignificance. If it can be said of a place that it exerted its will, this vast ruin would lure back bluecoat and butternut alike until the wet spring day in 1864 when the Southland's sons -- white and black, rebel and Yankee – would fatally converge.

Now it fell to the Yankees to try to figure out what, if anything, to do with it. Fort Pillow retained a certain plausibility on Union maps: a substantial fortification strategically situated, with vast entrenchments and well protected embrasures that appeared, at least, to command the Mississippi, even as the river itself receded from the foot of the bluff in the rising heat of late spring. But Fort Pillow had lost not just its garrison and its guns but its original *raison d'être*. The Union now enjoyed the free run of the Mississippi from Minnesota to Memphis, and in a matter of weeks its hegemony would extend all the way to the Gulf.

Inspecting this enormous ruin of the western Confederacy's giddy grandiosity, Davis, Ellet and Fitch judged that Fort Pillow's batteries and vast entrenchments "could not be properly garrisoned without a new armament and a corps of artillerists." But why bother? "For all practical purposes," Fitch reckoned, "one or two Gun Boats would be more effective than any command of infantry." So they did not linger long over their pyrrhic prize, but departed immediately for Memphis, leaving a mere company of infantry to pluck what they could from the ashes, as the gunboat *Pittsburg* kept watch from the river below.[193]

❖   ❖   ❖   ❖

Drawing on a stream of rumors and reports from the rebel deserters, Unionist refugees, and fugitive slaves who fled from Memphis to seek safety in the Union lines, the New York *Herald*'s reporter painted a picture of a city in the advanced stages of disintegration. Her blacksmiths were said to be manufacturing pikes for the new rebel recruits, "of which not quite a hundred men have as yet responded to the call of Governor Harris.

> The Governor, however, has disappeared from Memphis, and the Union men were abandoning the place, leaving all their property to be confiscated, as impressment at the point of the bayonet had become general. Men were driven from the streets and from their stores and dwellings to the rebel camps of instruction, and all who could escape from the city with their lives were glad to get away.[194]

After his flight from Corinth, Beauregard had removed all of his forces from not only Fort Pillow but Memphis as well, for the abandonment of the former dictated the evacuation of the latter. As the Confederates pulled out of the city, they hauled away teetering wagonloads of confiscated goods, burned thousands of bales of cotton and sweetened the waters of the Mississippi with thousands of gallons of molasses.[195] "We have no defenses at this point," the colonel in command had written on the first day of June, adding, with guttering hope, "We look to Fort Pillow."[196]

Two days later news of the fort's evacuation threw Memphians into a panic. "If not already done," Jeff Thompson urged Daniel Ruggles, who had been sent by Bragg to protect the Confederate depots and cover the rebel rear, "for God's sake, order the River Defense Fleet to defend every bend and dispute every mile of river." Thompson was willing "and believe I am able, to hold the river, if Commodore Montgomery will co-operate, which I believe he will."[197]

Montgomery would indeed cooperate, if only by default, but otherwise Thompson was mistaken. The city had no artillery, and though the citizenry held a rally in support of Montgomery's rebel fleet as it assembled off the city's riverfront, only ten citizens actually volunteered to stand and fight. Shelby County's Home Battalion announced that they would not "fight or defend," and desertions from the regular army were so rampant that the colonel commanding could not promise that he could hold onto even fifty armed men.[198] Meanwhile, the city fathers, defying not only the rebel officers who passed through but many country people who had always regarded the place as a den of iniquity and "Union hole," refused to allow the retreating Confederates to burn their fair city to the ground.[199]

On June 4th, the depleted, shell-shocked Fort Pillow garrison arrived at Memphis.[200] It had rained all along the way, but Lieutenant Lyons had kept himself relatively dry at night by sleeping on fence rails. They had trudged eighteen miles to Randolph and there boarded transports for Memphis, which Lyons had found so inhospitable three months before. Arriving before midnight on a riverfront heaped with cotton bales and overturned hogsheads of molasses, they camped just outside the city and the next morning, June 5th, boarded a train for Grenada. "My candid impression," wrote Lyons, "is that Tennessee is lost to us. I am still in good spirits and shall be the last to despair. Nevertheless, I know we will have to fight desperately."[201]

    Lyons did fight desperately for the remainder of the war. Brave, fair-minded, popular with his men, he was promoted to major of the 1st Confederate Battalion and survived to return to Florida and marry Amelia Horsler, the recipient of his letters from the front. He called her "Meley;" she called him "Marks." He never laid eyes on Fort Pillow again.

❖ ❖ ❖ ❖

Fearing that 54 days of grueling bombardment and the humiliating abandonment of Fort Pillow may have brought the ailing Villepigue to death's door, Beauregard praised the "skill, vigor, and intrepidity" with which the febrile and emaciated Brigadier "evacuated his command in the face of superior numbers with a success equaled only by the brilliancy of his defense."[202] Poor John Bordenave Villepigue would endure long enough to serve courageously at the Second Battle of Corinth in October, but end up once more covering a retrograde movement, protecting Earl Van Dorn's rear on his retreat to Holly Springs.[203] "An educated soldier," as Bragg described him, "possessing in an eminent degree the love and confidence of his officers and men," the gallant young Frenchman died a month later at Port Hudson, "the result of too great exposure to the weather, and over-fatigue in the performance of his laborious duties."[204]

    The Memphis *Avalanche* went so far as to depict Villepigue's evacuation as "what is generally regarded in military circles as a great triumph." Despite the garrison's exodus, the *Avalanche* insisted that "the river has not been given up." As for Fort Pillow itself, "we held it as long as we wanted to hold it," the *Avalanche* boasted, "and when we got ready, we left it in our own way and in our own good time."[205]

As a matter of fact, Villepigue had reported "a great number of desertions" along the march to Randolph. Though the precise number of men who evacuated Fort Pillow is not known, and some companies may have traveled to Grenada by other routes, he reported that only about 800 men out of the garrison's over 2,000 reported to Memphis, suggesting that desertions may have run into the hundreds. For all that, it was perfectly true that many of Villepigue's men, like Beauregard's forces at Corinth, had withdrawn in good order: a vast improvement over the rebel performance at Fort Donelson.[206] But Memphians were about to find out that as far as the Mississippi they knew was concerned, the *Avalanche*'s perfect truth that "the river has not been given up" was perfectly false.

Montgomery's desperate resistance the next day would seem at first to support the *Avalanche*'s editorial. But Montgomery and his rams were trapped. Back when his brand new fleet had departed from New Orleans, he had signed a note for 20,000 barrels of coal to fuel his steamers as they patrolled the waters off Fort Pillow. But General Mansfield Lovell had refused to pay for the stuff, and now Montgomery found himself stranded at Memphis without enough fuel to reach Vicksburg. Arriving from Fort Pillow a little before midnight on June 5, he ordered his men to scrounge up what little coal the retreating army had left behind in Memphis, but it was not enough. As the federal fleet made its appearance in the predawn gloom, Montgomery faced a grim choice: scuttle his fleet or stand and fight.

"I determined," he said, "to do the latter."[207]

❖ ❖ ❖ ❖

Davis had been the first to depart from Fort Pillow, steaming down to Randolph with his gunboat fleet and camouflaging his masted ships with tree limbs and foliage. Meanwhile Ellet rounded up his rams and moved downriver, anchoring off the Tennessee shore some 18 miles above Memphis. At Randolph, Davis found vivid evidence of the rebels' departure the night before: burned cotton bales, abandoned houses, spiked artillery. Since Memphis was said to be entirely unfortified, and Montgomery's rams had, after all, withdrawn from "a position whence they could choose their own time of attack, with Fort Pillow to fall back upon," the Yankees expected to take Memphis without resistance.[208]

On the morning of June 5, Ellet's armada steamed downriver with his flagship *Queen of the West* and three of his hardiest rams leading the way, and caught up with Davis's fleet in the channel above Memphis. Davis's lead pilot was Horace Brixby, who, like Montgomery, had helped to teach the young Sam Clemens and the future Mark Twain the art of steamboat navigation.[209] Stationing his rams on the Arkansas bank, Ellet was preparing to steam across to confer with Davis on the opposite side of the channel when a shot came arcing overhead, apparently from the rebel ram *Jeff Thompson*. As it crashed into the woods beyond, Davis wigwagged to his gunboats to gather in the middle of the stream, and Ellet ordered his fleet to attack by raising a banner on his flagship's mast. As Davis's guns returned the rebel fire "with considerable vivacity," Ellet's rams -- *Queen of the West, Monarch, Lancaster,* and *Switzerland* -- rushed out from among the gunboats like dogs unleashed.

Anticipating a spectacle and praying for a rebel victory, hundreds of white civilians had already lined the city's levee, cheering the three rebel rams that steamed "boldly upstream toward our fleet." Among the spectators was Jeff Thompson himself, who, after bragging that he could defeat Davis with a few men in skiffs, had left his headquarters at the Gayoso Hotel to stand beside his charger in full mufti and wave his feathered hat at his namesake ram as she and the *Lovell* bore down on the *Queen of the West*.

What followed was a classic game of chicken, and for a few panicked seconds Ellet feared that his wooden rams might get the worst of it in what seemed an inevitable head-on collision. But at the last moment, "as the distance between us and the enemy, short at first, became dangerously small," the two rebel boats, "apparently quailing before the approaching collision, began first to back water and then to turn, thus presenting their broadsides to my attack."

What may have happened was that the *Lovell*'s engines "got out of order," as Montgomery reported, and as it lost velocity and veered off, the captain of the *Thompson* followed suit.[210] Be that as it may, for a moment Ellet could not decide which rebel ram to attack, "for there was still a third ram within supporting distance" – the formidable *Sumter* – "to which I would be exposed if I struck the second, while the second would be sure to reach me if I selected the first." But the *Queen* herself, still barreling downstream, decided for him by plowing into the *Lovell*. The hastily mounted guns that Montgomery had removed from Fort Pillow and installed on his rams' decks exposed their crews to Yankee sharpshooters, and the *Lovell*'s gunners could manage only a single feeble round that was "lost in the water" as the *Queen* broadsided her just forward of her wheel-house.[211]

"The crash was terrific," Ellet recalled. "Everything loose about the *Queen* -- some tables, pantry ware, and a half-eaten breakfast -- were overthrown and broken by the shock." The *Lovell*'s hull crumpled, and her chimneys nearly toppled onto the *Queen*'s bow as the rebel captain and his crew jumped into the current and paddled for  shore. But Ellet was by no means out of danger, for within the next thirty seconds, as the *Queen*'s crew tried to clear the wreckage from her decks, her port wheelhouse was struck by the rebel ram *Sumter*. "This blow broke her tiller-rope," said Ellet, "crushed in her wheel and a portion of her hull, and left her nearly helpless."[212]

All this had taken less than eight minutes and littered the river "with the fragments of the rebel vessel." Charles Ellet emerged from the *Queen*'s pilot-house and stood on her deck to see how his experimental ram was enduring its first combat. But he lingered too long: long enough, at any rate, for a rebel signal officer to get him in his pistol-sights.[213] Firing repeatedly, he sent the elderly engineer-turned-colonel toppling to the floor of the deck, bleeding so profusely that the rebels assumed, and rejoiced, that he was dead. Within less than a minute of Ellet's emergence from the pilot house, his men were dragging their wounded commander inside.

By now the Yankee ram *Monarch*, with Alfred Ellet in command, had caught up to his wounded brother's disabled *Queen* and aimed his timber prow at the *Sumter*, colliding with such force "that piles of furniture were precipitated from the rebel steamer upon the forecastle of the *Monarch* and were found there in large quantities after the action."

Rudderless, down to one wheel, the *Queen* limped back to the Arkansas side of the Mississippi, landing not far, as it happened, from where the demolished *Sumter*, staggered by the blow from the *Monarch*, had itself ground up onto the bank. At the rebel crew's request, Ellet's officers took them prisoner as their shattered ram wheezed and sank in the shallows.[214]

What followed was a melee: iron turtles charging and swerving and sinking amid dense clouds of steam and gun smoke. The witnesses to the Battle of Memphis were like blind men trying to describe an elephant. Their only point of agreement was that the result of the battle was the near total destruction of the Confederacy's River Defense Fleet.

According to Montgomery, his flagship *Little Rebel* had been about to ram a Federal gunboat when a cannonball pierced her boilers below the water line, and she began to sink. "Myself and most of the crew," Montgomery reported, "escaped by swimming ashore." A few were killed by Yankee sharpshooters as they floundered in the current. Elsewhere, the *Beauregard*, pursuing a nimble Yankee ram, missed her, blundering instead into the wheel house of her comrade *Sterling Price* and disabling her. As only one ram, the *Earl Van Dorn*, and one rebel steam freighter, *The Paul Jones*, its decks laden with Fort Pillow's rescued stores, managed to escape downriver,[215] the *Bragg* ground up on a sandbar and fell into Yankee hands. Everywhere sailors were jumping into the dun-colored current and kicking their way ashore, littering the Arkansas bank for two miles with the wreckage and life preservers to which they had clung. Those who managed to reach shore tried to escape into the woods, but Yankee sharpshooters were said to have picked off more than a hundred.

Wounded, surrounded, overpowered, the captain of the *General M. Jeff Thompson* saved his boat from capture by charging her into the shallows and setting her ablaze. "The fire caught her magazine," wrote a Rhode Island gunner named Ezra Green, "and the burning fragments went into the air, I should think, 200 feet, and the bomb shells could be seen bursting up there in every direction." At Cairo, 200 miles upriver, "they thought it was the shock of an earthquake." As the roar receded, the *Thompson's* "armor of cotton bales came floating past us down the river."

The loss of these two boats must have shaken M. Jeff Thomson to the core. After watching the Yankees capture the *Bragg*, on which he had steamed up Plum Run only a month before, and mourning his own namesake ram, now blown to kingdom come, the "lank and colorful" partisan mounted his horse "and left for parts unknown." Reporting the affair to Beauregard, Thompson was "sorry to say that in my opinion many of our boats were handled badly or the plan of the battle was very faulty." The Yankee rams "did most of the execution, and were handled more adroitly than ours," because, he said, "the guns and sharpshooters of the enemy were constantly employed, while we were almost without either." Why the rebels lacked for sharpshooters, of course, was because Thomson had kept his "Swamp Rats" with him on Fort Pickering Landing at the insistence, or so he said, of his co-commander Montgomery, whom he now erroneously believed to be dead.[216]

This contest "was all on one side," concluded Ezra Green. The rebels "were whipped too easy," and he "did not think anything more of that battle than I should of a target practice." Green was especially pleased to have taken part in the capture of the *Sumter*, "the one that sunk the *Cincinnati* at Fort Pillow." But as his gunboat towed the crippled rebel ram toward the Memphis riverfront, her crew discovered that her fleeing crew had set a slow fuse in hopes of blowing up the converging Yankee fleet. "Lucky for us it went out," Green reported, "or she would have blown us out of the water."

After a Yankee crew drove the captured *Bragg* up to the city landing, a steamer heaped with cotton bales approached, mistaking her crew for rebels. "She wanted to know the news and came down to get it off the *Bragg*, not knowing she had changed hands." Added Green, "*She* was up a little creek."[217]

❖   ❖   ❖   ❖

Disembarking at Memphis's riverfront, a Hoosier infantryman named Eli Sink discovered that some Memphians had been so confident of a rebel victory that they had just raised what Sink called "the Stars and Bars of treason" in front of the Gayoso House hotel. But as Davis demanded the city's surrender and the Yankees poured into her streets, the local people fled the levees, many with tears streaming down their faces.

"A large crowd of people witnessed our landing," and stood by as a party of Union soldiers hacked down their makeshift flagstaff. But the "lesson of the morning and the yawning ports of our Iron Clads had a very salutary effect on the rebel population," and "no insults were offered to us." By the end of the afternoon the Yankees had taken over all the public buildings, and for the next ten days Private Sink and his pals enjoyed their respite from "the mosquitoes and the Bull gnats of the Arkansas swamps" in the comparatively "wholesome air and clean streets of Memphis."[218]

An Ohio infantryman witnessed a kind of investiture of the Stars and Stripes over the Overton Hotel which first the rebels and now the Yankees occupied as a hospital.

> As I approached, a flag presentation was going on in front of the hotel, the flag being a present from the Union ladies of Memphis to Col. Slack, the Provost Marshal. A Miss Majors presented the flag in a neat speech, which was responded to by Col. Slack in a neat and appropriate speech, when three bands which were on the cars discoursed sweet music to patriotic ears: "The Red, White and Blue." The flag was then placed on the train, which moved off majestically down the main street, the band playing the "Red, White and Blue" and the "Star Spangled Banner" as they proceeded.

❖ ❖ ❖ ❖

Prostrate from his wounds, Charles Ellet turned the command of his ram fleet over to his brother Alfred, trusting that the gallantry his crews had shown at Memphis would make up for the demoralization "proceeding wholly from cowardice" of two weeks before.[219] On June 22nd, Grant arrived at LaGrange, Tennessee, where he was greeted in Sherman's absence by General Hurlbut who, a temporary model of sobriety and decorum, showed him around the grounds of the Charles Michie plantation where, before proceeding to Memphis, Grant did his best to make a dent in the stash of cigars his well-wishers had sent him from all across the North to mark not only his victories but his recent fortieth birthday.[220]

The last of Montgomery's fleet, the *Earl Van Dorn*, would survive only three weeks more before the Yankees caught up with her on the Yazoo River and sank her in a burst of steam and flame, stranding her charge, the *Paul Jones*, up a tributary. Here the ingenious, impetuous Montgomery himself begins to fade from the record, a broken man abandoned by the army, hounded by his New Orleans investors, forsaken by the Confederate navy he had briefly outshone.

After the *Van Dorn*'s destruction, and the subsequent demolition of the rams to which General Lovell had laid claim at New Orleans, Captain Charles H. Davis, confident now that the Mississippi had been swept clean of the remnants of Montgomery's shattered fleet, departed from Memphis with four gunboats and six mortar boats, bound for the siege of Vicksburg.[221]

"FORT PILLOW STATION"
LAUDERDALE COUNTY

Convinced at last that the rebels had actually withdrawn not only from Fort Pillow but West Tennessee itself, a few local people timidly emerged from the woods. Though many of them declared themselves secessionists, they all expressed to Ellet "a desire for the old order of things," and seemed to at least tolerate if not welcome the Union flag as it fluttered from the bluff.[222]

When the Yankees first marched into West Tennessee, their personal appearance "made a very good impression upon all classes, whites as well as negroes, an impression that many had believed impossible on account of the description of 'Yankees' on which they had been fed by politicians and the newspaper press of the country in order to excite hatred of the North."[223] But like every conqueror before or since, they were about to find occupation not necessarily more hazardous but certainly more frustrating, confusing and ultimately corrupting than invasion ever was.

Moored below Fort Pillow's battered bluff, the *Pittsburg's* Commander Egbert Thompson sounded the first of what would become over the next two years a familiar and forlorn refrain. Writing Davis on June 9th, he reported that the local Unionists were afraid of the bands of Confederate guerrillas whose ranks had been swelled by rebel deserters. Finding

there was such a small Federal force in the camp, many professed Unionists had come down to the river to ask the navy to take them to safety. But the former navy inspector who, as a young midshipman, had helped put down a mutiny and chart the Fiji islands, was at a loss what to do.[224] "Will you please inform me," Thompson asked Davis, "what facilities will be afforded them for leaving?"

"Deserters and refugees continue to take refuge here," wrote a reporter, "and the arrivals are becoming more and more numerous.

> They are a filthy looking set, for the most part as ragged and unkempt and frowsy in appearance as any beings that can be imagined. Coarse jeans, shrunken and faded from long wear, constitute alike the uniform of the deserters and the garb of the refugees. Once in a while you will be able to find one who, in former days, might have seen a little civilization, but it is very difficult to single out from the motley crowd one that can give you an intelligent, detailed account of affairs in the Confederacy. They don't seem to know much about Jeff Davis' institution; some of them don't know the regiment to which they belonged. It is very easy to see how they have been wheedled and misled, but the ignorance of these fellows is appalling.[225]

Commander Thompson asked for a copy of the current Oath of Allegiance with which he hoped to sound out the locals' allegiance and dispense as best he could with the rebel deserters who beckoned from the riverbanks. With no room on board in which to incarcerate these half-starved absconders, he paroled them instead for three-day terms, and though they had so far duly reported back to him at the appointed time, he wondered what the future would bring.

The situation was impossible for occupied and occupier alike. The Oath of Allegiance became something of a standing joke, but a mordant one. Acting Master James Marshall of the U.S. Navy believed the oaths weren't worth "a particle," and again and again the Yankees would catch some of the most obdurate rebels with their loyalty oaths tucked in their pockets.[226] In Osceola, Arkansas, immediately across the river from Craighead Point, "rabid Secessionists" were said to be organizing themselves into guerrilla bands. Armed with some of their names and addresses, Commander Thompson sent a detail across the river to round up the most prominent rebel agitators. Local secessionists and retreating rebels had circulated reports among the locals that it was "dangerous for any of them to fall into our hands," so Thompson docked a captive rebel steamship at Fort Pillow's landing to act as a kind of clearing house and "settle the uncertain feeling of those residing here-abouts in regard to what course the Federal Government will pursue with them." Those who dared to come down to the river were apparently "pleased to learn that if they go home — attend to their own business and have nothing to do with the bogus Confederacy -- they will not be molested."

Thompson suspected that though many planters along the Mississippi were marking the evacuation of Fort Pillow and the fall of Memphis by putting their cotton to the torch, some of Lauderdale County's farmers had simply hidden their cotton in the woods along the Hatchie to see what the morrow might bring. "I have not made very strict inquiries of the civilians that have come in," Thompson confided to Davis, "in order not to alarm them" nor had he ventured "beyond the line of the fortifications or sent scouting parties beyond them," except to discourage local blacks and whites from scavenging the supplies that the garrison had discarded in the woods behind the fort.[227] But within a couple of weeks bales of cotton would begin to accumulate at Fort Pillow's landing for sale and shipment to Memphis.[228]

Other local whites came to inquire about the whereabouts of their slaves, many of whom had been requisitioned by the rebels as laborers, others of whom had escaped to the river to be employed on Yankee gunboats as roustabouts and stokers. Thompson wrote that contrabands were turning up at Fort Pillow every day. He told them that "they had better go home to their masters." But in the navy, as in the army, officers were conflicted about what to do

with refugee slaves. Sending them back to their masters seemed cruel to some, a waste of labor to others. Some naval officers directed their crews not to hand any such men over to their masters, and not necessarily for humanitarian reasons. At the end of April, 1862, as the hot season approached the Mississippi Valley, Union Secretary of the Navy Gideon Welles had jump-started the enlistment of escaped slaves whom he, like his Confederate counterpart, believed could better withstand hard labor in a hot clime. "The large number of persons known as 'contrabands' flocking to the protection of the United States flag," he said, "affords an opportunity to provide in every department of the ship, especially for boats' crews," what Welles called "acclimated labor." He had therefore encouraged his officers to enlist contrabands as "boys" for from $8 to $10 a month.[229]

Since then at least nine runaways and black prisoners had found employment on Davis's boats for $10 per month. After their masters repeatedly applied for their return, one officer warned his men that "if any officer, bearing a commission of the United States, delivered up a contraband" he would be dismissed from the service "at once."[230] On the other hand, and perhaps only for the record, Davis himself cautioned his officers against receiving contrabands "promiscuously on board the ships of the squadron."

On June 12, Davis sent the *Cairo* upriver to help Commander Thompson retrieve the abandoned rebel guns from Forts Randolph and Pillow that William Howard Russell had ridiculed a year before.[231] Its skipper, Lieutenant N.C. Bryant, reported that smoke presumably from a rebel boat had been sighted curling above Forked Deer River. Yankee patrols began to nose around Dyer County, passing through Churchton and Newbern, searching for rebel deserters and guerrillas and any vagrant companies of Confederate regulars their commanders may have left behind.[232] But no steamboat materialized, the Forked Deer appeared safe, and the guerrillas and stray rebels were at least temporarily cowed by the trainloads of federal troops that began riding the rails between Columbus and Grand Junction.[233]

Captain T.O. Selfridge kept the Cairo anchored off Fort Pillow all summer as his crews demolished the Confederates former ramparts with mortar fire and rowed in occasionally to pick through the ruins. Some four miles inland they came upon the saw mill that the rebels had established to  reinforce their magazines; now the *Cairo*'s crew put it to work sawing "a large quantity of heavy timbers, with which a very complete and effective barricade was constructed around our boiler, engines, and exposed portions of our vessel, making the *Cairo* invulnerable to ordinary projectiles," and all "without any expense to the government." The greatest menace aboard the *Cairo* that early summer was malaria, which claimed a number of its crewmen, including Secretary of the Navy Gideon Welles's nephew, who was buried with the others on the bluff.

But as the summer wore on, the *Cairo*'s crew ventured deeper into the interior. In early August, they arrested a man who lived behind the fort on suspicion "of aiding the guerillas who infest the country around us, and are continually making attacks upon defenseless transports on the river and small scouting parties in the interior." Less than a week later, they rounded up "several secessionists, neighboring planters, who own some hundreds of negroes" and brought them aboard the *Cairo*.

"They were defiant;" recalled George Yost, and "refused to take the oath of allegiance; but notwithstanding, as no evidence was addressed showing their active participation in the rebellion, they were set at liberty." On the 21st about a hundred men from the *Cairo* rowed downriver to Fulton, "where they advanced into the country in quest of a body of guerillas said to be in that vicinity," and "killing, wounding and capturing a large number without the loss of a man on our side." At the end of August, the *Cairo*'s ship's carpenter was shot while out on a hunting expedition, whereupon forty men set off to find his assailants. "After having explored the vicinity of the attack, and finding no enemy," the men destroyed the houses, barns and hay stacks which had sheltered the attacking party. "A large quantity of arms and ammunition was found in one of the houses, the proprietor of which was captured and brought on board."[234]

By June 23, the Yankees had occupied Dyersburg, from which they sent out patrols to confiscate the slaves of secessionists, recruit the sons of Unionists, requisition horses and mules, string telegraph wires, guard the railroad. But they met with mixed success. Masters hid their slaves, or drove them into Mississippi or Texas to prevent their falling into Federal hands. Boys fled from Union recruiters, and farmers kept their best horses and mules hobbled in the woods. Men the locals called partisans and the Union called brigands or guerrillas cut telegraph wire with tiresome regularity and began to take potshots at passing trains.[235]

In early July, 1862, the *Pittsburg* was ordered off to Cairo for repairs, to be replaced at what Davis now called "Fort Pillow Station" by James Edward Montgomery's former flagship, the *Little Rebel,* which had fallen into Yankee hands during the Battle of Memphis.[236] Lieutenant Bryant of the *Pittsburg* had gathered intelligence from fearful locals about "certain men who have been active in the cause of the rebellion and who now intimidate the peaceably inclined," and spotted a band of armed and mounted men trotting near the fort whose "pretended purpose was hunting negroes." Though Bryant did not have the necessary force to deal with them, he duly reported the names of four especially dangerous men to headquarters at Memphis.[237]

"However deeply we may lament the exposed condition of loyal citizens in the interior," Davis wrote back, "it will be wholly impossible to attempt any relief without an independent military force." Nevertheless it was "satisfactory to me to know that by the presence of your vessel and by your personal influence you do everything in your power to sustain and encourage the Union sentiment."[238]

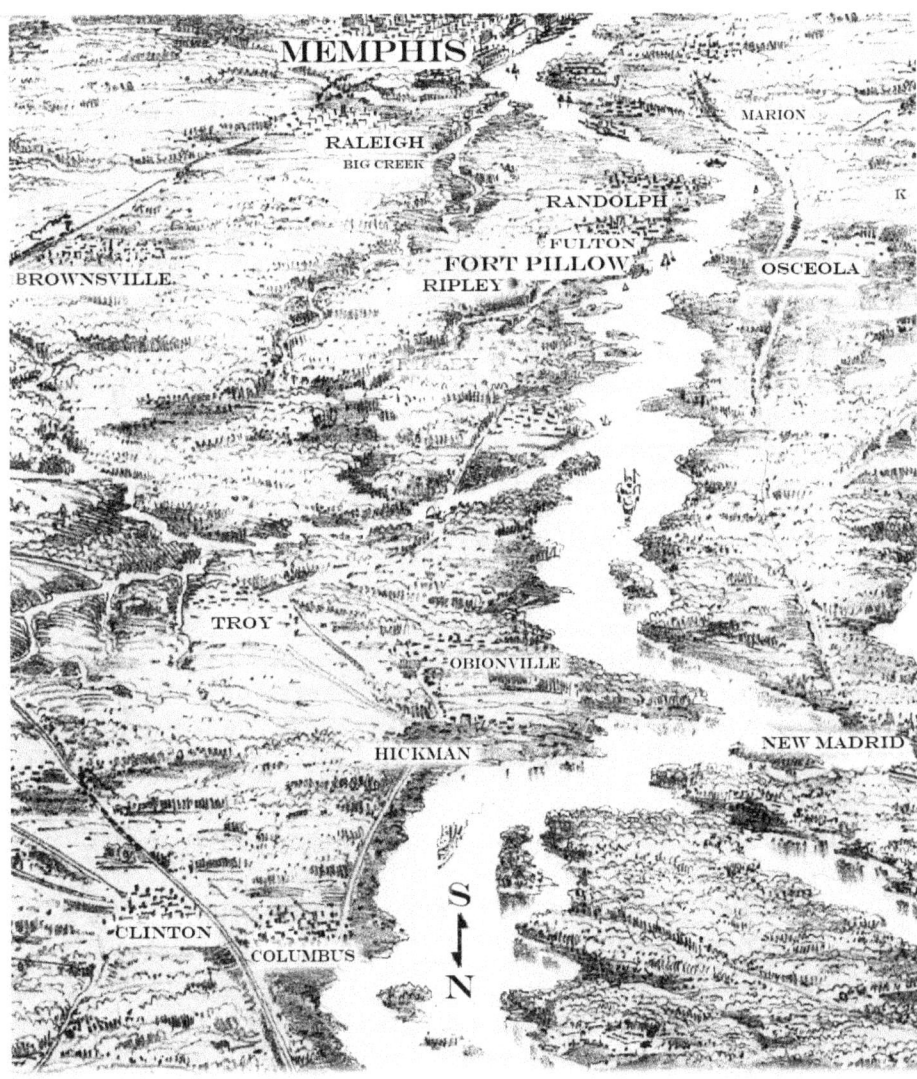

"LOOK LIKE THE DEVIL"
GUERRILLAS

What Union sentiment the Yankees could detect in Lauderdale County seemed primarily to consist of a wish for a return to law and order. Whose law and whose order did not matter much to many people anymore, and if the Union was on the ascendant, so be it. But in some quarters secessionist sentiment remained robust, and with Federal occupation, West Tennessee now entered its guerrilla period.

One of the first West Tennessee partisans to make a name for himself was a medically discharged infantry officer named Bill Dawson. An Irish Carolinian, he had saved up enough of his earnings as a flatboatman to buy 200 acres of farmland in Dyer County, where he was eventually elected sheriff. He had been perforated at Belmont and Shiloh, leading his Dyer County "Bell Grays" into the thick of battle. After recovering from wounds to his head and shoulder, and the loss of his left pinky finger, in late June he received Braxton Bragg's permission to recruit his own partisan band. One of his subordinates was a slaveholder from central Dyer County named Elijah P. Kirk, who commanded a company of his neighbors' boys. Almost six feet tall, he had entered the war riding his own horse and packing his own pistol. Fed up with the regular army, in which his brother had died at Columbus of what Kirk regarded as pure neglect, he was ready now to slip through the woods of West Tennessee, harassing Yankees and Unionists under his own guerrilla banner.

His chief nemesis was a Yankee named John Lynch, who at the time was captain of Company E of the 6th Illinois, a unit composed of battle-hardened men from the Wabash River Valley. Lynch would quickly enter West Tennesseeans' nightmares and the cautionary tales they told their children, his unfortunate name raising fears of drumhead hangings and ravaging hordes as his men ranged almost at will through Dyer and Lauderdale counties, snatching up livestock, forage and recruits. Dawson and Lynch would collide in mid August six miles north of Dyersburg, where Lynch's men captured most of Dawson's horses, arms and ammunition. Nevertheless Lynch came away convinced that hordes of well armed rebel Kentuckians and Missourans in flight from the Federal draft were pouring into West Tennessee to join bands like Dawson's.[239]

Only about half of West Tennessee's guerrilla leaders were Tennesseeans. The notorious Solomon G. Street was a Mississippi export, a thirty-three year-old former carpenter from Tippah County. "Hold them heads up!," he used to bark at the ragtag band he dubbed his "swamp angels." "Look fierce! Look mean! Look like the devil! Look like *me*!"

While serving in the eastern theatre of the war, Street heard of the fall of Donelson and immediately made plans to return home to protect his kin and keep his slaves out of Yankee hands. Under the terms of the Confederacy's new conscription law, Street promptly bought himself a substitute and hurried home. With Yankee units crisscrossing Tippah County, he went into hiding and began to organize the fugitives he encountered in the swamps and bayous into a company of partisan rangers.

In June 1862, Street led his men on a bold raid along the Memphis and Charleston railroad, defying and eluding the Yankee patrols that guarded it. Disguised in uniforms of Union blue, "Sol Street's guerrilla band" ostensibly served under Brigadier General James Ronald Chalmers, but operated with rangy autonomy from the backwaters of his boyhood, monitoring Yankee patrols, picking off stragglers, running off Federal mules and horses, catching runaway slaves.

Though it is not recorded what befell the slaves he captured, Street apparently regarded them as property too valuable to destroy. At one point, in the wake of the Emancipation Proclamation, Street would capture sixteen

Union soldiers – or "free Americans of African descent," as Chalmers sarcastically described them -- and return them to their masters. Street and his raiders did not always distinguish between Unionists and secessionists. Among his victims was a rebel sympathizer named Galloway whom Street shot down in cold blood after his men had set his cotton crop ablaze. As the whoops of Street's men faded off into the woods, Galloway's secessionist son Bob stood over his father's corpse in the glow of his incinerated fields and swore revenge.

Street's nemesis was not Lynch but a wealthy planter named Fielding Hurst and his 6th Tennessee cavalry, with whom his men traded punctures throughout West Tennessee. Released from rebel confinement in Nashville, Hurst had volunteered his services and his considerable resources to the Union cause and raised a regiment of Union Cavalry known as the 6th Tennessee  Cavalry. He was a man "of very strong prejudice," who, as a neighbor recalled, "had his enemies inside and outside of Purdy, and my candid opinion is that if his enemies had let him alone, that his course would have been far different."[240]

Be that as it may, Hurst proved to be one of the most ruthless Union commanders of the war in the West, rivaling even Jim Lane of Missouri in his scorched-earth depredations. However many of the stories that circulated about him were true, he was undeniably a terror to the secessionists of West Tennessee. At one point Hurst ordered rebel prisoners shot and had them buried along the roadside at one-mile intervals as markers. Another prisoner once offered to return the spurs he had stolen from the Yankees earlier in the war, remarking that he himself would not need them in prison. Overhearing the soldier's remark, Hurst said, with a laugh, "You mean you won't need them in hell," and shot him dead. Not long afterward, at a river crossing, he is said to have pointed to a white woman riding a ferry. "Watch her spread her wings," he said, and shot her in the back.

Condemning Street's partisans as spies and cutthroats, Hurst refused to treat them as prisoners of war. Chalmers insisted that Street and his men were regulars, and warned that if Hurst executed any of his captives, Chalmers would "retaliate upon your command, some of whom are now prisoners in our hands." In fact, the reverse scenario played itself out: it was Street's boys who first summarily executed two Yankee prisoners, and the Yankees who retaliated by shooting two rebel prisoners off a bridge. And so the reprisals continued. When guerrillas captured Hurst's nephew, they first trussed him to a tree and shot him between the eyes and then forced his sickly mother out of bed to view his remains, resulting in her falling and breaking her hip.[241]

Another Mississippian active in the area was a slave overseer named Milford Coe, a Mexican War veteran who made himself so disliked by his comrades in the 1st Mississippi Infantry that his captain, Frank Montgomery, discharged him. "He returned home," wrote Montgomery, "and early in the next year located himself on Island Seventy-Six, opposite the town of Bolivar, and gathered around him a gang of desperadoes, negroes and whites, and began systematically to prey upon the people on the main land, who finally organized a force, and, after capturing him, brought him over and shot him to death in a cane brake."[242]

When the Union army shifted a large portion of its western forces to Chattanooga, it created a vacuum in Mississippi and West Tennessee into which men like Dawson and Street and a native son, semi regular Colonel Robert V. "Bob" Richardson, eagerly rushed. Richardson was even more notorious than Street. Assigned command of the 14th Tennessee Cavalry, and eventually Forrest's West Tennessee Brigade, Richardson would fall in and out of Forrest's favor. Though the exact reason was never recorded, one trooper described his command as "not attractive or popular."[243] Condemned by both sides for his depredations, he joined forces with Street under Chalmers's ostensible command and spent the rest of the fall hectoring and eluding Yankee patrols, executing "Tories," and hunting for conscripts from Dyer County, Tennessee to Hickman, Kentucky.

Richardson was not the only man to straddle the line between regular army and rebel guerrilla. In October, 1863, Captain Lewis M. Kirk of Biffle's regiment was known as "a terror to all Union sentiment," having killed "several Union men in cold blood."[244] More prominent was the Kentuckian W.W. Faulkner, who commanded about three hundred Kentuckians and Tennesseeans, and led the Union Army a merry chase. Sometimes he rode under Forrest's banner, but he operated more or less independently until a couple of months before the end of the Civil War, when his unit would be folded into Nathan Bedford Forrest's command.[245]

Faulkner's was not the first guerrilla band Forrest succeeded in absorbing. After Christmas 1862, Sol Street and his gang joined Forrest's newly organized Cavalry Department, in which the formidable Forrest had the magical effect of turning Sol Street the bushwhacker into the obedient and disciplined Major Street of the 15th Tennessee Cavalry. But no sooner would Forrest's first West Tennessee campaign close than Street's old depredations would catch up with him. Riding into Forrest's camp at Bolivar one spring day, he was recognized by sixteen year-old Bob Galloway as the man who had murdered his father and burned his crops the year before. Raising his gun, Galloway blew Street out of his saddle, killing him instantly. An enraged General Forrest ordered a drumhead court martial to be followed immediately by a firing squad. But before the hour of his trial, young Bob Galloway escaped, eventually slipping into the Union lines at Memphis and steaming up to safety in Illinois.[246]

Every county had its allotment of rebel guerrillas. Some viewed themselves as sheriffs, deputies, slave catchers, posses. With Forrest's blessing, Captain George King of Obion County would organize a company of about 40 men in early 1864 in the vicinity of Kenton, Tennessee, to maintain order.[247] W. Bertram "Burt" Hays saw his role differently. The son of a

Hardin County planter, he had served with his brother in the regular army for a time. But after Hays received word that his secessionist mother had been raped by Union foragers, Forrest permitted him to resign from his escort to raise his own band.

    Their crimes were legion or legend, depending on whom you believed. Stories circulated that their men ravished damsels and hanged old ladies and dashed out babies' heads on stumps. Be that as it may, Burt and his boys were a dangerous set, and misery followed in their wake. By the end of the war his name would be printed in bold block font on Pinkerton's list of America's 100 most-wanted, where it remained until July, 1868, when Hays's bullet-riddled body was found moldering behind a barn in Hardin County.[248]

    Hays' Unionist trackers – local boys, for the most part, familiar with the lay of the land and nursing grudges against their secessionist neighbors -- committed depredations of their own, using their pursuit as an excuse to rob and harass anyone they suspected of loyalty to the Confederate cause. Among Hays's pursuers was the Unionist Elias Thrasher and his Buttermilk Rangers. Making their headquarters in Clifton, the men of his Second Tennessee Cavalry (USA) disgraced themselves preying promiscuously on the people of Hardin County. In March, 1865, five of his men rode up to the house of one William Johnson, who had been called away from his farm on Sugar Creek. They demanded $12,000 of Mrs. Johnson, and when she told them she had no money, "they hung her and her daughter several times," wrote a Union officer who had been sent to bring Thrasher to heel, "completing their diabolical work by each of them outraging the person of Mrs. Johnson." They next called on the wife of a local physician, "who gave them all she had."[249]

❖   ❖   ❖   ❖

Some guerrillas indulged in raping the wives and daughters of men who had gone off and joined the enemy. A former slave named John Crawford remembered when bushwhackers raided his mistress's house while her men were away, "taking things and having no mercy on the womens." Crawford's mistress and her daughters hid in the attic as the bushwhackers approached "swinging old muzzeloaders," and though the slaves told them the women were gone an infant's cry gave them away. The bushwhackers ran upstairs and "stay up there two or three hours, and then they come down and grab something to eat and ride away."

When the master and his sons returned "the womens tell them that they ain't seen no mercy. Grandpappy nearly tear his hair out. They go and get on they horses," and returned that night to report that the bushwhackers were "buzzard bait; they is hanging up in the air off a limb." But "the womens mooded to die." They sat on chairs, "not moving or talking a word," and ever afterward "the spirit all gone out of old Missus."[250]

Their victims were black as well as white, of course, and as the rebels grew more desperate for food, for funds, for shear survival, they targeted slave cabins as well as white farmhouses. "Thieves would come around and [take] everything they wanted," recalled a slave named Nancy Stewart of McNairy County. "One time they came and took all our bedding, and even tore up the floor to see if we had anything hid." Stewart was equally horrified by the way whites treated one another. "They cut one old man's ears off,

that lived near us," she remembered, "and another old gentleman that lived close by -- they made him get down on his hands an knees and spurred him just like a horse." Recruiters could be just as brutal. "We had another neighbor that had three boys that were too small to go to war. The rebels came and shot them down like dogs just because they were too young to fight. I went to their funeral," Stewart recalled, "one of the saddest funerals I ever attended. Those boys' little sister just went from one coffin to another."[251]

❖   ❖   ❖   ❖

Dipping down into West Tennessee from his native Kentucky, the rebel Champ Ferguson and his 9th Tennessee Cavalry gave no quarter. After their commander promised to spare a Union captain his men had surrounded, Furgeson dragged the Union officer down the stairs of his cabin and out into the yard and swiftly slit his throat. "We felt very mad that he did this," wrote John Weatherrede of the 9th, until Ferguson explained that the officer had torched Ferguson's house "and outraged his wife and daughter a few months before, and he had swore vengeance against him and his men who were at the outrage." He next found the officer's patrol sleeping in a cabin two or three miles from where their captain now lay, and, before they could roll out of bed, he cut their throats as well. Though Weatherred and his comrades could understand the depth of Ferguson's rage, "this was not our way of fighting," he concluded, "and we did not enjoy his company."[252]

"I was on a raiding expedition with about seven Confederate soldiers," recalled Sam Gilliam of the 1st Tennessee Infantry (CSA). "We came to [the] Tennessee River, and we held up our hands and swore that [if] one of our number should be killed, we would have revenge." Shortly afterward, a comrade was shot to death by a Unionist home guard who stripped off his victim's trousers and put them on, unwisely displaying one of the bloody holes his bullets had made to Gilliam's uncle. The uncle and his kin rode up to the home guard's home in the company of his kinsmen and asked him to come with them to Tullahoma to testify "against a prisoner that he had placed there." They all dismounted at a nearby church, where the home guard again showed off the bullet hole in his pants. The hole must have been somewhere along the belt line, because when they all fired at it, they killed him instantly."[253]

Some men would find out the hard way that they weren't cut out to be guerrillas. A Unionist named Jack Jones more than met his match in a self-possessed secessionist farmer named Cherry. Riding up to the dooryard fence of a local miller Cherry was visiting, Jones shouted, "Come out here, Mr. Cherry. By God, I am northern cavalry. I have come to take you off, you God damned rebel."

"Jack," Cherry politely replied as he emerged from the house, "I don't see how I can go today. My wife and children need some meal."

"Get over the fence, I tell you," said Jones, spurring and reining his rearing horse.

"All right," sighed Cherry, "if I must, I will." But as he approached the fence, he reached down and picked up a hoe, with which he proceeded to give Jones "such a beating as only a large stout man thoroughly aroused could do."

At last Cherry agreed to the miller's plea that he spare Jones, lest the Yankees retaliate. "Jack Jones," said Cherry, standing over Jones with the bloody hoe upraised, "if I conclude not to cut your head off with this hoe and throw it away, will you ever be seen in this country again?"

"No sir, Mr. Cherry," piped Jones, "I will not," whereupon the miller helped lift the Unionist into his saddle and watched him trot away, "his new federal uniform stained in his own blood, and his head and face much battered." Jack Jones was never seen in those parts again.[254]

❖   ❖   ❖   ❖

One way or another, rebel guerrillas made it hot for the Union Army's occupying force. One officer stationed in Tennessee reported that he had been required to keep his men garrisoned because every time he sent out a patrol the partisans would capture it. Not that keeping them garrisoned necessarily guaranteed their safety. "There was another one of our men got poisoned today and will die tonight," a Yankee wrote home, "and we have to be very careful about eating and drinking about here."[255]

The reprisals continued to spiral, until none could tell who was wreaking vengeance on whom or for what. By late January 1864, a question about the proper treatment of secessionist civilians in occupied territory would elicit from William Tecumseh Sherman a burst of Old Testament wrath. "The people of the South," he said, "having appealed to war, are barred from appealing to our Constitution, which they have practically and publicly defiled." With "a little reflection and patience," he continued, "they could have had a hundred years of peace and prosperity, but they preferred war.

> Very well, last year they could have saved their slaves, but now it is too late – all the powers of earth cannot restore to them their slaves any more than their dead grandfathers. Next year their lands will be taken; for in war we can take them, and *rightfully*, too; and in another year they may beg in vain for their

lives. ...To those who submit to the rightful law and authority, all gentleness and forebearance; but to the petulant and persistent secessionist, why, death is a mercy, and the quicker he or she is disposed of the better.[256]

"God knows, there was enough guerrilla raiding on one side and barn-burning on the other in our internecine conflict;" wrote the historian Fletcher Pratt, "but there was never any necessity for the Union to set up the classical device for repressing an antagonistic population, which is a chain of fortified posts, with heavy patrols working among them, and stern reprisal against anyone who moves without official order." Necessary or not, this was precisely what the Union Army set up along the Mississippi as it passed through West Tennessee: garrisoning the Confederacy's abandoned posts and patrolling the surrounding countryside in ever widening circles.[257]

These patrols were so demoralizing that for some Yankees it tainted the Union flag itself. Bill Mays of the U.S. 12th Tennessee Infantry recalled a grieving family he had encountered near Shelbyville, where the rebels were rounding up recruits.

The rebels would send guards out at night to catch any one of them that tried to go home. One night I went with the guard to a house where there was an old man and woman and children. The boy looked to be sixteen. They could not find the man that they were looking for. The officer of the guard went in and searched the house, tore up the beds and cradle, and found a little United States flag. He held it up to the guard like it was a great trophy. The old man looked like he was condemned. He said to the woman, who was crying, "Where did that come from?" The woman said, "Someone gave it to the children." So, they took the boy and old man and carried them to prison, for no other reason than finding that flag in the cradle. I hardly ever see a United States flag that I don't think of that scene.[258]

    Infiltration was another guerrilla game. Woody Robertson of the 14th Tennessee (CSA) recalled his close call with a Yankee guerrilla. In the fall of 1863, his company rode out towards Humboldt, and during a skirmish Robertson's horse got loose. "I was walking along to keep up when a soldier offered to take me up behind him on his horse, which I accepted. We did not go very far" when one of Robertson's comrades, "an old soldier, asked me if I knew whom I had been riding behind."

    Robertson told him, "No."

    "I have no doubt," the old soldier declared, "that he is one of Jack Hays's guerrillas and bushwhackers, and if he could have got you to one side, he would have shot you. He's pretending to be one of us, but my opinion is that when we leave, he will slip out and stay back here." And he did.[259]

    After the battle of Shiloh, when "the whole of West Tennessee was overrun by the federals and when the loyal unionists of our own country were extremely troublesome," a Henderson County man named Jack Briggance resorted to the "cover of the woods and night to save his life," and gained a certain fame as a one-man partisan band. "Many were the federals that he captured," recalled a neighbor, "unaided and alone, and carried across to Middle Tennessee or other places where he could deliver them to the Confederate authorities.

> On one such tour, traveling until late in the night before he came to the federal camp, the weather being very warm and raining all night, Jack was very tired and sleepy; so much so that on his return with his prisoner he became so fatigued that he called at the house of a friend for a short rest. Telling the Yankee to lie down and rest, which the fellow seemed very

anxious to do; after a few minutes Jack dropped asleep. The Yankee immediately took the gun, tapped Jack on the shoulder and told him, "We will now return to camp." Jack dreaded this very much, but there was no chance but to accept. After marching back a couple of hours, the Yankee became very tired and proposed to stop in out of the rain and wait until daylight. Briggance of course assented. This time Jack went to sleep and the Yank was guard. Pretty soon, the Yank went to sleep and Briggance took the gun, woke him and told him they would now return towards the land of Dixie.[260]

❖ ❖ ❖ ❖

Nevertheless, the Yankee noose kept tightening. The 6th Illinois Cavalry, acting on intelligence from Unionist spies, scattered a portion of Faulkner's Kentucky Cavalry encamped near Dyersburg as they slept, ate and played at cards.[261] Faulkner's men fled into the woods, but Yankee patrols scouring West Tennessee[262] encountered the remnants of Faulkner's command at a ferry crossing and killed a great many as they tried to swim away.[263]

Returning to her farm in mid August, a Lauderdale County woman found Union soldiers pilfering, requisitioning horses and persuading slaves to join them. After a Yankee squad persuaded a local slave to guide them to Ripley, five slaves from the same neighborhood tried to run away, but three were caught: one while trying to make his way to Fort Pillow.[264]

"For miles around Grand Junction, Bolivar and LaGrange," wrote a Union soldier in October, 1862, "the country speaks of a progressing revolution.

> Fields are laid bare; fences used up for fuel, corn crops long since appropriated; cotton fields half picked; houses standing here and there surrounded by desolation without a board, picket, or scarcely a post left to mark where a garden had been. No horses, no mules, no cows, no hogs, no cabbage, potatoes, or apples, no chickens, no nothing that is edible or that can be useful. Our trains went thirteen miles today for forage."

In the Hickory Valley anti-Union feelings became so strong that couples refused to obtain marriage licenses under Yankee auspices, leaving it solely to their preachers to sanction their weddings.[265]

THE RAILROAD REGIMENT
THE 52ND INDIANA INFANTRY

The first Yankee regiment to formally reoccupy Fort Pillow was the 52nd Indiana Infantry, composed of Hoosier farm boys from the south of the state and commanded by a tetchy ex-Kentuckian named Edward H. Wolfe whose orders were to prevent guerrillas from sharpshooting at river traffic from the bluff.[266]

In the months leading up to the outbreak of war, the predominant sentiment among Southern Indianans had been pro-slavery. Wolfe's father Joel -- like Lincoln's, and like many another southern Indianan – was a Kentuckian who had migrated northward. But, perhaps unlike Lincoln's father, many had left the upper south not necessarily to protest the treatment of slaves but to escape their proximity and "corrupting influence," and the political impotence and low wages the planter system imposed on poor whites. A Rush County haberdasher, Edward's father Joel was apparently not an abolitionist but a staunch Unionist nonetheless who spoke out boldly on behalf of the Northern cause at the Union meetings and patriotic rallies that flared up throughout the state in the late 1850s.

He met considerable resistance from fellow Hoosiers for whom Union, abolition and the widely distrusted Yankee were inextricably linked. "It is probable," wrote a county historian, "that few portions of the north were more deeply agitated than Rush County."[267] "I prefer to go with the Southern [slave] drivers all the time to agoin' with the Blue-Bellied Yanks," one Hoosier declared. In the little village of Boggstown, a speaker asserted that he would not side with the Yankees, who would rather steal a slave "from a good comfortable home where he was well treated and taken care of, than to pay some poor white man good living wages to do their drudgery."[268] Though the Confederate attack on Fort

Sumter turned many such white Southern Indianans against the South, most did not sign up to fight for the abolition of slavery but to preserve the Union as it was. As the war dragged on, Southern Indianans "opposed to further prosecution of the war" would don butternut symbols on their coats and jackets, burn draft enrollment registers, chase off recruiters, even shoot a Union provost marshal to death.[269]

Joel Wolfe organized Rush County's first company of Union soldiers and would go on to become a brigadier general. The previous October, his son Edward had been commissioned a major, and by April, 1862 had been elected Colonel of the 52nd Indiana Infantry, a regiment composed primarily of his kith and kin. The 52nd spent much of the war on garrison duty, venturing forth from time to time to guard the Union's supply lines. In fact, his men so often found themselves stationed at trestles and switches or roosting on freight cars with their muskets across their knees that the 52nd became known over time as the "Railroad Regiment." Their banner featured an angry eagle on a purple field under the regimental motto, "Clear the tracks."

They were a rough bunch. Addison Sleeth of Shelby County, Indiana recalled how a Captain McCorkle had assured his parents that if their "Ad" joined the 52nd he could not hope for a better class of comrades. McCorkle's company "was noted for morality and religion," he told them; the Captain himself was a Sunday school teacher, and many of

his boys were solid, church-going Christians. Addison's mother replied that if her son had to serve in the army, it should be with such men as that, and the next evening, at a patriotic meeting at the Little Blue River Chapel in Shelby County, nineteen year-old "Ad" signed up.

The following Monday he rode off to Camp Rush and asked for McCorkle's regiment. A couple of pickets armed with rusty muskets told him to go to the third company in the camp. "As I passed the first company," Sleeth recalled, "I noticed they were rather a rough looking set, and the second was not much different. But on reaching the third, to my amazement, I saw two or three groups playing cards and heard several oaths. I stopped and took a look. Surely some mistake here, I thought." But it was McCorkle's company, sure enough, and as he entered the Captain's headquarters, he "found the boys playing cards, telling stories, singing songs; and before night I'd made up my mind" that though "this kind of morality and religion was not my Mother's kind," he had "best not tell her anything about it.[270]

In early September 1862, Beauregard urged Bragg to retake Fort Pillow with what he predicted would be "a very small loss" and "resume the command of the Mississippi River," thus forcing the Yankees to fall back on Columbus, beyond which Beauregard himself intended to drive them.[271]

To forestall such a catastrophe, Sherman ordered the 52nd to steam down the Mississippi from its temporary encampment at Columbus and occupy Fort Pillow.[272] At the time there were so many Union troops in circulation, bound for posts along the Mississippi, that for a giddy moment it appeared to the Confederates that the Yankees had decided to evacuate Memphis regiment by regiment, in which case the rebels might pick them off one by one, and thus "clear out West Tennessee." But it was not to be; indeed, Sherman was busy fortifying Fort Pickering and slowly amassing a vast force with the ultimate intention of cutting his way to the Atlantic.[273]

At the outbreak of the war, Memphis "had been the second most important cotton mart of the South," wrote the

New York Herald. "No less than twelve regular packet and mail lines, embracing over forty steamboats, brought trade to her mercantile and industrial classes, and travelers to her hotels. Her population comprised the individual enterprising element of the North to an extent that told advantageously on her prosperity" and seemed destined to become "the rival of St. Louis." But all that ended with the war. "Perhaps no Southern city felt to a more pernicious and blasting extent the destructive service of secession."

The destruction proved more aesthetic than economic. Memphis's grand mansions became barracks and hospitals, its lush gardens muddy stable yards and roistering encampments. Though thousands of its 35,000 residents had fled from Yankee occupation, the Union Army and its attendant speculators, escaped slaves, sutlers, and whores had swelled the city's population to more than 45,000. The Gayoso House, to which Nathan Bedford Forrest used to bring his wife for luncheon, became a house of dissipation, its halls cruised by soiled doves, its balustrades busted out by the brawling, drunken Union officers who crowded its hallways.

By the spring of 1862, Memphis had resumed its promiscuous bustle. Dealers in staples refused to honor Confederate scrip and demanded Federal greenbacks instead. Meat and vegetables were at a premium, and many businesses appeared to be "drained of all goods." Apparently the rebel torches had missed a lot of freight on Memphis's riverfront, for a group of professedly loyal citizens applied to the army to provide transport to Cairo for 4,000 bales of cotton, a large supply of sugar, and 1,000 barrels of molasses. As a cool spell set in, it amused Yankees to watch the locals bundle up with hats and overcoats in what Northerners regarded as shirtsleeve weather.

The once secessionist Memphis *Avalanche* immediately began publishing Northern press reports, but the *Argus* clung a little longer to its rebel line, on the premise that the Union sentiment could be found only among the illiterate lower classes. The Provost Marshall, Captain Gould, had set up his office in the Planter's Bank and raised the Union flag over its roof. The Yankees looked forward to a performance by the Campbell Minstrels, and to the opening of the telegraph and the post office. But the locals were in a state of furtive anticipation, agitated by rumors of Forrest's cavalry and Jeff Thompson's Fort Pillow contingent lurking in the area, and rebels massing at Hernando and Grenada, where many fleeing Memphians had sought Villepigue's protection. The citizens who remained in the city "fear the sudden entrance of these men," reported the crew of the *Desoto*, knowing that their "utmost desire" would be either to burn the city down themselves "or compel Commander Davis to shell it, to drive them out."[274]

On October 17, guerrillas would fire on three more boats from the Arkansas shore, two of them a little distance upriver from Fort Pillow, a third six miles below Memphis. "In both cases," raged Sherman, "I will send and punish those who harbor and encourage such attacks. To reach the rightful parties will be an impossibility," he wrote, but "we must do something, even if every farm and plantation on the river is destroyed."[275]

Nor did Sherman spare Memphians his wrath. Indignant, frustrated, he vowed to "expel every secession family from Memphis if this mode of warfare is to be continued, and will, moreover, land troops on unexpected points and devastate the country into the interior." He threatened to exile ten to twenty Memphis families for every attack on a Union vessel. Among the first citizens Sherman banished was the family of an outspoken secessionist named Elizabeth Meriwether, whose advanced state of pregnancy did not prevent Sherman's provost marshal from ordering her to get out of the city within 24 hours or face incarceration in Memphis's notorious Irving Block Prison. Asked if she could take quinine for her children in the event they came down with a fever, her Yankee guard refused, remarking that "it was none of his business if rebel children got sick." Departing just under the deadline, Mrs. Meriwether drove her mule into Mississippi, pausing at Columbus to give birth to her child.[276]

Some Memphians suspected that the families the Yankees selected for banishment were not secessionists, necessarily, but people whose property the army coveted.

"You must not be surprised to see me at any time," wrote another Memphis matron. "My house is needed for the negroes," who were becoming "*very* numerous and troublesome."[277] Stories of expectant mothers banished into the wilderness outraged Southerners, but in fact some of Memphis's most effective spies and smugglers were women. When Sherman commanded Tom Gailer's mother to take the "iron-clad oath," she politely refused, "saying that she would help any sick or wounded man, whether he wore the blue or the gray, and that it was an outrage to ask her to be so cruel." Impressed by her pluck, Sherman gallantly wrote out a pass, not knowing that even as she stood before him, Mrs. Gailor was carrying in her bodice a message for Forrest stating the strength of the Memphis garrison.[278]

"All in Memphis who are hostile to us should be compelled to leave," Sherman wrote Grant from Memphis, "for so long as they remain correspondence will go on; and in case of military movements they will manage to convey the information to their friends." On the other hand, Sherman recognized that "if all who are not our friends are expelled from Memphis but few will be left." Therefore he intended to do "nothing hastily; only if any persons manifest any active hostility I will deal with them summarily." According to the Southern press, Sherman arrested the Memphis correspondent of the Chicago *Tribune* for disloyalty, and the Charleston *Mercury* gleefully reported that troops from Indiana, Illinois and Ohio got into a fight over "the negro question," during which fifteen men were killed.[279]

Sherman wrote that he had "found so many Jews and speculators here trading in cotton, and secessionists had become so open in refusing anything but gold," that he was forced to put an end to the traffic. "This gold has but one use," he had concluded, "-- the purchase of arms and ammunition." He intended to respect any permit Grant himself might issue, but in the case of what he termed the "swarms of Jews" whom he said were trading in merchandise of every kind, he intended to put his foot down.[280]

Trade, of course, was hard to suppress along a river like the Mississippi. Sherman officially restricted trade to federal posts, but the definition of federal posts was quickly if unofficially extended to neighboring towns and landings. At Iuka, Mississippi, wrote a correspondent for the New York *Jewish Messenger,* there was "quite a lively trade going on, though many of the shopkeepers are northern speculators and sutlers."[281] In Fort Pillow's case, it included not only the moribund little town of Fulton two miles downriver but Osceola, Arkansas across the river, where a local man named Bevel received a permit to set up a dry goods and grocery business.[282]

THE CRONY
STEPHEN AUGUSTUS HURLBUT

On November 20, Sherman summoned his old buddy, Major General Stephen Augustus Hurlbut, to take command at Memphis.²⁸³ Perhaps no one could have calmed and purified the waters the city's occupiers, profiteers, smugglers and secessionists had roiled and poisoned. But Hurlbut's transfer to Memphis would prove one of the most dismal appointments of the war.

His rise from Illinois lawyer to Union Army general had owed everything to Hurlbut's prewar friendships with not only Sherman but Abraham Lincoln himself. Before debt and dissipation had done their worst, Hurlbut had been the tall, dark, beau ideal of the up-and-coming young Southern attorney. His father was a Philadelphia schoolmaster with New England roots who had moved south to run an academy for the sons of Charleston, South Carolina's upper crust. As a boy, Stephen had been subjected to an austere academic regimen by his father, who instilled a Yankee federalism and secularism that, combined with an enthusiasm for cards and ostentation, made of Stephen a Southern Whig and impatient opportunist. Young Stephen joined the bar and, apparently, every club that would have him. Trading on whatever he could make of his brief and uneventful service as a volunteer in the Seminole Wars, he officiated at his company's interminable reunions where, all a-dazzle in his medals and ribbons, he befriended William Tecumseh Sherman, then a young artillery officer stationed at Charleston with the regular army.

To deny Democrats the votes of newly naturalized citizens, Hurlbut became a nativist, and credited his machinations with the election of the short-lived William Henry Harrison and thus the succession of Harrison's Vice

President, John Tyler. Hurlbut's attempts to get himself elected were less successful, however. He proved as sore a loser in politics as he was proving in his crapulous rounds of whist, in which he had taken to cheating so recklessly that he was forced to flee Charleston to escape a fellow clubman he had defrauded.

The elder Hurlbut had not only owned several slaves but sold one to pay his debts, and Stephen had obligingly auctioned slaves for his clients. Nevertheless, upon moving to Illinois, Hurlbut had proclaimed his lifelong opposition to the peculiar institution. Starting from scratch in Belvidere, he soon joined a distinguished law practice and set his sites on the legislature. Though his speeches tilted over into "pettifoggery and demagoguery,"[284] at the age of thirty he still cut an impressive figure. He first got to know Lincoln while campaigning for Zachary Taylor in 1848. When Taylor was elected, Hurlbut pressed for a South American ambassadorship on the reasonable grounds that, if appointed, he would be the only American representative who could actually speak Spanish. But such foreign posts eluded the undiplomatic Hurlbut, and he had to content himself with his law practice in Belvidere.

Missing the brass and dash of his Seminole War reunions, he got himself elected captain of a local militia company known as the Boone Rifles, garbing them in crisp blue uniforms, drilling them as conspicuously as possible, and showing off his own uncanny skill with a long rifle. But his political ambitions were dashed again and again by his

Whig nemesis, Elihu Washburn, who would go on to champion the fledgling Republican Party in Illinois. In 1857, Hurlbut campaigned hard for John C. Fremont, only to see his man defeated by James Buchanan. As the storm over Stephen A. Douglas's Kansas-Nebraska bill brewed, Hurlbut sided with the Free Soilers who opposed the extension of slavery into America's new territories. He championed the senate campaign of Abraham Lincoln, and during his friend's famous debates with Douglas, swelled the ranks of Lincoln's supporters with his Boone County Rifles. Two years later, Hurlbut stumped everywhere on behalf of Lincoln's campaign for the presidency.

By then, however, years of clubbing and campaigning had loosened Hurlbut's jowls, dimmed his eyes, and thinned his hair. Nor had his looks been improved by the chronic erysipelas that blotched and pimpled his nose and cheeks. Experience had been at least as unkind to his character. A skilled debater and backroom politician, he was nevertheless blunt, scathingly sarcastic, spendthrift, and a bingeing dipsomaniac.

❖   ❖   ❖   ❖

On Sunday morning, March 24, 1861, Hurlbut had slipped into his native Charleston, South Carolina on a mission for the newly inaugurated President of America's ever more tenuously united states. In the wan hope that there might yet be a way to avert a civil war, Lincoln wanted Hurlbut to sound out South Carolinian sentiment, a job for which Hurlbut must have seemed the perfect choice.

In truth, however, Hurlbut had oversold Lincoln on his South Carolinian connections. After riding along the Charleston waterfront and furtively conferring with old acquaintances, Hurlbut had reportedly devoted the rest of his mission to evading roving gangs of secessionist vigilantes and hiding from his creditors. Deeming himself lucky to have escaped in one piece, he returned to Washington to report that South Carolinians no longer felt any attachment to the Union; that their "separate nationality" was now "a fixed fact."

No less inevitable than the Civil War that ensued was Hurlbut's commission as a brigadier general of Illinois volunteers. But his appointment caused a hue and cry in northern Illinois, where he was notorious for his drunkenness. Perhaps to quiet his own doubts about his military ability, Hurlbut met his critics' expectations by drinking himself into a stupor. Reeling and reeking, he loaded his regiment aboard a train bound for the Mississippi River town of Quincy, Illinois, and along the way so disgraced himself in Chicago with another of his binges that word of it reached Lincoln.

In the wake of the ensuing scandal, a chastened Hurlbut tried to sober up and buckle down. But after his half-brother William was arrested as a Confederate spy, Hurlbut tried to gain a little fraternal distance by coming down brutally on secessionists, threatening civilians with execution should they try in any way to interfere with his planned invasion of northeastern Missouri. Outmaneuvered by the Confederate partisan ranger, Martin E. Green, Hurlbut blamed the subsequent failure of his campaign on the citizens of Hannibal and Palmyra, from whom he demanded thousands of dollars in tribute. On his retreat to Macon, Missouri, he drank himself insensible. Though his commander, General Pope, removed him from command for drunkenness, he did not dare bring formal charges against the President's crony. Nonetheless, according to the New York *Times*, Hurlbut had "done little or nothing except to tarnish as a soldier the brilliant reputation which he gained as a lawyer."[285]

In December 1861, Lincoln recalled Hurlbut to service, and Major General "Old Brains" Henry W. Halleck ordered him to St. Louis to drill new recruits. In this capacity Hurlbut apparently remained sober enough to elicit a commendation from his old friend Sherman, now a fellow Brigadier. In February 1862, Halleck ordered Hurlbut down the freezing brash and floes of the Mississippi and up the Cumberland to Fort Donelson, now in the possession of Union forces under a newly promoted Major General Ulysses S. Grant. Himself the object of rumors of drunkenness, Grant apparently ignored warnings of Hurlbut's inebriation and put him in command of the Fourth Division of the Army of the Tennessee.

Reunited with his old friend Sherman, Hurlbut sailed his division down the Tennessee River to take part in Grant's assault on Corinth, Mississippi. Buoyed by Sherman's company and heartened by this second chance to prove himself, Hurlbut tried to instigate a skirmish with the enemy at Shiloh Church, and bristled when Sherman pulled him back. His blood was still up on the dawn of April 6, 1862, when he valiantly led his men in a sortie to rescue General Benjamin Prentiss, saving what remained of Prentiss's command and holding his ground against repeated rebel assaults. It was as if Hurlbut had become possessed by some latent martial spirit, riding among his most exposed ranks to comfort and cajole his men, retiring in good order, and defending a ridge against more bloody assaults. The next day, while beating the stubborn Confederates back into their bastion, he had a horse shot out from under him and received a bullet wound to his arm. For these pains and services Grant recommended Hurlbut for promotion, and in September 1862, the Senate made him a major general.

The next month found Hurlbut a few miles downstream from Corinth, very nearly succeeding in surrounding a large rebel force under Earl Van Dorn until the battered Confederates broke through the Union lines and disappeared into the Mississippi countryside. Though he was criticized for not pursuing his foe, this engagement would have done him more credit had Hurlbut not celebrated his semi victory by getting drunk again and staggering out onto the battlefield, where, picking a fight with a teamster, he acquired a split lip and two black eyes. An embarrassed Grant relegated him to an administrative post in which Hurlbut salved his wounded pride with campaign-like tours of the Illinois regiments that had been posted in Tennessee. The tour must have gotten his political juices flowing, for Hurlbut asked Grant's permission to return to Illinois and run for office. But Grant refused, and at Sherman's urging, assigned him instead to command the District of Memphis.

Hurlbut set up his headquarters in General Gideon Pillow's abandoned suite at the Gayoso. Assisted by a staff of Illinois cronies, Hurlbut was supposed to keep order among a citizenry that was still predominantly secessionist, begin the process of reconstruction, protect the refugee slaves now massing behind his lines, pursue the Confederate cavalry that rampaged beyond the outskirts of the city, and abolish the black market in cotton that had bedeviled Sherman and Grant since 1861.

Secessionist planters and brokers furtively and profitably traded their cotton with Northern merchants for guns, rations, blankets, saddles and harness that made their way to the Confederate Army. It had been in hopes of putting an end to such trade that Grant had issued his infamous "Jew Order," refusing travel permits to any of Memphis's thousand Jewish civilians. Notwithstanding the condemnations heaped on Grant for his anti-Semitism, Hurlbut also portrayed the market as a Jewish conspiracy and set about arresting and harassing some of the Jewish community's leading citizens.

But what halfhearted measures Hurlbut took were unavailing, and he retreated into another alcoholic haze. He tried once again to redeem himself by declaring yet another campaign to stop the traffic in cotton, but ran up against one of Grant's less worthy pals, the merchant Joseph Russell Jones, who was making a fortune in the trade. Resigned to the cotton trade's nefarious persistence, Hurlbut decided personally to profit from it, delegating his staff to collect payments from black marketeers in exchange for his protection. According to Colonel W.S. Hillier, the rather compromised Provost Marshall of the Department of the Tennessee, at one point Hurlbut requisitioned $5,825.50 for "secret service" or purposes "unstated," over three thousand of it in coins.[286]

At first Hurlbut did what he could to meet the feints and sorties of such rebel cavalrymen as Van Dorn and Forrest. Following Grant and Sherman's design, he sent his 16th Corps down into Mississippi to tear up Confederate railway lines. But when his superiors took justifiable credit for the success of this expedition, Hurlbut returned to Memphis to campaign against prostitution: an enterprise so pervasive that his own Adjutant General, a former reporter for the Memphis *Bulletin*, was bold enough to reel up to Hurlbut's wife at the Gayoso Hotel and introduce a whore from Chicago as his wife.

The rebel hectoring took its toll on Hurlbut's besotted nerves, and after he refused to reduce his force at Memphis for fear of a rebel cavalry raid, Sherman had to drag him and his men into battle at Vicksburg, where, under Sherman's watchful eye, Hurlbut managed not to disgrace himself. But no sooner had he returned to Memphis than he resumed his rounds of drinking, extortion and graft. His corrupt subordinates collected ransom from wealthy families whose homes they ransacked and whose sons they imprisoned in the verminous dungeons of Fort Pickering. After the Union victory at Chattanooga, Hurlbut would pull up his socks long enough to escort Sherman around Memphis in lavish style. But by then Lincoln, Grant and Sherman had given up on reforming their old friend. Hurlbut, wrote Sherman, was "too easily stampeded by rumors."

ACTING NEUTRAL
THE LOYALTY OATH

Though its builders had intended Fort Pillow to accommodate 10,000 men and scores of cannon, and Villepigue had held out against the Yankees with perhaps 2,000 able rebels, Colonel Edward Wolfe reached its abandoned works with only one field piece, 610 Hoosier foot soldiers, and 381 troopers from the 2nd Illinois Cavalry.[287] Nevertheless, Wolfe's men were under orders to occupy the fortified bluff, pacify the neighborhood, chase down guerrillas, burn cotton, requisition supplies, and prevent the rebels from attacking the post from the east.

It fell to Union gunboats, however, and not Wolfe's 52nd Indianans, to keep the river safe for Yankee traffic. Thirteen miles downriver, rebel guerrillas – possibly a body of Faulkner's men from the Loosahatchie Bar – had recently fired on a Union packet from the abandoned works at Randolph,[288] whereupon an outraged Sherman ordered a gunboat to accompany the packet back up the river from Memphis. The packet was to act as a kind of decoy as the gunboat lumbered along well behind, ready to pounce should the guerrillas open fire again.

Aboard the gunboat was a detachment from the 46th Ohio Infantry, with orders from Sherman to destroy Randolph, leaving only one house to mark the place. "Let the people know and feel that we deeply deplore the necessity of such destruction," he instructed, "but let the place feel that all such acts of cowardly firing upon boats filled with women and children and merchandise must be severely punished."[289] Though the guerrillas did not attack the packet and the town appeared abandoned, by the time the Ohioans departed, all that was left of Randolph were ghostly rows of blackened chimneys rising like cemetery headstones above smoldering heaps of cinders.

Faulkner's subsequent attack on the steamer *Forest Queen* had convinced Davis, if he needed further convincing, that if the Mississippi were to be kept open to Union traffic, his gunboats would have to keep a constant lookout for guerrillas. On September 27, he sent the *Cairo* up to keep a vigil just below Fort Pillow and the *Cincinnati* to patrol between Fort Pillow and Randolph with instructions to exercise "discernment and discretion" in promoting legal trade, "and, secondly, preventing all illicit traffic."[290] Arriving aboard the steamer *Emena*, Wolfe was greeted by a third gunboat, the *New Era*,[291] the same vessel which, less than two years later, would be raked with fire from Forrest's sharpshooters as she tried, if only up to a point, to save the Yankee garrison.[292]

Almost as soon as he reached Fort Pillow, Wolfe came down with what his surgeon called a spinal infection, compounded, perhaps, by his grief over the death of his father at Richmond the previous August. So command fell temporarily to Major William T. Strickland.[293] The regiment's spirits were apparently low, for seven of Wolfe's officers, including even the regiment's chaplain, had gone absent without leave. If only to shore up morale, Strickland began to send squads of cavalry and infantry off into the interior to exchange potshots with Faulkner and Haywood, visit nearby farms, and command leading citizens to take the loyalty oath even as they hauled away their slaves, mules, wagons and supplies.[294]

The oath evolved eventually into this version, which Andrew Johnson circulated in March, 182 as Military Governor of Tennessee.[295]

I solemnly swear, that I will henceforth support the Constitution of the United States, and against the assaults of all its enemies defend it, that I will hereafter be and conduct myself as a true and faithful citizen of the United States freely and voluntarily claiming to be subject to all the duties and obligations, and entitled to all the rights and privileges of such citizenship; that I ardently desire the suppression of the present insurrection and rebellion against the Government of the United States, the success of its armies, and the defeat of all those who oppose them, and that the Constitution of the United States, and all laws and proclamations, made in pursuance thereof, may be speedily and permanently established and enforced over all the people, States, and Territories thereof; and further, that I will hereafter heartily aid and assist all loyal people in the accomplishment of these results. So help me God."[296]

Some took the oath as a safeguard against Yankee pillaging, though often the Yankees themselves would not honor it.[297] Most people "just *acted* neutral."[298] Union patrols often found signed loyalty oaths tucked into guerrillas' clothing.[299] Some took the oath under assumed names, for fear word would get back to their secessionist neighbors that they had broken faith with the Confederacy.[300] Nor was the oath freely administered. In April, 1863, General Asboth asked the Assistant Adjutant General's advice on whether two rebel prisoners who had recently had their legs amputated should be allowed to take the oath and go home.³⁰¹ When the provost marshal at Fulton required a Tipton County merchant named Petty to take the loyalty oath, he declined. "He says he is loyal because he cannot be otherwise, having lost his leg at Shiloh while in the rebel army" and now "wanted to be free, so that when he chose he could put down his stump leg."³⁰²

"What few [men] there are," wrote Surgeon Henry Eels of the 12th Michigan Infantry, "and the women that are left at home with any property, crowd the General's quarters at every stopping place to take the oath of allegiance, and get protection. They take the oath," continued Eels, "but as for protection, if there is anything on their farms our men want from chickens to beef cattle and forage it is taken."³⁰³ After a local rebel sympathizer emerged from the office of Colonel "Peg Leg" Moore at Union City, his friends asked if he had taken the Oath of Allegiance. "Yes," he replied, "but I have come out to vomit it up."³⁰⁴

❖   ❖   ❖   ❖

The Second Illinois Cavalry did its best to catch Faulkner and his men, but he was slippery. His main order of business was burning cotton bales to prevent their falling into Yankee hands, which should have smoke-signaled his presence to the Union squads that roamed the countryside. But he never lingered over his conflagrations. At one point the Yankees got a tip that Faulkner was at Covington burning cotton, but when they thundered into the town all they found was a heap of bales smoldering in the square.[305]

So the Second split up into two squads, hoping to catch Faulkner in a pincer movement. But they never found him, and perhaps out of frustration or, more likely, simple greed, at least one party of cavalry took the opportunity to behave "more like brigands than soldiers." They were certainly ingrates. After an elderly black ferryman transported them for free, they robbed him of almost $20. About ten miles from Fort Pillow, eight of them robbed an elderly widow of $13 in silver. After an old man who claimed to be loyal served them dinner, charging them nothing, they took his coat and bridle. They proved especially enthusiastic horse rustlers. Paid forty cents per day for the "use and risk" of their mounts, they rounded up steeds from nearby farms and refused to turn them over to the quartermaster. "Some of them changed saddles, turned in their own horses," and rode off on "fine animals that had been confiscated," claiming them as their own.

Some troopers took rebel resistance personally. On one of its forays out of Fort Pillow, a squad from the 2nd Illinois Cavalry encountered an invalided rebel trooper from Stonewall Jackson's command who, pistol in hand, tried in vain to escape. After the rebel was captured, a German private stalked up to him in a rage. "Point your pistol at *me*, damn you?!" he sputtered, and shot the captive rebel in the thigh. As he fell to the ground, a Yankee captain rode up and remarked that he should have shot him in the head, but for this they were both reprimanded by an Illinois colonel who had come along for the ride.[306]

As the 2nd Illinois Cavalry galloped hither and yon, the 52nd Indiana ventured forth by gunboat, disembarking at various points along the river. "Once we went up the river 50 or 60 miles," recalled Sleeth, "where a steamboat had struck a snag and sank.

> Rumor said the Rebs were taking off the cargo and hauling it out in the country. We reached the place late in the evening and landed. In our search we found among other things about twenty barrels of

whiskey and it was but the work of a few minutes to tap a barrel or two, and it was not long till two hundred and ninety of the three hundred boys were tight and singing, yelling and capering about, making things lively. A guard was placed over the whiskey, and we were ordered to load the goods we had found on the boat.

Sleeth and his comrades worked in teams of three or four, rolling the whiskey barrels the hundred yards toward the boat, when "all of a sudden" first one and then another of the barrels "leaves the road, goes tumbling out to one side into the bushes, landing on one end" with the other end soon caved in. As the Hoosiers filled their "canteens, coffee pots, tin cups and themselves," they whooped and yelled, drinking "to the success of the Nation," until "at last, late in the night, both men and whiskey was aboard," and they steamed back to the fort.

It was becoming obvious to most Union officers that infantry were not much use against mounted guerrillas. So Strickland sent the 52nd out to the neighboring farms to collect horses, mules, bridles and saddles for themselves.[307] One night two black men stole a mare from an ambivalent local farmer named Carter Whitson and took it to Fort Pillow, where Captain Ross Griffin of the 52nd Indiana laid claim to it. Whitson would later state that though he had "wanted the Union to stick together, his sympathy was for the men in the south engaged in war." Because he did not take the oath of allegiance until after his mare was taken, he was never paid.[308] Hiram Partee, the wealthy owner of four large farms who, according to his slave, Philip Mays, "was in favor of the Confeds, as he lent hands to help them build Ft. Pillow & Island No. 10" and had "one son in the Confederate Army," lost two yokes of oxen, a horse and four mules to the 52nd's roundup.[309]

Perhaps it was Partee's "large black mule" and "good bridle and fair saddle" that Addison Sleeth selected for himself in hopes of joining on a scout. But on the eve of the expedition's departure, he came down with a fever and had to turn his mule over to another man. Composed of thirty mounted men and forty-five infantry, the expedition returned a day and a half later with "much to tell." After the small force had camped for the night at Durhamville, some twenty-six miles southeast of Fort Pillow, perhaps a hundred rebels and guerrillas surrounded them at daybreak and opened fire.[310] Cut off by the rebels, two pickets from the 52nd tried to get back to camp, riding their horses side-by-side. The rebels opened a murderous fire as they rode past, killing the nearest boy and sending his horse tumbling to the ground with "between one and two hundred balls and buckshot" in its hide, while the other horse and rider returned unscathed. "The rebels charged them from all sides," Sleeth was told, "but our boys deployed, sheltering themselves as best they could behind trees stumps or whatever would stop a ball," and giving the rebels "a warm reception."

> The fight lasted till two or three P.M. when the rebels retired. George Stewart of our company said a rebel shot a slug of lead or iron at him that struck the ground by his side and plowed out a trench as big as a sheep trough. K. E. Derrickson had been fired at several times by a reb from behind a tree about fifty yards away and told one of the boys he was going to get that reb. He crawled off to our side while the reb was loading and the next time the reb fired, Derrickson put a ball through him, went and got his horse and gun, and took the spur off of his foot and rejoined his company.

After they returned to Fort Pillow, bragging ever more expansively of their victory over Faulkner's men, Major Strickland decided to mount Companies E and G of the 52nd Indiana Infantry which, combined with the 2nd Illinois Cavalry, would add up to "quite a mounted force for scouting purposes."[311] Not to mention foraging purposes, which the 52nd pursued with such enthusiasm that it was said that "they cost the Government nothing for subsistence, as they take horses, cattle, corn and cotton enough to pay all expenses."[312] Sleeth recalled one expedition in which he and his comrades rustled thirty head of cattle from an Arkansas farmer and tried to load them onto their boat. But the frightened animals broke through the railings and all drowned, "some of them swimming two or three miles without finding a place to land," so Sleeth and his pals had to content themselves with the rebel hogs they had stolen and butchered that day.[313]

This episode may have been the cause of a special order Strickland issued directing all foraging parties to obtain permits from the post command. But it is hard to know which orders were issued for the record, and which were to be obeyed, for the foraging continued at least into the early months of 1863. The 12th Michigan Infantry stationed in Hardeman County were also under strict orders not to loot, but as Henry Eels observed, "Our soldiers don't make very good guards." Eels knew Union troops "who couldn't see a Union soldier picking peaches in the orchard they were set to guard, and others who were kind enough to point out the best trees and then turn their back. The soldiers all go for fruiting the enemy as much as possible." Eels reported that his comrades "generally are not much troubled with scruples about stealing from anybody," but they never called it stealing. "A soldier never *steals*. Oh! No, certainly not. But sometimes he is suddenly taken with *cramps* in the fingers, so that he can't let go of anything that is in his hands."[314]

People in the North could "hardly form an idea of the extent of these depredations about here. The people are really afraid they will suffer this winter for the want of necessities." West Tennesseeans complained "a good deal of the soldiers foraging on them," Eels wrote, "but unless they can point out who did it in a particular case it is of no use, and, if they make much of a fuss, and get the ill-will of the men, it is bad for them. Their houses and barns are apt to take fire, or some other loss will be sure to happen to them."[315] In Iuka, Mississippi, an old lady chased a squad of Ohio soldiers from her well, telling them that creek water was good enough for them. She awoke the next morning to find that her "peaches, roasting ears, melons &c., were rather scarce..."[316]

"Every farmer in the South is doing his best to raise a large amount of corn & wheat," wrote an Ohio soldier from Elk River, Tennessee.

> Thousands of bushels of fine grain have been tramped in the ground, fed to the mules, and otherwise destroyed by us on this march and not a likely steer, calf, hog, goose, hen, or anything else in the eating line can be found in within 3 miles of one of our stopping places after we have left.

"Our boys sweep the country clean of everything," he boasted, "both Reb and grub." Nor were whites their only victims. Sometimes they would come at a free black's grocery "and present our case," the Ohioan continued. "They sometimes object, but the sight of our shineing beyonets argue the case. In fact, a bold face and a revolver at the side always wins the grub.[317]

Some damage the Yankees did was unavoidable. The camps of even the most benign Yankee commands wreaked havoc wherever they camped. It was common to see a large force occupy a hundred acres of land, crowding it with "troops, trains and animals, cavalry, artillery and infantry." As soon as the soldiers pitched their tents, they gathered all the fence rails within reach for their fires until "not a rail was left." Though the Yankees did not endear themselves to the farmers upon whose land they camped, many of the locals who saw them spread out over vast open ground came away convinced that the South could never defeat such a horde.[318]

Elsewhere in West Tennessee, Union commanders came down hard on looters. In nearby Brownsville, for instance, members of the 3rd Michigan Cavalry were compelled to pay $1300 to a merchant whose store they had pillaged. In fact, in late February, Colonel John Scott of the 32nd Iowa would order one of his officers to steam from Fort Pillow all the way up to St. Louis to return $280 to an Arkansan whose farm his men had raided.[319] But it was apparently not until May that any Indianans at Fort Pillow – all of them sergeants and privates – were prosecuted for "molesting the private property of a citizen without any authority."[320]

Mounted or on foot, neither the 2nd Illinois nor the 52nd Indiana could keep Lauderdale County safe for Yankees. On November 18, Dawson and his guerrillas routed a contingent of 4th Illinois Cavalry that had strayed into the area from its camp in Jackson. Suffering no casualties himself, he captured two Yankees, including their captain, and wounded eight more Union troopers before melting back into the woods. A week later, Dawson had less luck with 80 troopers from the 7th Illinois Cavalry based in Macon, Tennessee. Chased for several miles through Dyer County, Dawson's men entrenched themselves behind the banks of a dry slough, firing "very spirited but wild" shots at the better trained Yankees. When the Illinois troopers turned their left flank, the rebels "fled in confusion, throwing away arms, blankets, and everything," and abandoning 39 men, including two captains, to the Yankees.[321]

The 7th declared this a great victory, but as Major Strickland was well aware, it would hardly make a dent in Dawson's recruitment campaign. Even the capture of some 300 Dyer County rebel conscripts did not lift Strickland's spirits.[322] Bands that seemed to retreat from the Yankees in disarray would re-emerge the next day in the woods and bottoms of Lauderdale, Dyer and Obion Counties.

Strickland often indulged in almost comical overkill as he hunted down small partisan bands. Sleeth recalled accompanying 100 of his comrades on an attack on a church a little distance east of the charred chimneys of Randolph.[323] "We had gone about a hundred yds. when we came in sight of a church building and got the order. *Fire.* A hundred enfield rifles broke the twilight stillness," he wrote. "Fifty ounces of lead went whizzing through the walls of the church" and as many more where "the dim light of the campfires was seen. Then the order *Charge* sent us on the run to the church," where to their disgust they found only "six or eight rebels and about a basketfull of provisions with about enough powder and lead to kill a mess of squirrels with." Collecting the "little munitions of war" and setting the church ablaze, they brought their prisoners back to Fort Pillow."[324]

For the time being, Strickland begged off chasing after larger game, "for if I take a sufficient force to attack the main force, I leave the fort at the mercy of small bodies that are prowling around the neighborhood." He would move against them only if he could muster a cavalry force of 400.[325] Strickland's caution met with the approval of Hurlbut, who, pleading a lack of cavalry, had himself refused to pursue the renegade rebel Bob Richardson.[326] Other Union commanders were less trepidatious. Though a large body of paroled rebels from the Vicksburg campaign were "playing the devil" around the abandoned rebel post at Columbus, Kentucky, the volatile Union General Jefferson C. Davis mounted his infantry "to hunt these fiends" and with the assistance of both Unionists and secessionists succeeded in capturing and executing several guerrillas and keeping the number of murders in the area down to a manageable "half doz."[327]

❖   ❖   ❖   ❖

Strickland was probably wise to sit still, for among the rebels taking aim at West Tennessee that fall was none other than the Wizard of the Saddle himself, Nathan Bedford Forrest.[328] For weeks Yankee commandants had wired each other in growing panic: "Look out for Forrest." "Watch for Forrest." "Forrest preparing a raid into central Kentucky."

Their panic was understandable. Forrest was just about the boldest, canniest, and most tenacious cavalry commander in either army. Ordered by Braxton Bragg to cross the Tennessee and destroy the railway linking Grant at Columbus to his forces in northern Mississippi, Forrest had protested that his men were mostly green recruits, poorly armed and meagerly supplied. Which only makes Forrest's first West Tennessee raid -- one of the most spectacular Confederate successes of the entire war – all the more remarkable.

With a battalion numbering some 2500 men, he left Columbia on December 11, crossed the Tennessee, defeated a detachment of Union cavalry at Lexington, and then, as Bragg had instructed, began to chew up and spit out the railroad between Humboldt and Jackson. Following the rails up into Kentucky, his men gleefully burned and toppled railroad trestles. In mid December, a day after the local Yankee commandant had imposed martial law, Forrest thundered into Trenton and thundered out again, shooting up the Union camp and adding its livestock to his ever expanding herd of purloined hogs, horses and mules.[329]

As his future subordinate James Ronald Chalmers summed it up:

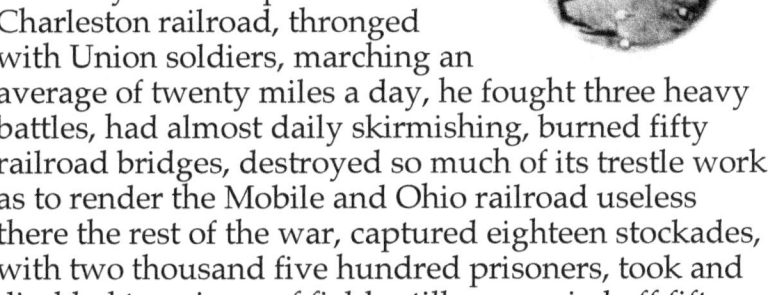

> In two weeks' time, with about three thousand raw and almost unarmed cavalry, in a small district of country, surrounded on three sides by the Tennessee and Mississippi rivers, and on the fourth by the Memphis and Charleston railroad, thronged with Union soldiers, marching an average of twenty miles a day, he fought three heavy battles, had almost daily skirmishing, burned fifty railroad bridges, destroyed so much of its trestle work as to render the Mobile and Ohio railroad useless there the rest of the war, captured eighteen stockades, with two thousand five hundred prisoners, took and disabled ten pieces of field artillery, carried off fifty

wagons and ambulances, with their teams, captured ten thousand stands of arms and one million rounds of ammunition, and then crossing the Tennessee river, seven hundred yards wide, in a few skiffs and one ferryboat, navigated by poles, his horses swimming, while an enemy ten thousand strong was attempting to cut off his retreat, he returned to his camp on the 1st of January, 1863, with a command stronger in numbers than when he started, thoroughly equipped with blankets and oil cloths, their shot guns replaced with Enfield rifles, and with a surplus of five hundred rifles and eighteen hundred blankets and knapsacks.[330]

Chalmers exaggerates. Forrest and his staff tended to keep a kind of exponential count of their victims and their spoils, omitting their failures. This was not just a matter of vanity, but part of his strategy of representing himself and his forces as more formidable than they were, the better to bluff his foe. Forrest had been unable to take Jackson, Tennessee, for instance, and had suffered a defeat at Parker Crossroads that cost him most of his loot. He did indeed recruit an enormous number of farm boys, but he had lost 500 men in battle, and many of his new conscripts -- some of them paroled infantry, others boys from Unionist families -- deserted as soon as they could, and worked their way home, only to fall into Yankee custody, pleading that "they were forced &c." ("What shall I do with such cases?" an officer asked Hurlbut. "They are mostly poor devils that are of no account to any body & say they have Families to support."[331])

The most significant unintended consequence of Forrest's destruction of the line to Columbus was that it forced Grant to move his headquarters southward to what turned out to be a far more advantageous position in Memphis. Nevertheless, Forrest's raid was so audacious and so shocking that as he galloped off it seemed almost biblical that nature should mark its close by convulsing West Tennessee in a terrifying earthquake, toppling trees and imbuing the sky over the Lower Mississippi with a strange, smoky haze.[332]

THE ABOLITION REGIMENT
THE 32ND IOWA INFANTRY

Living under fewer restrictions than its rebel predecessor, the Yankee garrison at Fort Pillow took full advantage of the neighborhood's extraordinarily rich supply of fish and game. Sleeth described hunting expeditions in which they shot wild turkey, groundhogs and woodchucks, and encountered, among other mysteries of the forest, a coil of snakes "as large as a washtub." Two or three miles from the fort they shot at the shy ducks that hid along the overgrown shore of Clearwater Lake, a creation of the great earthquake of 1811. "I had gone out on a log that ran out ten or twelve feet over the water," wrote Sleeth, "and was trying to get a shot with my revolver," when he happened to look down "and right under me was a large fish that certainly would have weighed sixty or eighty lbs." But just as Sleeth took aim, the great fish swam away, "leaving a wave for fully a hundred yards."[333]

Sleeth's Company G would have ample time to fish after it was assigned to Fulton to keep watch on the traders who pulled up at the landing to buy and sell whatever goods and produce happened to be available. At Fulton landing they rigged up a trotline and caught fish varying in size from ten to 120 pounds, "and we got a great many for the number of hooks we had." Company G, wrote Sleeth, "had a fine time: good houses to stay in, plenty to eat, and not much duty;" in fact, they would soon be accused of neglecting their duty or, worse, colluding with smugglers in exchange for bribes.

A treasury agent was stationed at Fort Pillow to purchase the bales of cotton brought in by local farmers and escaped slaves. "He has a permit from the provost marshal to buy," wrote a visitor, "but has to take a bill of sale of the men from whom he buys, and buys only from those who have taken the oath of allegiance" in which most Yankee officers put so little faith.[334] In fact it seemed to some locals that the Yankees' most mercenary officers judged a citizen's loyalty by the size of the bribes he offered, or his property's value to the Union cause.

Sleeth observed how mysterious little packets of cash – hush money, some of it, the rest shares of the graft their officers garnered – made its way into men's pockets. "We had been sent up to see if we could find any goods that had been taken from a boat that had been captured and burned some time before," Sleeth recalled of a trip to Craighead Point. "We found two or three boxes of shoes, a lot of ribbons and other goods, and confisicated seven guns. It was getting along in the afternoon, so we put the stuff we had found in the boat" and started back for Fort Pillow. But two or three nights later a buddy of his named Derrickson came to him "and handed me two dollars and said, 'Say nothing.'"

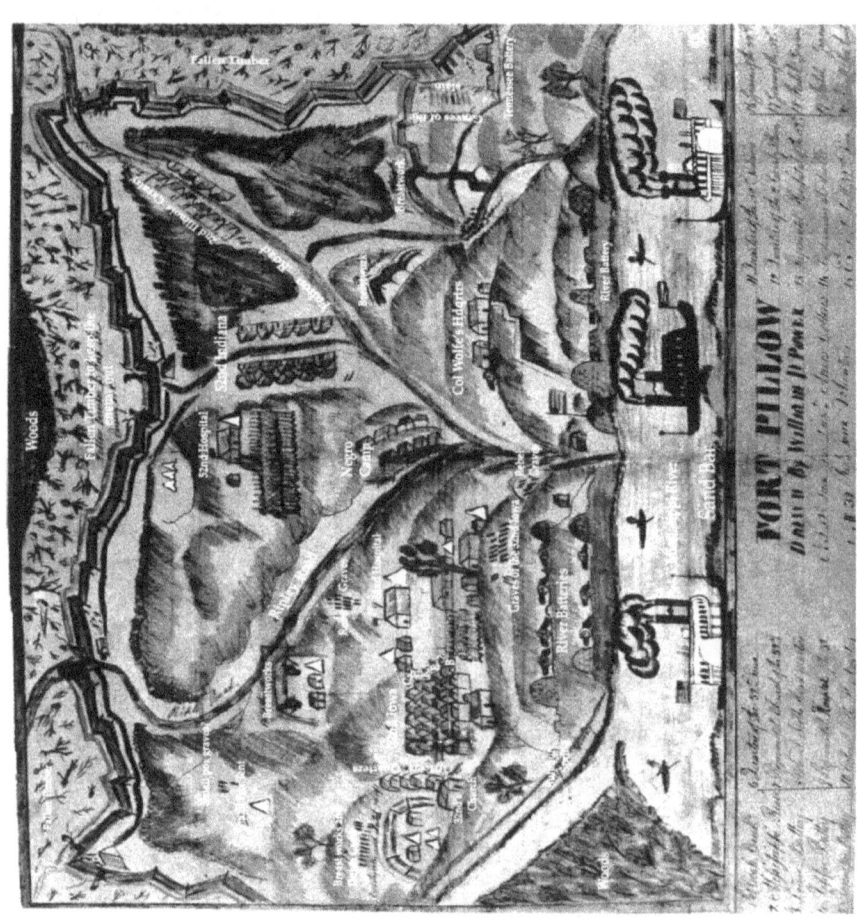

But next morning I asked him what that two dollars was for, and where it came from. He said, 'You remember that trip up the river? Now say no more about it.' And I never knew what went with the goods we found, nor who sent the two dollars, nor how much the other boys got, if any.

But "one thing I *do* know," concluded Sleeth, "somebody sent me that two dollars by Derrickson" who didn't "care to offer it to me direct."[335]

In December, a lieutenant from the 52nd was accused of falsely condemning a shipment of salt pork as unfit for human consumption and then apparently selling it to local smugglers.[336] "A great many Cotton buyers were scatered all along the lines of the Armey," recalled John Ryan of the 2nd Iliinois Cavalry, "and a goodly share of them were at fort Pillow.

> I noticed when ever we went out on a Scout we would meet a greate many wagons coming in to the fort loaded with cotton. I do not know if any post of the Union Army was used to protect those speculators, but circumstantial evidence was strong to that effect.[337]

In any case, trade was brisk, and the beneficiaries too numerous, and furtive, to count.[338] A correspondent for the *Jewish Messenger* deplored the "official huckstering" of the Yankee authorities that he had witnessed along the Mississippi, and "the vast cotton operations which have disgraced our management of the conquered territory, and enriched a class of speculators generally of doubtful loyalty. There are many means of gathering money," he concluded, "which are unknown or unenjoyed in the land of peace at home."[339]

Hurlbut, however, would claim to have known of only two Union officers who profited from cotton speculation. One of them, Colonel C.C. Marx of the 20th Illinois Infantry, apparently garnered $1500 selling cotton belonging to a loyal man named Strauss. Hurlbut arrested his accomplice and quartermaster and made them return the money, but he claimed he could not discipline Colonel Marx because he was no longer under Hurlbut's command. Hurlbut said that originally provost marshals, not commandants, had issued permits to cotton traders along the river. To most questions about profiteering on behalf of Union officers, Hurlbut either pleaded ignorance, implicated his former political foes in Illinois in the traffic in forged and otherwise illegitimate licenses, or refused to repeat the rumors he had heard, especially when the provost marshal he had recently replaced had kept absolutely no record of the hundreds of thousands of dollars that had passed through his hands.[340]

As the cold set in, Company G was sent back to help prepare Fort Pillow for the winter. Reluctantly concluding that his Hoosiers would not be transferred any time soon, Strickland began to construct a permanent post, and sent his men upriver to the deserted town of Osceola to find building materials.

He may have been inspired rather than discouraged by the remains of the rebel encampment, for they still bore evidence that the Confederates and their slaves had built their facilities with considerable care and expertise; here and there among the wreckage he could still make out the vestiges of stables, bakeries, and a blacksmith shop.[341] So his men crossed the Mississippi, more or less dismantled the entire town of Osceola, and piled it onto a steamboat: walls, beams, rafters, roofs, windows, furniture, and all. "As the town was deserted," Sleeth explained with a wink, "nobody objected to us moving it."[342]

Out of these purloined materials, the Hoosiers constructed a substantial military post. Each company's officers were provided with a "very comfortable" cabin, with four or five more for their men, laid out on either side of a little *cul de sac* that led eastward off the road to Fulton.[343] Near the two mounted companies' barracks, stables were constructed to keep their ever expanding herd of requisitioned horses out of the wind. Atop the central bluff, perhaps half a mile from his men's barracks, they built Wolfe a 16-by-22-foot headquarters and two more cabins for his staff, one of which – Provost Marshal J.H. Parker's headquarters – included a meeting room, an office, and a bedroom.[344] The 2nd Illinois Cavalry built barracks and stables southeast of the 52nd, on either side of the Fulton Road, just before it exited through the half-mile abatis of fallen timber.

In early November 1862, the gunboat *Louisville* was stationed at Fort Pillow with instructions "to break up the practice of smuggling along the river, whereby goods are carried into the rebel Confederacy," and to capture and send to Cairo "all vessels touching at points not occupied by United States forces, unless said vessels can show good cause for what they do." In a typically ambiguous incident, the *Louisville* had already encountered a Memphis steamer called the *Evansville* steaming twelve miles beyond its permitted range with a barrel of contraband salt in its hold, an "unusually large supply of wood on her guards," and a suspect body of horsemen following her along the bank. Lieutenant-Commander Richard W. Meade sent the *Evansville* to Cairo on suspicion of "engaging in some kind of illicit traffic."[345]

Though the Union might at least hope to keep rebel trading boats from operating freely along the Mississippi, its tributaries were another matter. In full flood, they afforded flatboats and skiffs a maze of swamped woods and bayous to shelter them on their rounds; and in the dry season, they were too shallow for Union gunboats to navigate safely. Thus the Hatchie, the Forked Deer and the Obion became the preferred supply routes for rebel partisans, smugglers, and farmers hoping to sell their cotton before the rebels could burn it or the Yankees requisition it.[346]

The rebels burned their cotton primarily to keep it out of Yankee hands, but also in part because Richmond believed that cutting down on the supply of Southern cotton would force Britain to side with the CSA. It was Confederate gospel that Britain's economy could not survive unless its textile manufacturers received a continuing supply of American cotton. But even though the shortage did give Britain pause, it merely proved a boon to the proliferating cotton growers of Britain's newly established Indian Empire.

In mid November Fitch asked Admiral Porter to provide his man Schermerhorn, the same young officer whose attempt at a land attack on Fort Pillow the previous June had been betrayed inadvertently by Ellet and then rendered moot by the rebels' subsequent evacuation, for a shallow-draft boat to explore the smaller tributaries. He asked specifically for a howitzer-mounted tug "to use as a feint up the Forked Deer River."[347]

On December 27, a "very much alarmed and quite nervous" Union General Thomas Alfred Davies claimed that Earl Van Dorn was at Brownsville, a few miles inland from Fort Pillow, which Davies announced he would reinforce with troops from New Madrid. According to an appalled Brigadier General Clinton Bowen Fisk, Davies had "withdrawn his force from Hickman; has destroyed all the guns and ammunition at Island No. 10; has ordered Colonel Scott, of the Thirty-second Iowa, to roll his guns into the river at New Madrid, burn carriages, blow up magazines, abandon his post, and remove his forces to Fort Pillow.[348]

❖   ❖   ❖   ❖

Six companies of the 32nd Iowa had spent the latter part of the fall of 1862 garrisoning the abandoned rebel works at New Madrid under the command of former Iowa state senator and future Lieutenant Governor John L. Scott. Scott had served with mounted Kentucky volunteers in the war with Mexico, where, in January 1847, he was taken prisoner with Cassius M. Clay. He was square-built, like Grant, with a full salt-and-pepper beard and a no-nonsense but not forbidding gaze. With six of his companies at New Madrid and four at Cape Girardeau, he had repeatedly and futilely urged his superiors to reunite his regiment and allow it to take the field.[349]

In 1860, Lincoln had carried Iowa with over seventy thousand votes.[350] But the state did not want for dissension. Long before Iowans began to smell gun smoke blowing up from the border wars to their south, the state's Democrats were already in splinters over "issues, patronage, and personalities." Some were no doubt outright Copperheads, though it was a label some Republicans slapped promiscuously on any critic of the Lincoln administration. But most were pro-Union; and, in any case, the Copperheads were nowhere as vital a force in Iowa as they would become in Indiana and Illinois. After June 1863, Iowan peace rallies would dwindle into insignificance.

Horrified by the border wars of the previous decade, and less invested in the slave economy than their counterparts to the southeast, many of the state's Republicans were both anti slavery and pro-Union out of sympathy for the refugee slaves who for years had fled to freedom from across the Missouri border. But their sympathy had its limits. Though Iowans generally welcomed Lincoln's Emancipation Proclamation, in the spring of 1862, the Iowa House refused to ratify a Senate resolution offering full citizenship to blacks who served in the Federal Army, and it would later vote down a resolution demanding that Congress take immediate action to end slavery. After the Union Army began to recruit blacks, the Governor of Iowa once remarked to General Halleck that when the war was over, "and we have summed up the entire loss of life it has imposed on the country, I shall have no regrets if it is found that a part of the dead are [black], and that all are not white men."[351]

In the election of 1862, only slightly less than half of Iowa's civilians voted Democrat, but almost 80 percent of the state's soldiers voted Republican. As the war dragged on, the Union and not Emancipation became the Iowa soldier's primary motivation, his initial abolitionism falling victim to his encounters with the slaves who converged on their camps. Ignorant, diseased, desperate, they did not conform with the cast of *Uncle Tom's Cabin*, and many a young soldier recoiled in disillusionment and disgust.

B.D. Everingham of the Thirty-Second Iowa wrote from New Madrid that "many soldiers who were formerly abolitionist and had favored enlistment of black regiments now hated blacks and said they'd shoot any black soldier placed beside them in the field." But Everingham probably overstated the case, for the 32nd would never acquire the Copperhead reputation of Iowa's 16th and 40th Infantry or 6th Cavalry. In fact, compared to the sullen Indianans and rampaging Illinois cavalry they were about to encounter at Fort Pillow, they were fanatical abolitionists.[352]

❖   ❖   ❖   ❖

The 32nd's post at New Madrid had been "surrounded by a ditch, in front of which was an abatis consisting of small, sharpened pine trees, though "from long neglect the ditch had in some places filled up and the abatis was considerably decayed." The post's little star-shaped fort was also flooded a foot deep when the 32nd arrived, but the industrious Iowans had "drained the fort, deepened and cleaned out the ditch surrounding the camp," repaired the abatis, thrown a gate across the one land approach from the east, and built themselves comfortable winter barracks.

Understandably proud of their work, they were appalled when an unsubstantiated rumor of a raid by Jeff Thompson and his rangers persuaded Davies to order the entire post destroyed and the garrison deployed to Fort Pillow to reinforce Wolfe's command in response to a similarly unsubstantiated report of an imminent attack by Earl Van Dorn.[353]

Columbus had recently sent Scott a company of German recruits from the 2nd Missouri Artillery, the same regiment from which a young Pennsylvanian clerk named Lionel Booth would be recruited to raise the regiment of black artillery he would lead against Forrest in his siege of Fort Pillow over a year later.[354] Now the Germans joined the 32nd as they piled aboard the steamer *Kenton* and her escort, the gunboat *New Era*, and turned to watch all their hard work brought to naught.

Colonel Scott ordered his adjutant, a future newspaperman named Charles Aldrich, to spike the guns and burn the carriages.[355] "It was very annoying," Aldrich recalled, "to see the fires lighted under the guns, which soon destroyed the carriages." The job of exploding the well supplied magazine was taken on by the men of the *New Era,* "who prepared long fuses, reaching perhaps one hundred or more feet to the powder in the magazine," and raced back to the gunboat.

> It was some minutes before the sputtering fire reached the three thousand pounds of powder. In the meantime, we had proceeded perhaps a mile when the magazine blew up. A great column of dirt rose, apparently two hundred or three hundred feet in the air. For an instant it was shaped like a bundle of wheat, and we could plainly see the shell exploding through the clouds of dust."

In the end it turned out that Van Dorn never had any designs on Fort Pillow at all, nor had Thompson intended to take New Madrid, and "aside from the mortification which this needless evacuation caused our men," groaned Aldrich, "there was the destruction of government property.[356]

More disheartening still was the predicament of the contrabands who had sought refuge at New Madrid. Scott would not leave them behind, but he could not bring them with him to Fort Pillow, garrisoned as it was by Indianans and Illinois troopers who were more than likely to abuse them. So Scott took it upon himself, apparently at his own expense, to arrange for their transportation by steamer to central Iowa, to be taken under the wings of the regiment's kith and kin.

Among these contrabands, wrote Scott, was the family of a young boy named John Lewis Waller. "Probably very few of the comrades have any remembrance of this colored family," he would write long after the war, "who, with others, were furnished transportation to Central Iowa. It may interest them to know that the boy, John, is the identical John L. Waller, late Presidential Elector from Kansas; later, United States Consul in Madagascar; and at present, November 1895, enjoying the hospitality of a French prison, under a twenty-years sentence of a Military Court," for aiding the natives of Madagascar in their fight to prevent the French from laying claim to their island.[357]

❖ ❖ ❖ ❖

Saddened by the needless destruction of their post, the Iowans steamed downriver as a "pleasant Indian summer" gave way to a cold and wet winter.[358] As if to underscore their sense of misery and dislocation, a hard rain was falling when they pulled up to Fort Pillow's landing, and their boots could hardly find purchase as they scaled the slick clay bluff.

With the coming of the 32nd, Yankees of two very different stripes were about to collide at Fort Pillow, enacting in microcosm the deep divisions that plagued the Northern cause. The pro-slavery 52nd Indiana Infantry and irrepressible 2nd Illinois Cavalry were an unhappy match for the comparatively well disciplined and high-minded 32nd Iowa.

Fort Pillow seemed "most uninviting," recalled an Iowan, whose comrades "had to shovel snow off the ground to prepare a place to sleep."[359] Charles Aldrich remembered that "the cold was constantly increasing," as they settled in, "and the men were without tents." Their supper of coffee, boiled cod fish, and corn bread had to be cooked in the open air "by our colored 'Aunty'" who had been permitted to accompany them from New Madrid. But Adjutant Aldrich's men, many of them recovering from the measles, had to sleep in the open, where they "suffered fearfully during the night."

As soon as possible, "lumber was secured, and a hospital shanty erected in which the sick men were provided for as comfortably as possible," but three of the regiment's invalids "took severe colds and died during the next two or three weeks," and over the next two months some seven more would join them in the little graveyard set aside for the Iowan dead a few yards west of Colonel Scott's headquarters.

"Thar is some more of our boys that is loucking bad," wrote James Jenkinson of the 32nd, "and i thinck ought to be sent home till tha get better for tha never will get well as long as tha stay in the South. Thar is but fue of us that is loucking as fresh as when we left Iowa. It seems as when a man gets sick here thar is know geting them up agane." Jenkinson declared that he didn't fear "anything of a soldiers life but sickness. *This* is tha dark side of a solders life."[360]

"There being no immediate prospect of removal from Fort Pillow," wrote Scott, his Iowans laid claim to a number of abandoned slave cabins "that had been discovered in the neighborhood, and removed them to the regimental camping ground, rebuilding them better than they had previously been, and occupying them as quarters." The cabins were sided with rough wood and roofed with battened sticks and clay, and each boasted a fine brick chimney. Some Iowans "split 'shakes,' in pioneer Iowa style, with which they covered the roofs in lieu of shingles," and one captain "even made his house more comfortable with green blinds—which he found somewhere."[361] Scott's headquarters – which would house the commander of the Fort's white Tennessee contingent a year hence -- were built from logs taken from abandoned slave cabins on the nearby

farm of Samuel Lanier, and illuminated by windows pried from the walls of his mansion.[362]

On a site just south of the northernmost earthen breastworks that black artillerists would one day occupy -- and into which the entire Union garrison would flee from Forrest and his cavalry -- rose barracks, hospitals, storehouses, and "a pleasant camp was the result." Within the breastworks themselves, Scott's company of German recruits from the 2nd Missouri Artillery occupied what the rest of the garrison called a "Dutch Camp." Germans from St. Louis, they were apparently so disconsolate about their transfer, enraged by the destruction of their batteries at New Madrid, and bitter about the scant allotment of warm clothing they had received, that with Teutonic resolve they refused to drill or perform any military duty whatsoever.

"They have no arms of any kind," Scott would later report to Columbus, "and would not use them if they had." By the end of April, Scott would ask Asboth to take this "burden to my command" and "useless expense to the Government" off his hands.[363] But one night the Germans simply packed up and left, leaving only three of their number shivering in their tents behind the breastworks. The rest escaped to St. Louis. "We have unofficial information," wrote Scott, that they "returned immediately to Saint Louis and reported promptly to the Comdg Officer" who received them so warmly "as to induce the others to escape whenever opportunity offered."[364] Scott sympathized with them somewhat, for "they were sent here accidentally without any intuition or premeditation," and should therefore "have been Settled in the State to which they belonged."[365]

By the time of the 32nd's arrival, the 52nd's Colonel Wolfe had recovered from his ills and resumed his command. After an inspection by a much despised General Davies, Wolfe declared that a certain laxity had set in during his absence and ordered his officers to "put their respective commands in fighting condition," and "see that the guns are in good order, and the cartridge boxes amply supplied."[366]

Afraid that Colonel Scott, who outranked Lieutenant-Colonel Wolfe, would begin to throw his weight around, Wolfe and his boys were not welcoming. "As far as I can see," Scott wrote to Curtis, "we are of no use here.

There is no artillery here, and the works are much extended. With a few pieces the place might be held against a large force. As it is, an attack from a largely superior force would be fatal. I know, of course, nothing of the policy that sent me here in such haste.[367]

Nor, as it turned out, did Davies's superior, Major General Samuel Ryan Curtis. Davies had apparently overstepped his bounds by ordering the 32nd to destroy New Madrid and come down to Fort Pillow, for Scott and New Madrid were part of Curtis's command, while Davies and Fort Pillow fell under Grant's. The result of Davies's panic was that, between Cairo and New Madrid, the Mississippi had been stripped of Union forces.

At first, Curtis directed his wrath at Scott for obeying Davies without conferring with his department. He demanded that Scott be arrested and court-martialed for abandoning "Fort Pillow," which he had apparently confused with New Madrid. Scott was therefore forced to depart from Fort Pillow to answer charges in St. Louis, leaving his men under the command of his subordinate, Lieutenant-Colonel Edward Mix.[368]

Curtis's subordinate, Brigadier Eugene Asa Carr, claimed he had issued Scott a countermanding order, and condemned Scott's acquiescence as "shameful and cowardly."[369] But the fair-minded and possibly guilt-ridden General Clinton Bowen Fisk, who had advised Scott to obey Davies, came to the Iowan's defense, insisting that the colonel had protested the General's "questionable" order, but that Davies, in a sweat about Thompson and Van Dorn, would not listen to reason. Cooling down at last, Curtis began to see that the culprit had not been Scott but Davies, who, Curtis had begun to realize, commanded in "a crazy kind of style" and seemed sometimes to be "quite possessed." In late February, Scott was at last found "not only free from culpability" but "honorably acquitted of all blame," and allowed to return to Fort Pillow.[370]

"ILLICIT TRADE"
FORT PILLOW

By now Fort Pillow resembled a trading post more than a military encampment.[371] A black market in salt, blankets, and other necessities developed along the post's periphery, and despite orders that "no steam boat should sell whiskey to soldiers while lying at this post," liquor seemed to flow fairly freely through the camp of the 52nd. (Some of the spirits they imbibed came in the form of medicaments like 94-proof Dr. J. Hostetter's Stomach Bitters, first marketed in 1853 and distributed throughout the Union Army to invigorate men before battle.)[372]

Wolfe blamed all this on his commissioned officers for not paying "that attention to exercising the authority over their men which their duty requires."[373] A Lieutenant Smith of the quartermaster's office who was already suspected of pulling the same trick with salt pork, was accused of condemning large shipments of uniforms and blankets and selling them to smugglers.[374]

Wolfe tried to put the best face on what was fast becoming a scandal, though a scandal by no means unique to Fort Pillow. He claimed that salt had been sold only by authorized merchants, and though he acknowledged that "blankets, shoes &c." had been smuggled through his lines, it was always without his knowledge "or, if so" he had found out "too late to capture the goods or party smuggling."[375]

All this apparently shocked the Iowans. Lieutenant Amos Collins of the 32nd wrote an insinuating letter to Memphis to inquire whether it was proper for Fort Pillow's provost marshal to pocket the 50 cents he charged for cotton trading permits, and whether it was all right for field officers to purchase cotton from the Quartermaster and sell it.[376] The implication, of course, was that this was common practice under Wolfe's command.

Perhaps to deliver his own men from such temptations, Lieutenant-Colonel Edward Mix, while commanding the 32nd during Scott's courtmartial, had sent its regimental chaplain L.S. Coffin to Chicago to obtain "Bibles and Testaments and Such other Religious reading matter for the men of this command as you deem proper." "Drill was not neglected," wrote Charles Aldrich, "but it is not to be denied that the surroundings were disagreeable to the officers, and would have had a demoralizing effect upon the men but for constant resistance, and the labors and prayers of the chaplain, Rev L.S. Coffin."[377]

Coffin was ordered to bring medical supplies back with his bibles, for they were hard for the Iowans to come by.[378] Indeed, it began to seem to the Iowans that Wolfe was intent on depriving them of their just allotment of arms and supplies and excluding them from combat. By now Wolfe had added Company E of his 52nd Indiana to companies A and G's mounted scouts, and sent them out with the 2nd Illinois Cavalry to "protect unionists and confiscate property of guerrillas and their supporters."

They were apparently getting a lot better at chasing guerrillas. Training was one key to their success, learning the lay of the land another, but perhaps the most significant factor was the intelligence they gathered from neutrals and Unionists and pragmatic ex-secessionists who had come to the conclusion that the Confederacy, and slavery, was doomed. Even local men like Samuel Lanier, whose livestock, produce, fence rails, slaves, slave cabins, and even windows had been requisitioned by the Union garrison at Fort Pillow, knew that if locals were to receive permits to trade in cotton, if they were to hope to keep their land and survive the war, they could not merely mutter the Oath of Allegiance with their fingers crossed.[379] If the Union was their master, and they were her slaves, that was a relationship they knew something about. To gain favor, obtain pay, serve the Union, wreak vengeance on rebel marauders, pursue old feuds, or perhaps just bring the nightmare of Civil War to as rapid a conclusion as possible, some of them volunteered to serve as the garrison's eyes and ears: its guides, mapmakers, spies and informers.

They did so at considerable risk. Colonel Faulkner of the 12th Kentucky Cavalry(CSA) had a novel way of flushing out homegrown Yankee informers. "His advance guard were dressed in federal uniform in order to protect themselves and evade the federal columns should they meet them," wrote John Carroll.

> Calling at the house of a unionist they inquired of him if there were any rebels in the country; he said there were and proceeded to give names, writing them down for the officers, noting as he wrote what should be done to this one and to that one. When he came to the name of my father, he said, 'Burn him out,' that he had a son in there who was a bad guerrilla, referring to me. When he had finished his memorandum, the officer told him to get over the fence and move along: that these were Confederates he was talking to. The mortification and downright fear depicted in his face was awful to behold. They put him under guard,

foraged on him, taking bacon, hams, chickens, etc., and he furnished a bountiful supply.

During the night the officer sent for me and, when I arrived, had the man brought into my presence and rehearsed in my presence what the old sinner desired done with his southern neighbors. I saw that those men intended to kill him; they told him they would. Having known the old rascal for years, I begged for his life and offered to go security for his good behavior during the war. He promised to leave the country and not to meddle again in such manner, which he did and kept his word faithfully with me.[380]

The old man was lucky to get off so lightly. Addison Sleeth remembered riding along the bank of a stream, searching for shallow water through which to forde when he and his buddies came upon the remains of a man on a rock in a stream.

> The skeleton had the boots still on but no other clothing was to be found and the bones were bare and dry. One of the citizen scouts with us recognized the boots as those of his father who had been missing for several months, and, on examining the teeth, it proved to be the remains of his father who had been murdered for giving us information concerning the movements of guerrillas. Such things had become so frequent all along the border that no one was surprised at them for there was no safety to life or property in Tennessee, Missouri, portions of Kentucky and West Virginia.[381]

After the Confederate Army abandoned his property on the bluff, an entrepreneur from New York named Edward B. Benton had returned to Fort Pillow and re-established his trading post under Colonel Wolfe's protection. According to his biographer, Benton rendered "many and valuable services to the Southern people in the vicinity, whom he knew by a previous residence in their midst, and whose respect and esteem he had secured by uniform kindness and correct deportment." Though he may not have converted any die-hard secessionists by his example, he probably helped persuade their more ambivalent neighbors that the road to survival began at Fort Pillow.[382]

Unlike the trepidatious Major Strickland, his second-in-command, Colonel Wolfe was eager to impress his superiors with large-scale forays into the interior. In late December, acting on a tip, a detachment from Fort Pillow caught up to Gus Smith, a wily turncoat who had once served as General Henry Halleck's scout, killing him and several of his men, with no loss or injury to themselves.[383] But their biggest success came a week later against the wily Irish guerrilla, Bill Dawson. "On the afternoon of Jan 7, 1863," recalled Sergeant John Ryan of the 2nd Illinois, Wolfe's mounted men were called into line by the 2nd's Captain Franklin B. Moore of Ryan's Company D. Moore had organized his company from his neighbors in Alton, Illinois, and taken part in a daring raid on St. Louis to remove the federal arsenal from the rebels' reach.[384] "Known to be hard on the civilian population and, according to his commander, just as hard on his horses,"[385] Moore told every man "to prepare himself for a hard ride and a fight" against 250 to 300 of Dawson's guerrillas. Half of Dawson's men were said to be well armed, and all of them, according to a local informant, encamped some 35 miles away at Knob Creek. "At 4 P.M. we marched out of the fort with 65 men and officers of Co. 'D' and 38 mounted Infty comanded by Lieut David Temple of the 52 Ind., making our forces 103 men," plus their guide: a young local man "disguised so his appearance was that of an old man of 65 yrs."

At 2AM they paused to rest in Knob Creek Bottom, within a quarter mile of the enemy's pickets. Advancing at daylight and firing on the rebels' campfires, "we moved forward over the road, yelling like Commanchee Indians," wrote Ryan, and "charged into there Camp like a freight train going through a village." Dawson's men were taken completely by surprise. "I never saw so much confusion,"

Ryan declared. "We mixed right in amoung them and compeled a great number to surender in thare Camp. A few of them got in line on the top of a steep hill. they fired a few shots-down at us in the camp and we could see the blazing powder down to the breach of thare guns on that dusky morning," but after a Yankee squad went after them their lines "melted away like snow in a hot sun."

One Yankee was badly though not fatally wounded in the affair, while Dawson suffered the loss of 16 killed and 14 wounded. When the detachment returned to Fort Pillow with 47 prisoners and 50 rebel horses, a delighted Colonel Wolfe fired his cannon in its honor. "It was about 10 Oclock at night," Ryan proudly recalled, "and the hills were lighted up with Bon fires by the Infantry boys, and cheers was given for the 2nd Ill Cav, and David Temple and his mounted Infty."[386]

❖   ❖   ❖   ❖

Dawson himself managed to slip away and within a week had joined forces with Richardson.[387] The Yankees believed that their combined strength was about 1200, but there was nothing much the Federals or their partisan foe could do that week, for on January 15 nineteen inches of snow fell on West Tennessee, and it took another week for it to melt away.[388]

Various other Union regiments passed through Fort Pillow that January, including the 178th New York Volunteers, a regiment that arrived in an almost mutinous state, its colonel's two senior-most officers having "arranged themselves" against him. Wolfe urged Memphis to court-martial the two insubordinate officers on "charges," Wolfe cryptically wrote, "of a very grave and serious nature."[389] Apparently, however, the court could not prosecute one of the officers because he had never been mustered in.[390]

On January 16, Grant suddenly announced his decision to reduce drastically the force at Fort Pillow and ordered the 52nd, the 2nd Illinois Cavalry and the 178th New York Volunteers to get out by the 19th.[391] Uncertain whether to risk the suspicions that had fallen on his Iowan counterpart for evacuating New Madrid, Wolfe would not entirely abandon Fort Pillow until the works had been inspected by someone he trusted. In the meantime, he kept six companies of Scott's 32nd in place.[392] Major General Charles S. Hamilton duly toured the fort on Grant's behalf and reported that there were no heavy guns at Fort Pillow, and that the old rebel "floating battery" was under water.[393] Nevertheless, at the urging of Brigadier General Alexander Sandor Asboth, the plan to abandon Fort Pillow was itself abandoned, no doubt to Wolfe's and Scott's disappointment, though at least they could console themselves that Asboth sent the mutinous New Yorkers of the 178th packing.

On February 8, Asboth would write to Hurlbut that "to secure the safe navigation of the Mississippi," he considered it "most important to hold strongly not only Island No. 10 and Fort Pillow, but garrison also Hickman." He intended "to strengthen Fort Pillow with some light artillery," and instructed Wolfe to do something to restore some of the abandoned rebel guns. Wolfe's men duly winched and dragged two guns out of the muck and remounted them on the bluff, assigning their maintenance and operation to Company F of the 52nd, whose men were to be drilled somehow as artillerists though the guns were to be kept unloaded.[394]

❖   ❖   ❖   ❖

Late in January 1863, Dawson and a battalion of about 100 men attacked a party of Ohio Infantry and Illinois Cavalry at Yorkville, Tennessee, only to suffer one killed and five wounded before he finally whistled his men back into the woods. A day later, Dawson was the object of a three-point assault by battle-hardened Yankee troops riding hard out of the Union garrison at Trenton and converging on his camp near the bustling town of Dyersburg. In the ensuing battle, a Union officer was severely wounded, but before sounding the retreat, Dawson lost two killed, four wounded, and seventeen captured. The Yankees pursued him all night, scouring Dyer County and capturing thirteen more of his men until at last their horses gave out. Four of Dawson's men took the loyalty oath, one succumbed at Fort Pillow, and at least one of them would die in Federal prison.[395] A few days later, Bill Dawson's wild chase ended when a patrol of Minnesota trackers came upon him hiding in the bottoms. On the 14th of February Dawson was sent to Gratiot Prison in St. Louis, and not long afterward, after his second-in-command was also captured, "Dawson's Band" scattered into a few ragged gangs of indiscriminate thieves.[396]

Richardson, however, remained at large, encamped at Bloomington in Tipton County and still capable of gathering at least a rumor of a substantial fighting force.[397] In late February, Captain Moore found his way to Richardson's abandoned camp, capturing eight men he had left behind the day before, while Richardson himself set off with the rest of his force to "capture, or 'confiscate' money & property of Union people" and plunder citizens who had taken the oath of allegiance. Armed with old muskets, U.S. belts and cartridge boxes, the eight had been detailed to "bring up persons that had been conscripted and had not reported to camp."

The eight guerrillas had holed up in an abandoned Methodist meeting house from which Moore led them out at pistol-point.[398] Setting fire to Richardson's camp, including the church and a set of comfortable old houses, Moore headed back to Fort Pillow. The captain had a reputation for allowing his men to forage at will, shooting game and wild animals on his way, but perhaps because he was being observed by the officers and men of other regiments, or because he feared that any firing might alert the rebels to his column's whereabouts, he disappointed the expedition in their hopes by halting the column as it started back to the fort and making "a little speech, in which he said we were not to fire a shot on our return, unless we were attacked." Seeing the disappointment in his men's eyes, Moore paused, however, and added, "But boys, remember that clubs will kill, and if you find anything that hasn't taken the oath, kill it." The expedition proceeded heavy laden with poultry that "hadn't taken the oath worth a cent in that region."[399]

Not every expedition enjoyed such success, however. "Those long marches" eastward toward Trenton and Jackson, groaned John Ryan, "became tiredsome, especially in the night," and Ryan could not remember "that we found any rebles in that direction," though they scoured the area from February to March.[400] Nevertheless, after Moore returned to Fort Pillow with his prisoners, wagonloads of rebel stores, and twenty-seven of Richardson's horses and mules,[401] Asboth praised the pyromaniacal young captain's "indefatigable zeal" and recommended him for promotion.[402]

❖   ❖   ❖   ❖

Perhaps in hopes of forcing Moore and his horsemen to hole up at Fort Pillow, rebel guerrillas caused a letter to be relayed to Wolfe warning him that a local partisan named Captain Albert Cushman was about to attack. The letter, recalled John Ritland of the 52nd, "rather funnily expressed" the rebels' "very strong desire to possess the place," but Colonel Wolfe took the threat seriously. "Come any time," he wrote back. "I have plenty of boys to fight you, and they are the best kind." His men "felt certain that they would come upon us in the night," and "waited while the dogs howeled and the lightning played back and forth on the heavens, and at three o'clock all fires were extinguished, but no rebs came then, nor at dawn, when we thought surely they would have hurled themselves at us."[403]

Nevertheless, Wolfe kept his men on the alert, and refused to grant them furloughs. The result was a spate of desertions. Private William B. Goodman of the 52nd fled home to Rotterdale County, Tennessee, about twenty miles from Fort Pillow, in order to attend to his wife, who was "lying very low with sickness at the time" and subsequently died. Because Rotterdale County was itself aswarm with rebel guerrillas, a military court found that this mitigated the length of his absence and commuted his sentence of three months' imprisonment to loss of pay.[404] Denied a furlough by his Captain, Manliff Malson of Co. F deserted to join his ailing and expecting wife. Though he said he had intended to return in two weeks, he did not turn up until six weeks later, and was sentenced to a year at hard labor.[405]

The garrison's sundry grievances found their focus in the matter of pay, and there was plenty to complain about. The 52nd Indiana Infantry and the 2nd Illinois Cavalry had not received a penny since August, and the 32nd had not been paid at all.[406] Staring at the beckoning current of the Mississippi, shivering in their cabins, their pals expiring of pneumonia and diarrhea, some simply decided to return to hearth and home.

One night, with the help of some local citizens, a boatload of Union soldiers obtained civilian clothes and fled by skiff across the Mississippi to Arkansas. But as they neared the opposite bank, they were overtaken by a steamer commandeered by a Union lieutenant who raised a bullhorn and ordered them to paddle back to his boat. "They refused to obey," however, "and swung their hats in defiance and proceeded to make their escape by running the skiff ashore on the Arkansas side, where two of them jumped out in the back water," and three more tried to follow. The Lieutenant ordered his men to open fire, and Private James A. Raney of the 52nd Indiana Infantry "fell wounded on the skiff, where he was taken aboard of the steamer and brought to Fort Pillow."

Raney claimed that one of the other deserters had prevented him at the point of a pistol from surrendering. Besides, he argued, other men had deserted for brief periods "and nothing had been done about it." But the army ripped off his insignia and imprisoned him at Alton, Illinois for the remainder of the war. (In November 1864, his mother would beg Lincoln to release her dying son from prison because she didn't "think he colde stande the fare thare a nother wintere,"[407] but the President refused.)

Scott of the 32nd was more liberal in granting furloughs, which probably only deepened the discontent among Wolfe's Hoosiers. Apparently in response to a complaint by Wolfe, General Asboth declared that under rules that had not yet been published, Scott had no right to grant furloughs and that every man to whom he had granted a leave of absence was to be "immediately recalled."[408] Scott protested that regimental commanders had always granted furloughs, and declared that it "advance[d] the public interest" to grant to at least "a *small* number who have exhibited much merit in the discharge of duty short periods to visit families and transact business."[409] But Wolfe overruled him, commanding his rival to call all of his furloughed Iowans back to their post.[410]

Hard though they were on Contrabands, Iowans, secessionists, and one another, Wolfe's sullen Hoosiers could nevertheless muster some sympathy for Man's Best Friend. "One day," wrote Sleeth, "a hunter came across the river from Arkansas in a canoe so small it didnt look like it would float with a baby in it."

He went out in the country and got one of the noted hunting dogs and placed [it] in the bow of the canoe, then got in himself and pushed out into the river. Just then the dog's mate came running down to the edge of the water and kept walking up and down by the waters edge till the canoe had got a hundred or two [hundred] yards from shore, when he put out into the river after the canoe. The river was nearly a mile wide and the canoe had to go down stream angling across the river, so that it was over two miles to the landing on the opposite shore. On went the canoe and the dog swimming apparently about the same distance behind it till they reached the main current then it was evident the dog was losing, and the distance growing greater between the two. They were now over a mile away and it took close looking to see the little dark speck we knew to be the dog's head.

By this time some two or three hundred men were standing on the bluff, "watching with almost as much anxiety as if it had been a human being instead of a dog. Presently the dog threw his neck and shoulders above the water and remained in this position a second, then went down, and a number of voices said, in a breath, 'He's gone.' But in an instant we again saw the dark object moving toward a point of land that projected out from the Tennessee shore about two miles below, and after a long anxious watch we had the satisfaction of seeing the dog reach it and climb upon the bank," as a hundred voices shouted, "Bravo!"[411]

With his garrison at nearly full strength, Wolfe sent an expedition under Captain Moore to kill Cushman, whose "evil nest, wrote John Ritland of the 32nd, lay "not far from camp."[412] A well educated Swiss German, 35 year-old Captain Albert Cushman had been detached from the 12th Tennessee Cavalry to forage and recruit in Lauderdale County, where he had fast acquired a reputation as "a robber, guerrilla, regular land pirate" and the "dread of the whole county."[413] He had been active around his hometown of Ripley for the past three months, evidently delighting in "burning cotton, robbing cotton buyers, stealing horses, making threats, and committing acts of violence against loyal citizens," not to mention "shooting down as many Union officers as he could safely get a bead on."[414]

Colonel Wolfe sent three companies under Captain Moore to search the surrounding country for Cushman, but first Moore paid a call on Cushman's wife and children. "One cold evening," wrote John Ryan of the 52nd, Moore ordered Cushman's wife and children out into her yard, "and then set the house on fire, burning it to the ground. I am willing to give Capt. Moore much praise as a industerious officer," wrote Ryan, "But I Condemed the act then and I Condem it now as I think of that poor woman with her children standing in the street in the Snow, Crying and Shivering with Cold. Capt Moore may have done this By order of Col Wolf, But it was not nessesary. It was cruilty: only that and nothing more."[415]

As the flames consumed Mrs. Cushman's house, Moore spurred his men toward Durhamville, where, at around 10 o'clock on the night of February 7, they crept up on a house on the Fitzpatrick plantation. Peering through a window, they spied Cushman and three of his men bundled up in purloined Union overcoats, warming themselves by a fire with their rifles and revolvers apparently hidden about the house. Moore burst in and took them all captive, finding on the rangy captain's no doubt gamey person correspondence

from Earl Van Dorn and Richardson, who had sent Cushman to Ripley to burn cotton and recruit conscripts. The notorious Switzer was brought to Fort Pillow in irons and taken into the custody of Provost Marshall Ross Griffin who escorted him to Columbus for trial, while the three others, described by Federal authorities as "young and human appearing men" who deeply regretted their involvement with Cushman, were spared hanging and sentenced to hard labor at Alton, Illinois for the duration of the war.[416]

An indignant Richardson warned that if the Yankees put Cushman in irons he would put five of his prisoners in irons, and that if Captain Moore did not repay Mrs. Cushman for the torching of her house, he would shoot ten captive Yankees.[417] But put Cushman in irons they did, and Mrs. Cushman never saw a dime.

Ryan, of course, was not the only Yankee to recoil in horror from their own comrades' behavior. "Hit is a shocking sight," wrote a Union Private from Camp Sill, Tennessee, "to see how the soldiers starve the farmers."

> They take everthing before them. I saw them today go in to a hous and take everthing they could lay thaer hands on, and then went for the chickens out a doors, and the worst of all hit was a poor widow woman with fore little children. I was mity sorry for her. She beg them not to take her things for her little children wood starve if they took her provishion, but they went ahead and took. I hav saw a heepe such cases as that till I am tired out of such doings.[418]

The Yankees were not always as harsh with their guerrilla captives as the rebels had been led to expect. Two captive Dyer County chieftains were surprised by the treatment they received by the 42nd Minnesota. They were "a pretty good set of fellows," wrote Captain Walter Grizzard, who had been captured on foot with a self-styled major named Algee. "They let us ride their horses, until they got tired, then two others would dismount and let us ride their horses & so on until we reached the rendezvous."[419]

Nor were all rebel guerrillas the monsters the Yankees made them out to be. Bob Richardson's men once caught a trader named Cones in the act of transporting cotton to the Yankees and brought him to their commander's headquarters a few miles from Fort Pillow. Richardson asked Cones the usual questions: "whether he had served against the Confederate States, &c." Apparently satisfied with Cones's answers, Richardson declared, "Well, sir, I'll parole you."

"Why, Colonel," protested Cones's captor, "you ain't a goin' to parole that infernal cotton-buyer, are you?"

" Well," Richardson replied. "I've got to parole him or shoot him. You'd rather be paroled than shot," he asked Cones, "hadn't you?"

Cones replied in the affirmative, and, allowing him to keep his watch and his money (though not his cotton), Richardson gave him leave to proceed on foot to his home in LaGrange.[420]

But the Yankees' noose continued to tighten. On May 2, the 15th Illinois Cavalry would capture yet another Dyer County guerrilla leader, the "notorious" Captain Parks. "Thus another guerrilla company is destroyed," a delighted General Asboth trumpeted from Columbus, whose prison now contained some 300 "of our own men, disloyal citizens, and guerilla Officers and Soldiers." The General exulted that he had "four noted guerrilla leaders here: Scales, Cotter, Cushman, and Parks: all to be tried as highway robbers."[421]

MISFORTUNE'S PROFITEERS
FORT PILLOW & FULTON

The "infernal" cotton speculators who plied the Mississippi and its backwaters would elicit from Edward M. Main of the 3rd United States Cavalry a blur of mixed metaphors. "Following in the wake of every army," he wrote, "as sharks follow a doomed ship, are always found a horde of human vultures, who, hyena-like, prowl over battlefields, despoiling the dead, preying on the defenseless and profiting by the misfortunes of others.

> Whenever and wherever any portion of the army moved, he was sure to be present. When the army advanced, he followed. When the army fell back, he took the lead. Like his prototype, the coyote, he took precious good care to keep out of danger. His ambition was cotton, to get which, either by fair means or foul, was the dream of his life. His suave

and fawning manner, his boasted patriotism and pretended love for the Union, won favor at headquarters, giving him the freedom of the camp, and, in fact, about all other privileges he felt inclined to take. The man of doubtful or unproclaimed loyalty was not permitted to ship his cotton, the value of which at current prices, if realized on, would make him comfortable, and so in sight of all this wealth he and his family starved for the ordinary necessities of life, while our bunko man, the "loyal cotton" buyer, could ship his cotton, and no questions asked. When and how he got the cotton, the price paid, etc., were known only to himself and perhaps one or two others.

"The glitter of his gold corrupted officers and men," Main concluded, "tempting them from the path of duty and rectitude, and bringing many to shame and degradation."[422] To remove the temptation of the glitter of gold (and the burble of whiskey, on which they had recently drunk themselves insensible), Wolfe ordered the comparatively tame Company B of Scott's 32nd (32/B) to take their place downriver at Fulton.[423] Captain A.B. Miller was to "examine carefully the approaches to the place, familiarize yourself with the ground and location," deploy night pickets "to prevent any surprise, keeping always ready and at hand some means of speedy Communication with these Head Qrts. You will not allow any of your Command to straggle off through the country," Wolfe cautioned Miller, "and will positively forbid unauthorized interruption or molesting of the private property of any Citizen."[424]

At Fulton 32/B followed a strict regimen: up at 5:30AM, breakfast an hour later, mounting of the guard at 7AM, morning drill at 8AM, lunch at noon, three and a half hours of keeping tabs on trade, and then afternoon drill, followed by more monitoring. Supper at 5PM, dress parade at 6PM, at which patriotic letters were read aloud, then another three-hour gap, then tattoo at 9PM and taps a half hour later.[425] There were inspections every Sunday, and voluntary prayer meetings.

Though Fulton was a tiny outpost for a full company to occupy, they found plenty to do. "Our company is alone, but well situated here," wrote an Iowan. "It is a verry pretty place on the river and would have ben a large town had it ben in a free state, but it now has two stores, a one horce tavern, a little meating hous, and a school in it, and four or five houses. I have bin so luckey as to make the acquaintance of the school marm," though he said he did not know "whether she wants to marry or not. Will tell you next letter. The Pa is rich. He gave me a polite invitation to come and see them. I will go."[426]

A "good many boats" had landed recently, Howard continued, "and it was thought by the Commander of the post at the Fort that a good deal of Contraband trade was going on here, so he ordered us here to put a quietus on it." They were trying to draw "the reins pretty tight on the people of this vicinity.

> They can not purchase any thing Contraband without a permit from the Deputy Provost Marshall and paying 50 cts., then they have to have a Bill of all the stuff that they buy, which they take along to the Picket lines. Here the Guard carefully examines their goods and compares them with the bills, and if found all right, why, we let them go on their way rejoicing. But if we catch them trying to smuggle goods that are contraband through the lines, then we take their goods and turn them over to the Quartermaster, arrest the persons and send them up the river to Columbus or some other stronghold, where they receive their reward according to the deeds done.[427]

In April, a member of the 32nd would report that some of his comrades had settled into a warehouse rather than share a shanty with "so many together. The boys are divided up in Squads of eight to twelve for eating purposes, their food cooked by "a couple of 'cullud people,'" as he wrote. The most notable of these eating clubs was a group known as the "'Wisdom Squad,' so called on account of the gigantic intelects of its members, partly, and partly because of the

Literary Institution connected with it." They had "lively times in their sanctum every now and then." A soldier named James Jenkinson was "the best appearing soldier in our Co. He is as straight as an arrow with his clothes brushed boots blacked and arms and accoutrements always in good order. In fact, 'Jim,' or 'Colonel,' as the boys call him, is a perfect Soldier." In all, he said the Iowans were "good soldiers," though there was "a marked difference in their manner and appearances."[428]

Occasionally a few men from Company B would be sent after an escaped prisoner or a rebel guerrilla, otherwise they did not venture far from Fulton. Their duties entailed laying claim to the skiffs the rebels abandoned and salvaging the cargos of the ships that were always running aground on Flour Island. In May, they were ordered downriver to salvage cargo from the wreck of the steamer *Majestic*.[429] And it was left to the 32nd's officers to figure out what to do about a barge that had become stranded just south of Fulton during the Confederate evacuation, "still having coal in it, mixed with mud," to which various traders laid claim.[430] On May 12, Wolfe stopped a local citizen from shipping the coal downriver, but allowed two steamers to burn about 1,000 bushels of the stuff.[431]

Disentangling valid claims from false claims drove officers to all but implode with frustration, for no sooner would one claimant present himself than someone else would turn up to insist that the property in question belonged to his neighbor, now in the service of the Union Army, or to the widow of a Confederate officer. And what to do with the abandoned property belonging to the estate of a deceased old farmer of indeterminate allegiance whose trustee served in the Confederate army but whose sons were Union officers? Wolfe must have taken some grim satisfaction as the priggish Iowans haplessly entangled themselves in the convoluted snarl of wartime river traffic.

It apparently still pleased Colonel Wolfe to bar the 32nd from taking any active part where there was any prospect of killing or capturing guerrillas. That privilege he reserved for his Hoosiers and the Illinois cavalry companies he had come to regard as his own. Scott tried to go over Wolfe's head and plead for a transfer to Northeastern Kentucky, where he had lived for eight years before the war. "I know the men who are now over-running that locality, from Humphrey Marshall to John C. Breckenridge," he wrote, and he "would like to meet them" in battle. "As well as I can decide myself, our command is not needed here—and we are all Anxious to take part in an active campaign against live rebels. My Regiment is in good condition and might be made very effective."

Scott and his men were nonetheless compelled for the time being to stay put, which, combined with a number of deaths from disease, now led to desertions in his own regiment. In fact, his force was so reduced that he offered his extra arms to Wolfe, who agreed to take the Enfields he was offered, but declined a stack of Prussian muskets.[432] Wolfe was loath to allocate ammunition to the 32nd, and in mid April Scott had to make a special request for 54,000 rounds for his men.[433]

All the while, the bold Captain Franklin Moore continued to hunt Richardson and Faulkner, galloping at the head of his Illinois cavalry and mounted Hoosier infantry, ranging as far as Dyersburg, Double Bridges, Key Corner.[434] At Eaton they had to cross the Forked Deer to reach an encampment of about 80 rebels. "Thare was a high bridg at the town," wrote John Ryan, "but the rebles had taken up some of the flooring of the bridg and was on Guard thare to prevent our forces from getting over." So Moore ordered a small detachment to swim across the river below Eaton while the rest tried to cross the bridge.

"Two of Co. E's boys and Harry Crawford and myself volunteered," wrote Addison Sleeth. "The command started off down the river, and we four boys stripped ourselves and unsaddled our horses, mounted them, and swam across, intending to take an old boat that was tied to the bank and go back for our clothes, saddles guns &c." But the boat had been busted through by the rebels.

> Our horses stood shivering on the bank; our clothes, guns, and saddles were seventy five yards away; and there was fifteen feet of ice water all the way from where they lay to where we four boys stood in a cold biting wind without as much as a pocket kerchief to cover or protect us. Up the river at the other end of town stood a sawmill. To this we must go and get lumber, build a raft and go for our clothes &c.

Stark naked, they "climbed up the bank and with a series of wild warwhoops we went flying through the streets as if the old Nick was after us." Passing a schoolhouse "just as the teachers and scholars were coming out into the street," Sleeth and his pals "had no time to be polite or lift a hat if we had had one to lift. We had a hard race, but we got there and soon had a raft on which we brought over our saddles, guns and clothes." The rebels guarding the bridge soon found themselves "caught in a trap by our men who Crossed the river below the town," wrote Sleeth. Falling upon them from behind, they caught half the rebel force and all their horses.[435]

By the end of April, Union forces from posts up and down the West Tennessee bank of the Mississippi were ranging throughout Dyer and Gibson County. At Eaton they managed, after "stealing everything along the way," to capture a guerrilla named Cotter who had been harrying Yankee expeditions for months. Captain Moore broke up another remnant of Dawson's old command under Nathaniel Porter, a wealthy planter, slave owner and justice of the peace who barely made his escape slipping across the Forked Deer in a skiff.[436]

On April 26, Captain Moore captured 24 more of Richardson's recruiters, including their captain, with no casualties on either side. "Harry Crawford and I got the lead," Sleeth recalled, and, just as they galloped into the town, they saw "a Rebel officer mount his horse and start at a keen run down the street. We gave chase and were getting close on him when he left the main street, Harry following close behind, while I made for the next crossing to head him off." But after Sleeth "rode around two sides of the block and looked down the street, there was Harry with his revolver in Mr. Reb's ear." For this feat Crawford was allowed to keep the officer's fine revolver "as a trophy."[437]

Rebel conscription continued.[438] On May 1, a band of recruiters broke up a Methodist meeting in Bethesda, dragging off 16 males for military service.[439] (In fact, both sides found churches convenient recruiting stations, swooping down on congregations in mid service and impressing their men folk.) Fielding Hurst and his 6th Tennessee Cavalry (USA) roamed around Tipton and Haywood counties to enforce a decree by Colonel M.K. Lawler of the Union post at Jackson. Lawler extended a pardon to all men, including Richardson's guerrillas, who had styled themselves "partisan rangers" on condition that they "deliver up their arms, subscribe to the oath of allegiance to the United States of America, and return to their peaceful pursuits." But if "any of these bands were reorganized or new ones should spring up," warned Lawler, "I would hold those persons who had not taken the oath of allegiance, or who had not faithfully observed the same, responsible for any act or deeds perpetrated by such bands."[440] Lawler's decree sounded generous enough on its surface, but Hurst saw it as a further license to kill.

The 52nd's mounted infantry enjoyed disrupting classes at the schools they passed. One private rode up to a schoolroom window, treated the schoolmarm and her students to the apples he had collected in his haversack, and departed with this admonition: "Now I want you to be good," he told the children, "for I tell you, you've a splendid, good looking teacher."

Sleeth fondly recalled his wartime encounters with Southern hospitality. One afternoon, he and his comrades came upon a school at recess, and were greeted by a row of children who handed them holly branches. "This little thing," wrote Sleeth, "so simple in itself, had an effect none but those who were there can realize. Most of us had been little more than school children when we went in the army," he explained, "and, if this touched us in one of the tender places left in our hearts, just remember it had been many months since we had seen or felt the influence of childhood's warm true friendship and love."

On another occasion, "after an all day's ride in the mud and rain," recalled Sleeth, "we reached Ripley on our way to the Fort.

> The officers decided we should remain here till morning and gave us an hour to hunt up supper for ourselves and horses and be back at the courthouse. Three of us rode out about a mile into the country, put up at a house, got supper, and fed our horses. The rain was coming down in torrents so we decided to stay till morning. The old man and his three daughters were all fiddlers and they had three fiddles. After supper they gave us a treat in the way of music. About 10 o'clock we were shown to a room and good bed and after recapping our guns went to bed and slept till morning. It had been about two years since we had slept on a bed before.[441]

Even the Iowans penned up at Fulton and Fort Pillow sometimes got to experience the special warmth and security of a Southern household. One of the wealthiest planters in the area, Judge James L. Green, "occasionally invited members of the Field and Staff to vary camp fare by eating buffalo-fish and the accompaniments at his table. On a certain occasion it is said that some officers of the 32nd Iowa had their legs under the good Judge's mahogany" when a detachment of rebel guerrillas "arrived unnoted to the place.

The judge requested his guests to remain seated; interviewed the strangers, who departed, 'casting longing, lingering looks' upon a number of valuable steeds near the house! It was nicely done. The Judge was a man of character, respected by all parties, and his home may be said to have been within the Union lines. These officers were his guests.[442]

Sometimes the locals' hospitality was downright disorienting. "We got an invitation," recalled Sleeth, "to participate in a Fourth of July Celebration out near Ripley.

> We went out the evening of the third and spent the night near the picnic ground. The Fourth came bright and clear. We went early to the grounds and had a fine day's enjoyment and a splendid dinner. The strange thing about it was Union and Rebel citizens and Federal soldiers all met on this day under the old flag with the kindliest feelings and celebrated the anniversary of our Country's Birthday.[443]

The region's most apolitical inhabitants were not so hospitable. A scourge of the scouts that circulated through West Tennessee that spring was the fiery bite of the buffalo gnat, an insect "about the size of a housefly, a little darker,

 perhaps slightly heavier, and more active in its movements." Roaming in swarms along the Mississippi, "they had long ago switched their dining preferences from the now vanished bison to the white man's livestock." They compelled farmers to build greenwood fires and drive their stock into the smoke, where they were sometimes joined by wild turkeys and deer seeking the same protection.

These fires infused the entire Lower Mississippi valley with a silvery haze. When horses, mules and oxen had to venture out beyond the smoke to assist in the spring planting, farmers coated them in something called "gnat oil." Even in Memphis, where smoke was an almost constant presence, the mules that pulled the street cars had to be liberally daubed as well. The gnats were at their worst just before dusk, and a traveler recalled having to rescue his horses one evening by covering his own head in a handkerchief and scraping the gnats off his horses' bodies with a buggy whip. Unprotected animals, wild and domesticated, used to run for deep water when the gnats descended and stand until nightfall with only their noses breaking the surface. [444]

The gnats were not merely annoying; in sufficient numbers they could harry an animal to death. "The Buffalo gnats were swarming everywhere," Sleeth recalled. "They covered our horses, crept in their nose and ears, gathered in great bunches in every tender or unprotected part." One morning Sleeth and his comrades came upon five or six pickets of the 3rd Michigan Cavalry whose horses "all lay dead, killed by the gnats."

In some places, houseflies were so thick that officers had to station pickets to protect their company's rations. The flies "contest our right" to eat "to the last," wrote a soldier in Nashville. "We therefore have a skirmish quite often in order to capture the tough beef steaks, butter that could outrun a rebel on retreat," a few grounds of coffee "that are like a bad creditor and would never settle," and a "large quantity of nothing."[445]

The "trumpet-tongued" Mississippi mosquito – enormous, multitudinous, insistent, and armed with a proboscis of unusual length, posed a graver threat. Though Fort Pillow appeared at first to be "reasonably exempt from malarial influences" and "a nice location for a camp," Colonel Scott wrote that "there was considerable sickness among members of the Regiment, quite a number of cases proving fatal. The streams that entered the river at this point were sluggish, and those in the rear of the bluffs were of the same character, and the seeds of future attacks were here sown, which developed later, causing many deaths."[446] No-one, at that point, had linked malaria to mosquitoes, and the 52nd's surgeon, James W. Martin, would theorize that Fort Pillow's "malarial influence" arose from the flooded lands "along the banks of the Mississippi river, Coal Creek & Hatchee river," whose "stagnant water is slowy drying up on the overflown lands along the Streams. In September, 1863, the number of men suffering from malarial fever at Fort Pillow would reach 181.[447]

Malaria brought with it sweats and chills and delirium from which many men never fully recovered, their fevers recurring through the war and even into old age. One Iowa regiment could always tell when its bugler was having another of his febrile spells by the way his notes wavered as he blew.[448] The 52nd's surgeon at Fort Pillow reported 178 cases of such intestinal disorders as diarrhea, dysentery, and constipation, arising from everything from eating spoiled food to drinking water tainted with human waste. Other men complained of rheumatism, bronchitis, pink-eye, ulcers, toothache; and in one month 25 would be diagnosed with syphilis and gonorrhea.[449]

By the outbreak of the Civil War, the Lower Mississippi had acquired a reputation for pestilence, emanating, so it was believed, from the foul miasmas arising from its bogs and bayous. Its climate was called "sickly," especially in late summer and early fall. For much of the war in the West, a quarter of the Union Army's Department of Tennessee languished on the sick and disabled list.

Among the straws at which the Confederates grasped after the fall of Vicksburg was the hope that, just as the Russian snows defeated Napoleon, Dixie's pestilences and muggy heat would turn the Yankees' triumph into disaster, requiring "the enemy to maintain -- cooped up, inactive, in positions insalubrious to their soldiers -- considerable detachments from their forces." Disease did prove at least as lethal an obstacle to the Union occupation of West Tennessee as guerrilla depredations and Confederate cavalry raids. Fifty-eight men of the 2nd Illinois Cavalry stationed at Fort Pillow would be killed or wounded during the war, but 175 would die of disease.

In mid May, Hurlbut, whose constant complaint to Grant and Sherman was a shortage of cavalry, summoned the audacious Captain Moore and his 2nd Illinois Cavalry battalion to Memphis, along with every other detachment of cavalry under his command.[450] "We were Sorry to leave Col. Wolf and his 52 Indiana and the [Iowa] boys," recalled John Ryan. "While we were getting ready many of those Infantry boys Came to our Camp to bid us good bye and wish us good fortune." Ryan had never met "a better and kinder lot of officers and men." Strict discipline "and good order was a standing rule with Col Wolf," Ryan concluded, "and his officers and those rules were obeyed not becaus the men feard those officers but because they loved and respected them."[451]

The men of the 32nd would not have concurred. By keeping them dismounted, Wolfe had rendered them incapable of taking any meaningful role in the raids that had brought Captain Frank Moore such fame. They suspected, perhaps rightly, that Wolfe simply did not want them to witness his own men's corruption. Ordered to stand guard over prisoners, establish pickets on the fort's periphery, inspect boats coming in and out of Fort Pillow, they felt exploited, wasted, humiliated, and Scott began to complain to Memphis about Wolfe's corrupt and slovenly command.

When he wrote to Hurlbut that a number of local people had complained to him that they had been robbed by

Wolfe's men, Wolfe tried to knock Scott down a few pegs by accusing one of the Iowans' surgeons of taking "from a Mrs. Ross of the Village of Osceola, State of Arkansas, Two Hundred Eighty 50/100 Dollars in gold coins."[452] But Scott retained the moral high ground. W.J. Ross, the woman's husband, was a smuggler, Scott explained, who had recently been arrested at Island Number Ten. Furthermore, the surgeon had immediately relayed the money to Scott, who, in turn, had deposited it with a Treasury Department agent in St. Louis.[453]

One effect of Grant's prolonged siege and ultimate victory at Vicksburg, and his subsequent advance into Mississippi was to reduce his reliance on West Tennessee's railroads for his supplies and thus the need for Wolfe's Railroad Regiment's services.[454] None of Captain Frank Moore's glory seemed to have redounded to Wolfe. Stranded, sullen, idle, the men of his garrison grew slovenly, strewing garbage around their camps.[455] After Captain Moore's departure, the garrison fell into a rocky, contentious period marked by soldiers taking "French leave," and engaging in fistfights and drunken sprees.[456] Without Moore to lead them, Wolfe's scouts indulged in a round of depredations, stealing cash from local farmers.[457]

One day Addison Sleeth and twenty of his comrades dashed twenty miles "to an ex Rebel Major's whose two sons were said to be at home recruiting and collecting supplies for the Rebel army." The major was home when the scouts rode up, but his sons were nowhere to be found. Sleeth and his buddies "fed our horses, helped ourselves to the major's peach brandy, and had a good dinner in the negro quarters." It all seemed routine until the next morning, back at the fort, when Wolfe placed them all under arrest. Sleeth and sixteen privates "were put under a strong guard and allowed to speak to no one, nor hold any conversation" with one another.

"The Lieutenant and the three non commissioned chaps including myself were paroled on condition we held no conversation with each other or any member of Co. G. or E.

A court was convened to try us and we now learned we were charged with stealing $1800.00 from the old ex-Rebel major's house. The Lieutenant and non commissioned officers were examined but none of us knew anything about the money" until at last one of the privates from Co. E. not only confessed to holding a third of the money but informed on a comrade, James Harnet, who had apparently committed the theft. "The money was returned to the Rebel Major," recalled Sleeth, the informer was let off, another boy who was found with $400 was sentenced to six months' hard labor on the fortifications at Columbus, and Harnet was sent "to Alton prison for his term of enlistment, where he died."[458]

Perhaps this small windfall was what encouraged the Treasury Department, which was itself widely suspected of graft, to assign an agent named Peter Casey to act as Fort Pillow's one-man Board of Trade. He was instructed to restrict sales only to people who intended to put the goods they bought to their own private "use and consumption." Furthermore he was not to allow more than $10,000 worth of merchandise per month to be sold at Fort Pillow.[459]

Allegations of impropriety began to swirl around Wolfe himself. The colonel had by now fallen out with his second-in-command, Major William I. Strickland, who had been assigned by Asboth to circumvent the post's Provost Marshall and inspect Fort Pillow's records and report directly back to Columbus. Shortly thereafter, Strickland accused Wolfe of allowing a man named Garner to sell goods from his boat at Fort Pillow, apparently in exchange for a share in his profits.

Wolfe demanded an immediate investigation into the charge, recalling that Hurlbut himself had given Garner permission to trade at Fulton, which was what had necessitated his stationing a company there. Wolfe conceded that some of his soldiers had broken into a store of whiskey and drunk themselves into a stupor, but the Colonel had ordered all 40 barrels of whiskey seized and placed under guard. To the charge that he had traded with the enemy, he answered with what was perhaps a non-denial denial, "My father fell upon the battle field of Richmond, Kentucky last," he wrote, "fighting for the Flag of his country. My only brother served his term of enlistment with the 16th Indiana in Virginia, and there is not a man living who can with truth say that I have by word, thought or deed expressed or implied, committed any act that would justify or afford foundation for such a charge," which had been "circulated by wicked and designing men and done for the purpose of accomplishing some selfish *end*." ⁴⁶⁰

Other officers weighed in, however, and the cumulative accusations of corruption began to gather over Wolfe's head like a toxic cloud. They charged that Wolfe had allowed traders to bring some 23 barrels of whiskey into Fort Pillow "by Government Teams and Guarded by soldiers at this post" and eventually escorted down to Fulton to be sold. It was also "believed and asserted by some" that Wolfe ordered his "cavalry and Mounted Infantry" to escort a trader to the Fort, and that officers had received illegal payments for captured horses of from $35 to $40 a head. But the taint of corruption extended to Strickland himself, who was accused of seizing some 39 bales of cotton that was apparently never turned over to the government. In addition, it was said that Strickland had allowed 150 barrels of salt to pass through the lines to a trader who sold the shipment in Covington, Tennessee.⁴⁶¹

Seeing his chance to vent his outrage over Wolfe's management of the garrison and his dismissive treatment of the 32nd, Colonel John Scott weighed in with his own

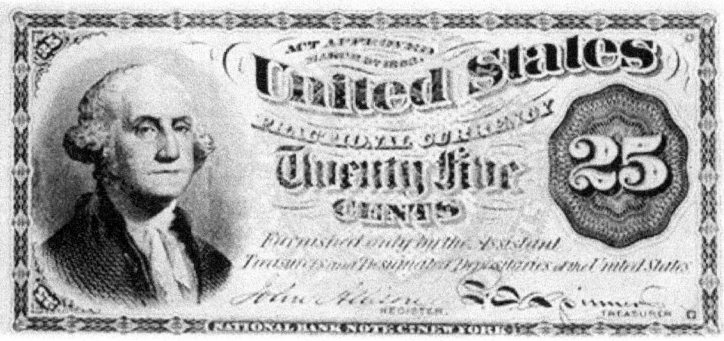

charges against the commandant. Though Scott primly prefaced his allegations by asserting that he had not "encouraged criticisms of my immediate Commanding officer," nor kept a "black book of his administration of affairs," he alleged that Wolfe had "the confidence of the disloyal of this section to a degree that is especially uncomplimentary to a man professedly loyal."

In the meantime, Asboth ordered Captain Franklin Moore to return to take command of the cavalry at Fort Pillow, where he knew "all the country and people of my district."[462] But within two days Hurlbut had again overruled Asboth and ordered Moore back to Memphis with all the cavalry companies that had apparently collected at Fort Pillow over the past few days.[463]

On Moore's departure, Wolfe paid tribute to "Capt. Frank Moore of Co. "D" 2 Ills Cav.

> And also to the gallant men under his command. The zeal and energy manifested by this company since its connection with this Post in capturing and scattering the lawless band of guerillas that has infested the vicinity together with the prompt discharge of their and all military duties, seldom equaled [and] never excelled, must commend itself to the special attention of all. In leaving this Post the company both Officers and Men take with them the good wishes of all, satisfied that, wherever placed, they will gallantly maintain their reputation as brave men.

CONTRABANDS
FORT PILLOW

Scott saved his most vehement denunciations for Wolfe's treatment of Contrabands. He accused the Colonel, the provost marshal, and other officers of the 52nd Indiana of a "want of sympathy" for the contrabands that was both "openly expressed and its expression encouraged." Scott backed up this allegation with several instances of neglect and abuse. The first involved a former Confederate soldier named Jones who manacled two runaway slaves who had taken refuge in the fort and led them off to a whipping post with the intention of flogging them to death. "They were rescued on the following day," Scott reported, but despite the incident's widespread notoriety, Wolfe had initiated "no investigation of this matter."

In another case, a black man was "enticed without the guard lines and carried into slavery." His abductors were briefly imprisoned but "released with assurances that their conduct was not improper." And finally, though an officer's servant was shot while traveling upcountry to visit his family and his murderers were "known and could be arrested without difficulty, no notice has been taken of the outrage."

At the end of May, Colonel Wolfe detailed Colonel Scott's adjutant, Lieutenant Charles Aldrich, "for the purpose of collecting and enrolling all able bodied male persons of African descent within my Command who are desirous of enlisting in the Military Service." He appointed the 32nd's Captain Joseph Cadwalader Post Superintendent "of the Colored Men that are in the Fort or that may hereafter come within our lines."[464] Wolfe may have regarded these assignments as yet another odious duty he could pawn off on Scott and his men, or perhaps by now he realized that only the 32nd had enough credibility with the local contrabands to recruit black solders successfully.

Scott accused Wolfe of providing "no assistance or protection" to negroes who reached his lines, nor any assistance in retrieving their families "though frequently asked for and by men who wish to be enlisted as soldiers as soon as their families can be rescued." Wolfe refused to allow officers of the 32nd Iowa to round up slaves who wished to escape from rebel masters, and discouraged recruitment of black soldiers. When an officer of the 32nd Iowa volunteered to recruit black troops, one of Wolfe's lieutenants remarked in the Colonel's presence that he ought to be shot," to which "Wolfe expressed no dissent or reproof."[465]

Such charges were difficult to investigate, let alone prove. As Lorenzo Thomas would conclude after trying to get a handle on the illegal trade in cotton that June, "My operations in this respect were of little practical value, and I only excited opposition, and I discovered that this opposition acted injuriously upon the third and most important part of my duties:" recruiting blacks.[466] Asboth similarly concluded that rather than pursue such charges against Colonel Wolfe or, for that matter, Major Strickland, he would endeavor to avoid further scandal by relieving

Major Strickland of his duties as post inspector and second-in-command and replacing him with Lieutenant-Colonel E.H. Davies.

❖   ❖   ❖   ❖

Scott hoped that reuniting his six companies at Fort Pillow with the four companies that had been stationed at Cape Girardeau might cheer his men up, and again raised the matter with Asboth. "The Separation causes many embarrassments," he pleaded "and a tendency towards demoralization that I very much deplore."[467] Asboth himself declined to reunite Scott's fractured command, but on June 3, General Hurlbut overruled him, in order, he said, to "relieve a regiment I wish to send Grant."[468]

Asboth then summarily transferred Colonel Scott and his 32nd Iowa to Columbus with all their "camp and Garrison Equipage and Stores."[469] Wolfe took a certain pleasure in recommending the dismissal from the service of the 32nd's revered Chaplain Lorenzo S. Coffin, whom he accused of being absent without leave.[470] An outspoken abolitionist and New Light, Coffin had been a thorn in Wolfe's side. Certainly not disloyal, but probably corrupt and certainly precipitous and neglectful, Wolfe had allowed traders, informers, smugglers and spies to infiltrate Fort Pillow, and in the process made a good many enemies out of men who should have been -- if not his friends -- his allies.

According to one charge, Wolfe had ordered the provost at Fulton "to pass the goods of a man who buys large quantities of 'family supplies' every month. I saw the June supply at Fulton to-day. Under his statement it is a shameless farce, and the man is indubitably disloyal."[471] Whatever the truth of the matter, Fort Pillow, under Wolfe's command, had become a leaky sieve out of which wagonloads of contraband salt and barrels of whiskey were frequently and mysteriously hauled off into the interior, and

blankets and shoes that passed through the post were routinely found scattered around captured rebel posts.

However earnestly Scott may have wanted to see Wolfe brought to justice, as he prepared his regiment for the transfer to Columbus, he made no more accusations: delighted, under any circumstances, to be out from under the Hoosier's thumb. But the 32nd's transfer was bad news for the contrabands, who were now to be overseen by Lieutenant B.K. Logan, one of Wolfe's least sympathetic officers.

Nevertheless, it was with a giddy sense of renewal that John Scott and his Iowans departed in stages on June 17 and 18, 1863, bidding Fort Pillow and the busy smugglers at Fulton Landing a hearty good riddance:[472] relieved, as one of their captains put it, that they would no longer have to allow a "Hoosier colonel to abuse and vilify us."[473] Scott and his men may have hoped that the army or the fates might reward them for their longsuffering service in West Tennessee. But as their steamer pulled away from the landing and chugged upstream around Craighead's Point, they could not know that after leaving Fort Pillow they would spend many months guarding bridges "and doing very irksome garrison duty," until April 9, 1864, three days before Forrest attacked the garrison at Fort Pillow, when the 32nd Iowa Infantry would lose almost half its men in a battle at Pleasant Hill, Louisiana.[474]

"The 32nd, which had hitherto been confined to garrison duty, until all connected with it were impatient and indignant at such treatment," one of them wrote, "has at last been tried in the severest shock of battle, and the long list of killed and wounded demonstrates what Iowa men do when their blood is up."[475]

❖   ❖   ❖   ❖

Hurlbut worried that having transferred the 32nd, Asboth would remove the 52nd as well and thus abandon Fort Pillow altogether. "General Halleck has directed that, in case of a movement in force on New Madrid, Asboth shall throw his whole force there, even to the abandonment of Columbus and Fort Pillow," but Hurlbut would "dread to trust"

Asboth "with such discretion," for he had "very little judgment," and if he did evacuate Fort Pillow, Hurlbut was convinced that the rebels would immediately reoccupy it.[476]

Lacking actual cavalry, his men stretched thin performing the garrison duty he had once so gleefully assigned to the now departed Iowans, Colonel Wolfe would have welcomed a transfer to New Madrid, or anywhere else it might please the Union Army to send him. Now the day-to-day idiocies with which John Scott had contended piled up on Wolfe's desk, and it did not matter how many adjutants and assistant adjutants he might appoint; he could never stay ahead of the industrious smugglers who could operate more openly and expansively now that the less corruptible Iowans had departed.[477]

As the summer heat intensified and weeds began to overgrow the ground the rebels and their slave laborers had cleared, morale plummeted.[478] An Army inspector would find little to praise on his tour of the camp of the 52nd. Its guns and accoutrements were in poor shape, with very few bayonets and all of them badly rusted.

> The sinks not in good condition. Company books and papers in bad condition. The roads leading out from the Fort need work before the Fall rains to make them passable during the winter. Companies E & G are mounted, and are very efficient as scouts, but not equal to the task of keeping the guerrillas out of the counties of Lauderdale, Haywood & Tipton.

Wolfe had bothered to muster in only his staff and five captains. Though all his other officers had been promoted from non-commissioned officers as far back as April 1862, they were not yet officially recorded in the army's books, and Wolfe would not request a mustering officer from Memphis until September.[479] Wolfe's men had still not been paid, and to make their situation more desperate, the local produce merchants were gouging them with exorbitant prices.[480]

The Hoosiers' mood inevitably turned foul. On July 1 alone, five men were court-martialed: one for stealing $500, three for deserting.[481] A few days later a corporal and two privates were accused of allowing a prisoner to escape from the Provost's Guard House.[482] Some of the Hoosier's antics verged on Mutiny. When Major Strickland refused to allow his men to drink from a stream after a long, hot scout, threatening with his upraised sabre any man who dared to try, Private William Butler of Company G drew his revolver and aimed it at Strickland's heart, "swearing if he didnt put up his sword he'd put a hole through him." Butler was arrested, but, perhaps reading his men's mood, Strickland released him.[483]

On one of their scouts toward Ripley, Addison Sleeth and his comrades came upon three or four barrels of whiskey. Their captain ordered them to haul the casks back to Fort Pillow, with instructions "to let none of the boys have any except by order of a commissioned officer." But every few miles "the officers came back for a drink, and they always treated the guards," until "long before we reached the Fort, we were gloriously light and imagined or really did have an immense amount of fun. We reached the Fort after dark and turned the three full barrels over to the hospital." Captain McCowick of Co. E. "took the one we had tapped to his quarters, and that night Co. E. got on a general drunken spree," during which a corporal named Mattison Cox proposed to his comrades that they attack McCowick's "shanty."[484] "Let us put the thing through tonight," he said, "and turn over his shebang."

A rattled McCowick testified that around midnight he rose from his bunk to the report of a gun and the sound "of rocks or bricks coming through the windows of my quarters" and landing at his feet. When his sergeant gathered the company together and demanded to know who had done it, an apparently intoxicated Private Thomas Koons stepped forward and declared, "I can tell the Captain who was in it. I was in it, and I threw bricks. I threw four." Koons and Cox were found guilty and sentenced to six months' hard labor and loss of pay,[485] and Wolfe banned all sale of "Vinous Malt or Spiritous Liquors" at his post.[486]

Gambling for money among officers and men became so prevalent that Wolfe had to entirely prohibit his men from playing at cards.[487] But more court-martials followed: John Roe for getting drunk and calling his captain "a goddamned son of a bitch;" a German artillerist for refusing duty; a citizen for smuggling medical supplies through Federal lines; Private John T. Lewis for desertion.[488] Within a month two more men would be sentenced to hard labor for "Larceny" and "Pillage and Plunder."[489]

Wolfe could hardly afford to lose any of them. His garrison was down to 580 men, of whom 112 were on the sick list or otherwise out of commission. When a small squad of his mounted infantry returned from Brownsville to report that Colonels Jacob Biffle and Jesse Forrest had trotted into the area with about a thousand Confederate cavalry, Wolfe pleaded that he had "not sufficient force to operate against them" and asked Asboth for "two full companies of Cavalry immediately."[490]

What gave the Yankees the jitters that July was an increased level of rebel activity in the Jackson Purchase area of Kentucky. On July 10, Asboth sent part of his Columbus garrison off to Union City, Tennessee to check a reported advance by rebel cavalry. He should have kept them in Columbus, for the so-called advance was a sly diversion. While Asboth's cavalry galloped around chasing ghosts, rebel horsemen raided not only Hickman but Columbus itself, looting stores, capturing a steamboat, and forcing Asboth's garrison to retreat into its fortification.[491]

The wily Bob Richardson, too, began to reassert himself, leading the 4th Illinois Cavalry a merry chase and losing them in the bottoms near Colliersville before crossing into Lauderdale County with 400 men.[492] Fielding Hurst and his 6th Tennessee Cavalry (USA) encountered some 1,500 rebel cavalry under Biffle, Forrest and Newsom eight miles up the Forked Deer from Jackson. "They fled before us in great haste," Hurst reported, "destroying all the bridges they crossed on, giving me such difficulty in crossing streams in 40 miles travel that I found myself 10 or 12 miles in their rear without any hope of overtaking them this side of our lines." Nevertheless, Hurst took 20 prisoners (though five or six escaped because, as he explained, his rear guard was so "worn out with fatigue from hard marching and crossing streams by fording, swimming, &c."). Hurst believed that the entire rebel force, "out of ammunition" and "low-spirited," had fled toward Shiloh, so "badly torn up" that they could have been easily captured "by a small force from Corinth."[493]

Be that as it may, they were not captured, and had done more damage than they had sustained. Indeed, Forrest's cavalry seemed to many southerners to be the most active in the entire Confederate Army, for the Confederate "cavalry everywhere," groaned one secessionist, "save in West Tennessee, seem to be doing little else than picketing and scouting."[494]

❖ ❖ ❖ ❖

In early July 1863, a soldier correspondent for the New York *Jewish Messenger* described taking the steamer *Belle of Memphis* up the "smooth, expansive bosom" of the Mississippi to Fort Pillow. Apparently oblivious to the 52nd's upheavals, he described an idyllic encampment. "Summer has given the Pillowites brighter materials wherewith to rear their cities;" he reported, "and royal arches of cedar boughs, festooned with flowers and wreathed with the glistening leaves of oak and maple adorn the entrance to shady bowers, and rural retreats, beneath the verdant palaces of our soldiers." He found Wolfe's headquarters "delightful, a model of rustic elegance," and found that "many of the officers there have families with them, and the presence of women and children add not a little to the peaceful enchantment of military life as at present displayed at Fort Pillow."

Apparently paid by the word, he waxed on about how "feathered warblers" paid "great nature's god their evening homage" and "the rush of waters 'neath the 'painted thing of life'" -- his boat -- drowned "to nothing the angry croak of quadrupeds" -- frogs – "building earth houses close by the shore." Before his boat had even landed, Fort Pillow had already elicited several columns of poetic references and quotations, but his "soliloquy" was finally and mercifully interrupted when "the gang plank is shoved out, the revenue guards board the boat, and my pass is demanded." As his papers were inspected, he gazed up along the bluff at parapets "bristling with 'dogs of war' in the shape of 'thirty-twos' and 'sixty-fours.'"[495]  (In fact, according to Wolfe, the fort's entire battery consisted of two 24-pounders, one 32-pounder, a 52-pounder, and one smooth-bore 12-pounder that Colonel Scott had rescued from the demolition of New Madrid.)[496]

The garrison's repairs had served "to render this stronghold stronger than any other in our possession, and to remove all apprehensions of any hostile 'ram' which might venture within range of its guns. The appearance of Fort Pillow is now in happy contrast to that presented when the 'Stars and Bars' were lowered from its flagstaff, and our troops marched in triumph through its sallyports."

Though the adjacent country was "a beautiful region at this season," the correspondent could see the "marks of desolation everywhere, and few of civilization, except such as accompany the army. There are few inhabitants left, and within the fort there has not been the slightest attempt at planting or sowing, though the soil is favorable to cultivation." The locals, he said, were "wise, as they do not wish to sow for the 'Yankees' to reap. A fence is anomalous here. The able bodied white men are mostly in the Southern army, while the negroes have either been run off south or have seceded to the Yankees."[497]

One of the 52nd's most unwelcome duties was to help local authorities enforce the law. After a civilian court sentenced a black man to death for joining two white men in the murder of a white resident of nearby Covington, "the sheriff sent a request for the mounted force at Ft. Pillow to come," recalled Addison Sleeth, "and keep down any disturbance that might otherwise occur.

When we reached Covington, a large crowd of citizens-- men, women and children; white and black -- had collected there. The sheriff and the two deputies took the prisoner from the jail and placed him on a mule and led the way. We boys followed in column of fours and the citizens brought up the rear. When we reached an elm tree in the edge of a grove, we halted and formed a hollow square facing inward with the prisoner and officers inside and the crowd outside. The negro was told that he had to die and was asked if he had anything to say. He then told the story of how he and the two white men committed a murder so horrible that it made ones flesh creep to listen to it. When he had finished his talk, a rope was thrown over a limb of the tree and fastened, and the mule led from under him, and his career in this life was ended.

A few days later the sheriff sent a message that one of the white murderers had been captured "and there was danger of his friends and the outlaws making an attempt to rescue him that night." So Sleeth and his comrades returned to Covington, and after standing guard over the prisoner watched as "the sheriff and two guards brought out a slender rather fine looking young man who looked to be not over twenty two or three years old. As I remember him, he had a worn look and was pale and nervous, but there was nothing in his looks to denote the depth of wickedness and crime into which he had fallen." As the 52nd escorted him to the same tree from which the black man had been hanged, the prisoner turned to Sleeth and his comrades. "Boys," he said, "it looks hard to jerk a man up and hang him without giving him a trial." But he refused to say if he was guilty or innocent, and the 52nd drew him up to the tree, where he was mounted on a mule with his hands tied behind his back. His wife approached and, holding his tied hands, began to speak to him when the sheriff asked him if he had anything to say. The young man again refused to reply.

"We are not fooling," the sheriff told him. "We *are* going to hang you. If you have anything to say, say it now." But the prisoner said he had nothing more to say, and "the sheriff drew the black cap over his face, [and] placed the noose around his neck. His wife gave one wild scream," Sleeth recalled, "and fell in the dust at the feet of the mule, apparently lifeless." After some of her neighbors stepped forward and dragged her away, the mule was led out from under the prisoner. But "the rope slipped its fastening to the limb, letting the victim's feet touch the ground."

He tried to draw them up to hasten his death, but "his knees touched the ground before the rope could be drawn up," and it took him five minutes to die. "We remained till life was extinct ," wrote Sleeth, "and left behind us one of the most trying scenes on the nerves we had to witness in the four years of service."[498]

LAND PIRATES
PARTISANS & SCOUTS

At last, on July 27, 1863, Hurlbut announced to Colonel Wolfe that he was no longer commandant at Fort Pillow and that Fort Pillow itself would no longer be considered a Union post.[499] This may have been done because Memphis deemed Wolfe unfit to command any but his own Hoosiers, or to keep him from interfering with the 2nd Illinois Cavalry, which was ordered briefly back to Fort Pillow to prevent Richardson and his guerrillas from holding an election on the first thursday of August.[500] But the message got lost between Hurlbut and Asboth, who relayed his commands to the 2nd through Wolfe and expected the Colonel to continue making his reports as before.[501]

It must have been exhilarating for Wolfe and his men to have Captain Franklin Moore and his 2nd Cavalry back among them. Wolfe quickly allocated a herd of captured Tipton County steeds to the men of his mounted companies, enabling two of them to take part in a raid near Denmark, Tennessee at the end of July that resulted "in a total rout of the enemy."[502] On August 8, a Federal scouting expedition to Dyer County resulted in the murder of a man named Lucius Wilkins as he tried to hide his horses near Trenton. Apparently the Yankees – or Unionist Home Guards -- mutilated his corpse in a manner "so barbarous and revolting to the refined feelings of humanity and civilization, so much like the work of demons and savages," that his fellow Masons vowed never to forget it, entering a "Solemn protest, as an evidence of our indignation of such a wanton, atrocious and unfounded murder."[503]

On August 11, two members of the 2nd Illinois Cavalry who had been captured a month before by General James Chalmers were paroled and returned to Fort Pillow.[504] The 2nd continued its forays in groups of 25 to a hundred men. On August 11, they killed eleven and captured 40 of one Major Solshect's 150 guerrillas at Merriweather's Ferry in Obion County.[505] On one of these expeditions the 52nd demonstrated a certain lack of awe for Captain Moore. Riding with five Hoosiers in the extreme front of his small force, they charged through a rebel skirmish line with their guns blazing, only to be chased for several miles until at last the rebels looped around in front of Moore's column and formed a battle line, threatening to charge. As his troopers caught up to him, "the Captain became excited," wrote Addison Sleeth, and kept up "a continuous string of orders and a wild waving of his sword," commanding Sleeth and his comrades to move off the road. But Sleeth's Sergeant Wilkes "gave the Captain a cursing and told him, if he was scared, to get to the rear;" for the 52nd would "attend to the Rebels in front." The rebels, however, thought better of it, and melted back into the woods.[506]

These Union raids resulted in hundreds of fugitives "skulking in the woods" around Fort Pillow: disabused rebels whom Lieutenant Temple of the 52nd deemed "ready and eager" to join the Union Army.[507] Ready and eager or not, local boys who had managed thus far to elude rebel recruiters or desert from Confederate regiments now found themselves pursued by Union press gangs. Carroll County proved especially fertile ground for Union recruiters, for as one of the 52nd's Tennessee conscripts put it, all the young men had "turned Yankee."[508]

While the Wizard of the Saddle raced off with his main force to Chickamauga, John Brownlow of Forrest's 19th Tennessee Cavalry pulled his horse off the line of march and made for home. The Yankees had preceded him into the area, however, taking livestock and conscripting two boys named Yokley. Brownlow and seven of his comrades gave chase, capturing several Yankee pickets, but could not catch up to the patrol that had captured the Yokley boys. By the time he reached home at Lawrenceville his father had been shot in the bowels by a Federal soldier; he died in agony five days later. Though Brownlow managed to remain in the vicinity a few days after his father's death, the countryside teemed with Federals "arresting every reble they could heare of" while "Some of our own people were piloting them." He and his pal Polk Lovell, riding in the company of Brownlow's slave Landen, "ran into the federals several times befour we got out,"[509] and in early September local people often remarked that "the boys are skedaddling" from rebel conscription.[510] "No man in all that country is safe," wrote the empathetic Union Colonel Isaac Hawkins. "The confeds are conscripting: hunting men and boys down with hounds – and in some instances young men are so torn up by the dogs, as to be unable to travel. When the people are thus hunted on one side, it does seem to me that they should not be plundered by the other."[511]

In August, Grant had summoned most of the 2nd Illinois Cavalry's companies to Vicksburg, thus demolishing Asboth's hopes for the success of his two-pronged campaign against the elusive Bob Richardson for which he had deployed cavalry from Fort Pillow and Union City on coordinated scouts between the Hatchie and Obion Rivers.[512] Though the 2nd's Fort Pillow deployment was now down to four companies, Hurlbut ordered them across the Mississippi to Arkansas to protect shipping from "guerrillas well mounted and armed" who had been reported hauling cannon twelve miles above the dismantled settlement of Osceola.

Wolfe chose to deploy some of his own mounted infantry to Arkansas and send Moore off on a scout in the direction of Jackson, Tennessee in hopes, again, of sweeping Richardson out of West Tennessee. The 52nd found no cannons and only managed to bring back a few captives of dubious allegiance, and Moore's expedition yielded a handful of prisoners,[513] "it being impossible," as Moore reported to Wolfe, "to prevent the numerous 'Bands of Guerrillas' that infest the country from receiving information of his approach." On September 23, Asboth again commanded Captain Moore and his troopers to pull up stakes at Fort Pillow, this time to hunt guerrillas around Union City.[514] With forty of his men on the sick list, Moore and his frustrated troopers departed five days later, leaving a single company behind.[515]

The guerrillas harassed Union boat traffic from both sides of the Mississippi. Taking their cue from their prewar counterparts in Missouri, Mississippi steamship captains stacked their decks with cotton bales as a barrier against rebel sniper fire. A few boats sustained some damage from Confederate sharpshooters, but it was not enough to destroy them. Rebel arsonists, however, were more effective. In late September, at Milliken's Bend, Louisiana, saboteurs set fire to the steamer *Robert Campbell* so expertly that before the boat could reach shore its passengers were forced to leap into the river to avoid the spreading flames; twenty-two drowned, including several federal officers.[516] After this catastrophe, rebel arsonists were suspected of causing every maritime mishap on the Mississippi, including the wreck of the steamer *Sunny Side* in November. Entangled in a notorious antler-like snarl of driftwood off Dyer County known to boatmen as the "Rack," the sinking of the *Sunny Side* claimed the lives of some 35 passengers and took with it 12,000 bales of cotton.[517]

On September 13, Wolfe received an inquiry about a curious application that Asboth had received from Dr. A.G. Bragg of Saint Louis, upon whose land much of Fort Pillow lay. Bragg had demanded that the Union Army compensate him for the thousands of cords of timber that had been felled to clear the site. Wolfe replied that the rebels and not the Yankees had felled the trees, and that, besides, Bragg's claim to the property had been disputed by a Chicago firm to which he owed money.[518]

Wolfe's relations with his new Lieutenant-Colonel E. H. Davies were no better than they had been with Strickland. "There is trouble in this regiment," wrote Army Inspector

Burns, "between the Colonel & Lieut Colonel, charges having been preferred against each by the other. The feeling exists between the two and their adherents. Their cases should be brought to trial."[519]

On October 14, Wolfe sent out another scout through Ripley and Brownsville consisting of the lone company of 2nd Illinois Cavalry and the beleaguered Captain J.W. McCowick of the 52nd and "every available man of his command properly Armed and Equiped and provided with ten days prepared rations."[520] But no sooner had they set off than Hurlbut wired that Colonels Biffle and John F. Newsom of Forrest's command were about to descend on Fort Pillow with 3,000 men, having already inflicted heavy casualties on the Yankees at Colliersville.[521] And so the expedition turned around and rode back into Wolfe's fortification, removing their saddles and harness from their horses and mules and bracing for attack, though by now they must have had their fill of Hurlbut and his false alarms.

A tense but uneventful week later, Wolfe received word that a Union man named Captain Hays "who for some time has been engaged in recruiting and organizing a company of Tennessee militia" was captured and shot by Faulkner's guerrillas, his corpse "entirely stripped of his clothing, and thrown into the Middle fork of the Forked Deer River, near Lee's Mill, in Gibson County. "Captain Hays," Wolfe wrote, "by his personal bravery and daring, and by his indefatigable zeal in hunting down guerrillas" had made himself and his little command "a terror to that class of lawless men." Wolfe urged "prompt and decisive" measures to "avenge this inhuman and barberous outrage."[522] On October 29, after Hurlbut's alarm had died away, he sent Company E to Tipton County under 2nd Illinois Cavalry Lieutenant Curtin Dement to track down Hays's murderers, and in early November another expedition to hunt down the killers of a Dr. Joseph Bragg, a Union man murdered near Covington. Neither met with success.[523]

In mid November it was Sol Street who came roaring into Dyer County, this time with his own battalion of guerrillas and most of the 15th Tennessee cavalry, and fanned out to conscript soldiers for Forrest. Operating out of Union City,

Captain Franklin Moore and his 2nd Illinois Cavalry "attacked the devils at Merriwether's ferry" in Obion County on the 15th. "I whipped them and killed 11 men," Moore boasted, "and took Col. Solomon Street and 55 men, also one wagon of arms and some horses" at a cost of only one Yankee wounded. Street's brother was among the dead, but Street did not remain a captive long and after slipping out of Yankee custody was foraging back in Dyer County.[524]

Reading that Hurlbut had ordered the Unionist citizens of Memphis to organize themselves into Home Guards, Wolfe decided to try the same thing at Fort Pillow, drilling the speculators, barbers, sutlers, millers and refugee farmers who had collected along the bluff in the use of the musket and the bayonet.[525] He figured he might need them, as Hurlbut was now circulating a report that Forrest was in Okolona, Mississippi, just south of Memphis, shoeing horses, issuing arms and uniforms, and preparing to raid West Tennessee with a horde of seven thousand men.[526]

On November 21, Hurlbut sent an expedition after Colonel Faulkner, who was reported to be encamped some 25 miles from Fort Pillow. Awakened by the strains of "Boots and Saddles," they mounted up and headed east until they encountered a rebel picket. "The picket halted our advance guard and asked, 'Who comes there?' The Lieutenant in command replied that they were in the service of a rebel colonel named Marshall who, in reality, was their quarry. The picket ordered them to dismount and give the countersign, whereupon the lieutenant shouted to his men, "Ready. Aim. Fire. Charge," and "six or eight carbines broke the stillness of the morning and away we went as fast as our horses could run."

Finding their route forward blocked by Forrest's men, they turned back, though by now they had been told that the picket they had fired on was part of a cavalry encampment of some 800 men. As the Union rear guard collected the wounded rebel pickets, the rebels opened fire, "but the boys returned the fire as promptly as if we had fifteen to their one instead of them having fifteen to our one," and eventually returned to Fort Pillow with the captive pickets. They tried to comfort Wolfe with the news that during the encounter about sixty conscripts had escaped from the rebel camp, but Wolfe had by then received reports that Faulkner was approaching with 2,000 men. As Colonel George E. Waring reported the next day from Union City, Faulkner intended to make "a demonstration upon Memphis or Fort Pillow at some day not very far distant." His plan was apparently to attack Fort Pillow with a small force in order to draw out a scouting party and then attack in force.

Recalling his men from the field, Wolfe again urged Memphis to send him more cavalry,[527] but Hurlbut replied that he could not "at present increase the cavalry force at Fort Pillow, as every available man is needed to protect the working parties in taking up the iron on the Paducah and Hickman Railroad:" a priority which must have struck Wolfe as both curious and ominous.[528] Then would the 16th Army Corps at least send him bayonets to replace the scabberless blades that had by now rusted out?[529] And what was Wolfe supposed to do about the traders and sutlers who were pecking him to death now that he was no longer post commander and Memphis had decreed that all trade at Fort Pillow should cease?[530] Lest he be accused of colluding with smugglers, he came down hard on agents of Harris & Company, one of the more enterprising concerns to have set up a trading post at Fort Pillow. Before the year was out he informed Harris & Company that he was urging the local Treasury agent to punish them for smuggling liquor and horses through Union lines by stopping "the issuing of any further permits to your house."[531]

It had not entirely ceased, however. On December 8, Sleeth was ordered to take on one of the more tedious garrison duties formerly performed by the 32nd.[532] It was a curious appointment for a soldier with an already well demonstrated taste for liquor. Detailed as a pass clerk for the Provost Marshal's office, he was "to write passes through our lines and examine baggage &c. so that nothing contraband got out into the country or aboard any boat on the river. So I turned over my horse, saddle and everything except my gun and accoutrements to the Company Commander and moved down to the landing in the Provost Marshals building." He and a buddy named John Purcell "had the building -- two rooms and a cellar -- all to ourselves most of the time, as the Marshal had a private office. The duties of the office necessarially brought us in contact with many citizens and gave us much information we could not have gained with the company. In examining baggage we found more intoxicating liquors than all other contraband good together. Our orders were to turn all liquors over to the hospital, and we did," except, Sleeth confessed, for "what we appropriated to the use of the office, for in those days," he explained, "we were not teetotalers." One evening they knocked in the heads of five or six barrels of potatoes to find "a ten gallon keg of whiskey in the center of each." On another occasion they "got hold of a lot of canned peaches that had been expressed to one of the boys. We opened these cans and Lo! the peaches had turned to second class whiskey" which Sleeth appropriated for "office and hospital use."[533]

THE WIZARD
FORREST'S FEINTS

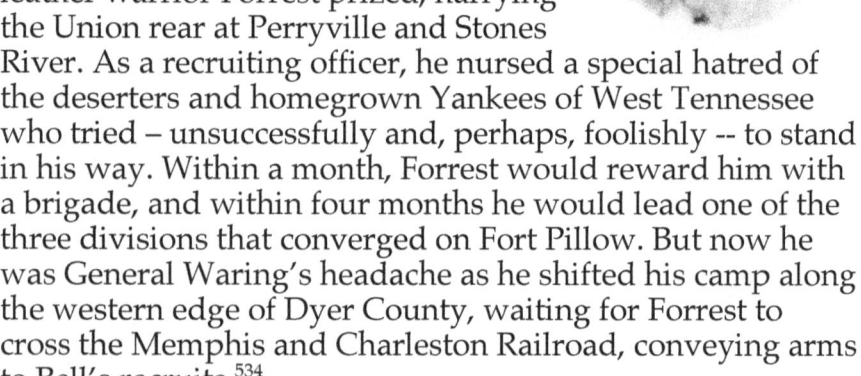

In Dyer County, Colonel Tyree H. Bell of the 12th Tennessee Cavalry had established a recruiting station near his home at Newbern, where he would eventually collect five companies of horsemen for his lord and master, Nathan Bedford Forrest. Forty-six years old, a Kentuckian turned Tennessee tobacco planter, he had moved to Dyer County in 1859. After casting his lot with the Confederacy, he proved himself the kind of hell-for-leather warrior Forrest prized, harrying the Union rear at Perryville and Stones River. As a recruiting officer, he nursed a special hatred of the deserters and homegrown Yankees of West Tennessee who tried – unsuccessfully and, perhaps, foolishly -- to stand in his way. Within a month, Forrest would reward him with a brigade, and within four months he would lead one of the three divisions that converged on Fort Pillow. But now he was General Waring's headache as he shifted his camp along the western edge of Dyer County, waiting for Forrest to cross the Memphis and Charleston Railroad, conveying arms to Bell's recruits.[534]

Forrest crossed into Tennessee at Saulsbury, which either his advance scouts or the town's fleeing Unionists set ablaze.[535] With some 5,000 men in the field, he somehow eluded Hurst's patrols and established his base camp at Jackson on December 6.[536] Dubbing it the headquarters of the Confederate Department of West Tennessee, he reported to Joe Johnston that by New Years he hoped to have swelled his forces to 8,000 men. He asked his commander, Stephen D. Lee, to keep up his feints along the railroad and thus distract the Yankees from Forrest's intention, which was to cut off Memphis by "effectually" destroying the railroad to Charleston, to build a bridge across the Hatchie, and to then rustle some 5,000 head of "good beef cattle" for the rebel army.[537] By mid December he was " conscripting every man capable of bearing arms and taking all negro men fit for soldiers" to serve as teamsters and prevent them from joining the Union Army.[538]

All this thoroughly rattled Hurlbut, who was convinced that Forrest intended to take Fort Pillow and prove "of serious injury on the river." He urged Brigadier General Andrew Jackson Smith, who had taken command at Columbus, to send "any spare infantry" to Fort Pillow at once, for, even if Forrest did not move on Wolfe, Smith would thereby relieve the 52nd, which Hurlbut wanted to send into the field.[539]

For the moment, Forrest had no intention of taking Fort Pillow. He hoped instead that Smith would deny Hurlbut's appeal, for though he thought he could withstand an attack from Union City, "should they move from Fort Pillow also" he would have "more than I can manage with the raw and unarmed troops I have, and especially so should they move from below at the same time." In fact, it was said that at this time only 200 of Forrest's men, primarily the veterans who served in his escort, were even armed.[540] At his headquarters at Jackson, his nostrils filled with the aroma of the 50 tons of smoked bacon he had appropriated from local farms, Forrest begged Stephen E. Lee to send "at least two brigades of cavalry up here without delay," for he had received reports that Hurlbut was mounting his infantry and preparing to send them to Fort Pillow under the command of the fearsome Benjamin Henry Grierson, whose raid through Mississippi the previous spring had initially convinced many Northerners and Southerners alike that he and not Forrest was the greatest cavalryman of the Civil War.[541] And well he might have been had he served under another commander, for Hurlbut had no intention of depriving himself of Grierson nor any part of his own "exceedingly light" force of infantry, and thus the two sides shadow-boxed to the end of the year.[542]

Forrests's biographers would make a great deal of Forrest's escape to Mississippi, the way he wove his way among the Union patrols sent to find him.[543] Few of them were strong enough to challenge him, however; in fact, they were in considerable disarray, responding to false alarms from Memphis, Columbus, and Union City. Forrest's pickings were a great deal leaner than he had promised Richmond. Nevertheless, along the line of his hasty retreat Forrest displayed his gift for sly improvisation and unblinking bluff that would repeatedly save his command from catastrophe. With a series of his detachments' feints, he tricked the Yankees into thinking he would escape via Bolivar or Purdy, and on Christmas Eve bluffed his way out of a jam at Estenaula. Trotting well ahead of his main column, he and an escort of sixty men encountered a force of some 600 federals. Under cover of night, Forrest spread his 60-man escort across a field of dried-out cornstalks and, shouting commands to phantom detachments, led his men on a charge through the field. They made such a racket that the Federals, mistaking the crackling stalks for the rattle and clatter of muskets, retreated into the night,[544] freeing Forrest to ferry his men and horses across the flooded and fast-moving Hatchie.

From Estenaula he veered toward Memphis, sent five hundred men across the Wolf River railroad bridge, and held the Yankees back at Collierville until the remainder of his force – 3,500 unarmed men – had dropped down into Mississippi, where, without a hitch in his step, he and his escort came to the rescue of a hard-pressed Bob Richardson, charging into the midst of his outnumbering Yankee attackers and firing their pistols into the blue-coats' faces until the survivors commenced "a confused and precipitate flight," strewing the countryside "with turkeys, chickens, ducks, geese, Haversacks, &c..[545] And arms, for it was here that Forrest's escort equipped itself with abandoned Yankee "Sharps Carbines, Colts, Repeaters & accoutrerments" that would aid "so materially to make the Escort a terror to the Enemy."[546]

Greeting Forrest at Okolona, the 2nd Tennessee Cavalry celebrated a "Southern Christmas," shooting their guns and passing the jug.⁵⁴⁷ On December 30, Forrest proposed an exchange. "I have in my hands forty-five or fifty Federal prisoners," he informed Hurlbut, "among them two Captains and three Lieutenants. I suppose that I have lost some men also," he said, "and owing to the fatigue and expense necessary to send your men to Richmond," and Forrest's "desire also to get my own men" he asked if Hurlbut would exchange any Confederate soldiers you may have in your hands," beginning with Forrest's own troops, for Forrest's prisoners "at any point you may designate on the Rail Road between Lagrange and Memphis."⁵⁴⁸

On December 18, Wolfe received word that General Smith had sent Colonel Edward Wehler and his 178th New York Volunteers to Fort Pillow.⁵⁴⁹ Recruited on Staten Island, they arrived by steamer in the early afternoon of December 22, and settled into what remained of the 32nd Iowa's old camp. The 178th was another of the Union Army's garrison regiments, having spent the war as military police in Washington, DC and vicinity and Columbus, Kentucky. Colonel Wehler immediately decried the lack of facilities at the post, especially the necessary means of hauling water and firewood. There were only six wagon teams at Fort Pillow, which Wolfe had reserved for his Hoosiers and the provost marshall.⁵⁵⁰ Wolfe and Wehler were soon colliding over matters of discipline. After Wehler arrested one of his officers, a Major Selden Hetzel, Wolfe released him, allowing him "the limits of the Fort" as he awaited court-martial.⁵⁵¹ One of Wehler's more literate privates deserted in early December and turned up serving as a clerk on a hospital boat. "It is very probable that the said Matthasi has pleaded sickness and forged a Descriptive List," Wehler warned the Provost Marshall in Paducah. "He is a most dangerous character" and "if not properly secured he will very likely escape."⁵⁵² His officers were ordered to hand over the wages of the deceased men of the regiment (208 of Wehler's men would die during the war, 190 from disease) so that they could be relayed to their rightful heirs and assigns.⁵⁵³

Though 1863 had been a good year for the Yankees in the western theatre of the war, it ended at Fort Pillow on a tragic note. The elements marked New Year's Eve with a severe winter storm that came hurtling down the Mississippi with paralyzing winds and icy snow, killing several men just below Cairo, and ten black laborers at Island Number Ten to which Wolfe had exported his contrabands that fall. Indeed the entire Mississippi was closed to shipping, and the Ohio clogged with ice.[554]

In the morning, Wolfe received a report of a trading boat moored above Osceola and supplying rebel guerrillas with "medicine and other contraband goods." So he dispatched Lieutenant Edward Alexander of the 52nd to equip eight men with a day's rations and forty rounds each of ammunition and lead them on what was by then a routine mission to interdict illicit trade.

There was no hint of a storm as they rowed off in their yawl. A dense fog obscured the Arkansas bank and soon Fort Pillow itself receded into the mist. The oarsmen tugged them across to Osceola and then further upriver, to the designated spot where – it was now late afternoon -- they found no trace of a trading boat. Picking up a boatman named E.D. Leizure, Lieutenant Alexander ordered his men to turn the boat around, and they began to work their way back toward Fort Pillow in the swift current of the swollen river.

By now a strong wind was blowing, carrying with it a cold rain, and as the wind turned frigid the rain turned to sleet. By nightfall they were nine miles above Fort Pillow, struggling to keep the wind and the current from sweeping them away and to prevent the bitter brown chop from swamping their yawl. Leizure, manning the helm in the dark, made for a sandbar he could just make out in the dark: a thin strip of white snow assailed by waves. The waves slapped the yawl's hull high upon the bar, and the ten men disembarked to search for firewood. But everything was saturated with water, and when they tried to launch their yawl to make for the Arkansas shore, the rope slipped out of their frozen hands and the wind yanked the boat into the current.

Leizure and an Indiana soldier squattered out and managed to scramble aboard, but the boat spun helplessly away as their companions' beckoning voices faded off into the wind. The water splashing over its side quickly turned to ice, freezing the infantryman to his seat. But Leizure somehow managed to steer the boat onto the Arkansas bank, and he and the frozen soldier, begging by now to be left to die, found enough kindling in the deep woods to build a fire.

Captain Ross Guffin of the 52nd was at Fort Pillow that New Year's Eve, and gave this description of the festivities.

> The commander of the garrison had given a supper, and the large dining-hall was filled with happy people; brave officers, respectable citizens, and charming women.
>
> It was the farewell of loyal hearts to the year that gave freedom to the slave—that brought the first real success to our arms—that gave us Vicksburg, Gettysburg, and Missionary Ridge—that had brought promise of the rebellion's overthrow. The perils and escapes, the achievements and hopes, the rewards and promises of the closing and of the coming year were earnestly and eloquently discussed; and so the old year went out, carrying with it the blessing of the loyal millions, and the new year stepped in.
>
> The party broke up, and we walked out into the cold, dark night. The thermometer was now seven degrees below zero.
>
> "Captain, have Lieutenant Alexander and his men reported?" asked the Post-Commander, Colonel Wolfe, as he drew my arm in his, and we walked away to our quarters.
>
> "Not yet," was my reply.
>
> "What can have become of them?" he rejoined. "I fear for their safety if they are out this dreadful night.

"And well you may, my brave Colonel," wrote the grandiloquent Guffin, "for even now, as we walk, where are they?"

Upriver, the Lieutenant and his men tried to keep alive by marching the length of the bar, but as the snow eased off, the wind turned even colder, and one of the men toppled to the ground. His comrades tried to revive him, but he had frozen to death.

"Boys," concluded Lieutenant Alexander, his beard a nest of ice, "there is no use striving any longer; it is now only about midnight, and one of our number is already frozen to death. We cannot hold out till morning; there is no hope, we must all die." And with that he drew his cape over his head and lay down.

Within a few hours, in temperatures as low as eight degrees below zero, he and four of his men lay frozen to death in the snows of the bar, while their comrades staggered on in circles, clothes stiff with ice. Finally a local Arkansas farmer – a Union man – spotted the men stranded on the bar, set off in his skiff, and rowed out to their rescue. Retrieved from the skiff by a Union steamer, they were all transported – the living and the dead -- back to Fort Pillow.

"I think the only tear Col. Ed Wolfe shed during the war," wrote Addison Sleeth, "was when the boat touched the wharf and brought him face to face with the frozen dead."[555] By Special Order Number 200, Wolfe ordered new blankets distributed.[556] But it brought them scant comfort. On New Year's day, one of the two of the survivors who had lost their frozen feet and hands to the surgeon's saw died of exhaustion and shock.[557]

ABANDONED ABSOLUTELY
THE UNION EVACUATION
OF FORT PILLOW

January 1864 was perhaps the most uneventful month of the entire war. In fact, some of the hottest fighting that cold month was against Native Americans in California and New Mexico. A kind of blood-weary ennui seemed to settle over the country, North and South, interrupted only by the trumpeting of politicians and the occasional guerrilla sortie. But the coming year would see momentous battles for which both armies tried as best they could to brace themselves.

As William Tecumseh Sherman prepared for his Meridian campaign and the long march eastward, there seemed to him no reason left to man Fort Pillow. After all, the Union Army's hold on the Mississippi was secure, vouchsafed by the destruction of the rebel river navy and the occupation of other river bastions – among them Cairo, Paducah, Columbus, and Union City – of greater strategic value, rendering Fort Pillow nothing more than a troublous relic of Confederate pretension.

General Hurlbut would later plead that he "never had any orders to evacuate" Fort Pillow. He claimed that his orders had been "to hold certain fortified points on the river." And that he "never had any instructions with regard to Fort Pillow one way or the other that I recollect. I considered it necessary to hold it, and never intended to abandon it," for he believed that Fort Pillow "should be held always, and there is nothing in my instructions that requires it to be abandoned."

But Sherman could not have been clearer. "Abandon Corinth and Fort Pillow absolutely," he commanded on January 11, "removing all public property to Cairo or Memphis; also leave all black troops and such of the local Tennessee regiments as can be employed, with minute instructions to the commanders of posts at Paducah, Columbus, Cairo, Memphis, and such others as you judge best to have fixed to organize and arm the loyal citizens for self-defense:" thereby replacing the veteran troops Sherman was scooping up with Unionist Southern blacks and whites[558]

Hurlbut may have believed personally that Fort Pillow "should be held always," but he at least initially followed Sherman's orders to the letter. He immediately commanded Wolfe to "send forward to Memphis the two best of his three batteries of light artillery," transport "all public property" to Cairo or Memphis, completely abandon Fort Pillow, and evacuate his garrison to Memphis.[559]

Wolfe was delighted to comply. Perhaps now the accusations of theft and bribery, Contraband abuse and smuggling would cease. He assured a jittery Hurlbut that the way was clear for such divestment, for "the surrounding country is at present unusually quiet," and "free from marauding bands with the exception of a very few guerrillas that still infest Tipton County."[560]

Hurlbut sent a company of black artillerists of the 1st Tennessee Heavy Artillery up from Memphis to assist Wolfe in dismounting the fort's heavy guns and loading them onto steamers.[561] For some of these troops this would be a homecoming of sorts. Back in June, Lieutenant-Colonel W.R. Roberts had sent First Lieutenant David C. Mooney to Fort Pillow to recruit Contrabands for his 1st Tennessee Heavy Artillery (African Descent).[562] Eager to rid his camp of Contrabands, Wolfe commanded all of his officers to render Mooney every assistance. "It is desired that these Regiments be filled as speedily as possible," Wolfe wrote, "and all Able Bodied Colored men that are now employed in the Regiment as Cooks must be allowed to enlist without hindrance. [Their] places can be filled by those who may hereafter come within our lines."[563]

When Lieutenant B. K. Logan was appointed Post Superintendent of Contrabands, he was ordered to deliver to Island Number Ten all of the Contrabands who had gathered at Fort Pillow since the last evacuation and hand over 14 new recruits to the 2nd Regiment Heavy Artillery.[564] But apparently the Contrabands kept pouring in, for within the month 38 more men had been recruited at Fort Pillow and transported down to Island Number Ten, while Colonel Roberts picked up more recruits from among the slaves of a local Secessionist named W.R. Carr, and another twenty from farms and plantations around Tiptonville,[565] while Wolfe continued to relay their kith and kin to Island Number Ten.[566]

On January 24, 1864, on an island two miles north of Helena, 250 rebel cavalry had "fired upon a party of black woodchoppers, set fire to their shanties, and stolen some two dozen mules and oxen."[567] So it was decided to evacuate all the remaining Contrabands at Fort Pillow to Island Number Ten, with a garrison of black troops to protect them.[568]

Soldiers' families posed another problem. "Twelve or thirteen Tennessee boys had enlisted in our Company," recalled Addison Sleeth. "Some of these were married. Then some of our old Yankee boys had married Dixie girls," so "most of them sent their wives to Northern homes."[569] In the meantime, the garrison's supplies and equipage, "horses, Mules, Bridles, Saddles, and Wagons," supplies, equipage, surplus tents and clothing were collected and inventoried and turned over to the quartermaster.[570] Finally, on Tuesday, January 19, Wolfe and his Hoosiers saluted their dead and crowded aboard the steamer *Thistle* for a three-day journey to Memphis down a river still littered with ice.[571]

Colonel Wolfe and the 52nd Indiana would spend the rest of the war in the Third Division of the 16th Army Corps, fighting at Tupelo and Oxford, and most notably in December at the Battle of Nashville, where they formed a line a couple of regiments down from their old nemeses -- the Iowans of the 32nd. "With a shout," as Wolfe reported, "peculiar to this corps," the Hoosiers charged the rebel

works. They captured enumerable rebel guns and several Confederate officers, including Major General Edward Johnson, for which Wolfe's seamy command of Fort Pillow was apparently forgiven or forgotten, for Wolfe was brevetted in March, 1865, and a statue erected in his honor. After the war, he would resume his mercantile business, accept a perhaps unwisely offered appointment as Indiana state auditor, and die in Rushville in 1916.

❖   ❖   ❖   ❖

According to Addison Sleeth, his fellow Hoosiers "left the keeping of Ft. Pillow to others." But to whom? Before the seemingly unaccountable arrival of the black artillerists and white Unionist troopers that in less than three months would meet their doom at the hands of Nathan Bedford Forrest and his cavalry, the post's civilian contingent apparently dwindled down to a few merchants and their servants. Without the Union Army's protection, they probably would have evacuated the premises altogether.

But on February 4, with the approval of William Sooy Smith, commander of cavalry for the Department of the Mississippi, a Tennessee Unionist named William Bradford arrived at Fort Pillow from Kentucky, where he had run into trouble recruiting men for his cavalry regiment. Deeming the Fort Pillow area a richer vein of Unionists to mine, he arrived with his embryonic regiment, the 14th -- though more commonly referred to as the 13th -- Tennessee Cavalry (USA).

As Bradford and his troopers moved into the tightly built quarters the Hoosiers and Iowans had left behind, the civilians returned to do business under the 13th's protection. From here Bradford would send foragers out to the already hardpressed neighboring farms, and expeditions against local squads of guerrillas, and develop in a few months a reputation as a zealous Unionist but also a rank amateur. Soon the post was bustling once more with smugglers, sutlers, moonshiners, cotton-buyers, grocers, Contrabands: even a daguerreotypist set up shop. Against Sherman's orders, Hurlbut added to the mix a company of the 2nd USC Light Artillery and the entire 6th USC Heavy Artillery to the mix. Some were men who had first set foot on the bluff as slave laborers for the rebels, who had experienced freedom in the conquered post's sprawling Contraband camp. For many of them Fort Pillow would be the setting not only for their enslavement, liberation, and conscription, but their death.

POST SCRIPT

Born in civil war, and reborn in civil war, we Americans may always have the seeds of civil war within us. What continues to astonish observers of this country is how readily we have been willing to denounce, exploit, and even kill one another over our opposing conceptions of our nation's destiny, identity, and ideals.

The Union conquest of the Upper Mississippi was like the invasion of a wholly alien force. Each side was an almost total stranger to the other. And the divisions within each of the opposing sides were almost as deep, with the fate of the African American serving as the wedge. It is what divided slaveholder from non, and, as with the Yankee garrison at Fort Pillow, the Southern Indianan from the ostensibly abolitionist Iowan.

Nothing was quite so manifestly vital to the defeat of the Confederacy as the conquest of its broad and meandering lifeline. Had it not been necessary for the Union to control the Mississippi so early in the war, and the Union Army had not been compelled thereby to occupy the counties along its banks for years on end, perhaps the wounds inflicted by both sides in that byzantine theatre of the war would not have festered for so long. But war itself is a squalid enterprise. It is the ultimate failure of a nation's political will, and in a democracy there can be no greater failure than that, unless it be a war over slavery in a country that has dubbed itself the land of the free.

On April 12, 1864, an outnumbering host of Confederate cavalry under Nathan Bedford Forrest overran Fort Pillow's garrison of white Tennessee Unionists and escaped slaves turned Federal artillerists. The result of this collision of Southerners was the Fort Pillow Massacre, the most notorious and hotly debated atrocity of the Civil War. It would owe a measure of its infamy to the machinations of

Radical Republican congressmen who delectatiously broadcast such lurid details as rebels slaughtering soldiers in their hundreds after they surrendered, of wounded men murdered in hospital tents, of men burned and buried alive. The South in turn responded much as it had to the prewar brickbats of the abolitionists: by hunkering down and denying it all.

Blaming Hurlbut for the massacre in April 1864, Grant would transfer him from Memphis to New Orleans, where he continued his pattern of inebriation and corruption in the Department of the Gulf. Though he did not save a dime of his army pay, he would return to Belvidere a rich man. Despite continuing charges of corruption and inebriation, in later years he would realize his ambition of being elected to Congress and subsequently serve as Minister first to Colombia and then to Peru where, after disgracing himself and his country in a drunken altercation with his American counterpart in Chile, he died in 1882.

The dearth of surviving correspondence in Hurlbut's archives relating to Fort Pillow's last garrisoning suggests that in the wake of the catastrophe that followed, Hurlbut may have destroyed it. Going by his history, and the post's, it may well be that the hundreds of Unionist Southerners, black and white, he stationed at Fort Pillow would die not in defense of the Union, nor the end of slavery, nor for the

security of the Mississippi, but merely to protect the nefarious commerce from which Hurlbut and his cronies were profiting so handsomely. If so, greed as well as racism must be called to account for the massacre that would taint the Mississippi with so many young men's blood.

Footnotes

[1] Regarding Pillow's cowardice, "The said Brigadier General Pillow did in the 2nd day of January, 1863, [screen] himself behind a large tree whilst his Brigade was advancing on the Enemy and remained there until the line had passed when he was ordered to leave by the Maj Genl Commanding." (R.E. Graves, Maj & Chief of Artillery. Maj Gen Breckinridges DW. Witnesses – St. Darragh, [St.] W.D. Gilman. Breckinridge, "Charges and Specifications" in the John Cabell Breckinridge Collection, Chicago Historical Society.)
[2] According to the New York *Herald,* Pillow was "famous for digging his ditches on the wrong side of his defenses." The New York *Herald,* April 24, 1862.
[3] In late April 1861, in order to insure Kentucky's "neutrality," Governor Magoffin had ordered Buckner, then head of the Kentucky State Guard, to fortify Columbus on the Mississippi so that neither Union or Confederacy could establish control of this strategic point on the Mississippi. Forrest C. Pogue Public History Institute, *The Civil War in the Jackson Purchase Region of Kentucky: A Survey of Historic Sites and Structures.*
[4] The New York *Herald,* November 12, 1861.
[5] On his arrival at Fort Pillow, a military band played "God Save the Queen" in Russell's honor, requiring the Irishman to doff his hat and stand in the midday glare. "I would not broil *my* skull in the sun," a bystander told him afterward, "not if General Washington was standing just before me." Italics mine.
[6] D. Wintter/Leonidas Polk: October 19 and November 12, 1861 in RG 109, Compiled Military Service Records, Sappers and Miners, Capt. D. Wintter (MC).
[7] Stevenson, *Thirteen Months in the Rebel Army.*
[8] The vast majority of veterans interviewed after the war testified that though their families' owned slaves, they labored hard. TCWVQ.
[9] McPherson, *The Negro's Civil War,* p. 39.
[10] WR1:7:698, 711, 733.
[11] Hopping, *Life of Andrew Hull Foote,* p. 565. The following recruiter's manifest gives some idea of how planters resisted sending their slaves to Fort Pillow: ""List of parties notified by me on [Decr] Creek Washington County Miss.: Louis Thompson: 20 men refused to send. Miss West: 20 men refused to send. Stephen Banefield: 2 plant, about 50 men, swears he

will not send a hand until compelled by force, has large wealth and has never aided the confederacy to the amount of $100 dollars such men ought to be reached in some way. William [?] Smith: about 50 men, sent his hands under [illegible]. [illegible] Hill 16 men goes up with his hands. Est. A. C. [Downs]: about 40 men. [A. J. Payton] 18 to 20. Col. George [B. Hall] sent before about 25. Mr. [Simes], 30 will not send. Doct J. P. Thomas about 50 men. E. H. [Paer] 12 men will send this time. Silver Lake: Douglas [McHatton] 30 men will send. C. G. McHatton, 18 or 20 men will send. Blackmor & [Oglisby] 30 men will send. William Ferriday 18 don't send. Mr. Wildon 10 don't send. J. W. [Woolfol], 35; J. W. Vick, 75; M. Cameron Overseer, 55; C. Goodloe, 40; Dr. Jackson, 10; M. W. Brown, 9; W. P. Bernard, 25; Henry Bernard, 8; W. Britton Overseer, 35; Helen Johnston Overseer, 70; J. R. Chisholm, 20; E. Mount, 30; L. Tillman, 4; Samuel Parks, 15; Wade Hampton Overseer, 130; S. Spencer Overseer, 25; Robert Fitz, 25; Andrew [Turnbull], 150; Marshall Spencer Overseer, 40; R. J. Turnbull, 190; Isaac [Heile], 14." No attribution (MC)

[12] Lewis P. Williamson/Leonidas Polk: September 29, 1861 in RG109/CSR (NARA).
[13] Italics mine.
[14] A. M. Rafter/J. A. Rogers: December 17, 1861 (MC).
[15] Richard Martin (SN).
[16] Metcalfe, *Cotton Plantation Record and Account Book*, Mississippi Department of Archives and History.
[17] Lewis P. Williamson/Leonidas Polk: November 9, 1861 in RG109/CSR (NARA).
[18] Montgomery Lynch/Major General Polk: October 30, 1861 in RG109 Compiled Service Record, Montgomery Lynch (MC).
[19] Wharton, *The Negro in Mississippi: 1865-1890,* pp. 14, 124-125.
[20] WR1:7:739.
[21] Tines Kendricks in Botkin, *Lay My Burden Down,* p. 73.
[22] S.L. Phelps/Andrew H. Foote: December 10, 1861 (OR).
[23] James A. Rogers/Leonidas Polk: October 23, 1861 (MC).
[24] J. M. Brett/[unknown recipient]: October 25, 1861 (MC).
[25] Stevenson, *Thirteen Months in the Rebel Army.*
[26] Montgomery Lynch/Major General L. Polk: November 26, 1861 in RG109 Compiled Service Record, Montgomery Lynch (MC).
[27] The varieties of trees they felled is stated in a letter from E.H. Wolfe, the commandant of Fort Pillow in the fall of 1863. E.H. Wolfe: Henry Binmore: September13, 1863 in 52nd Regiment Indiana Infantry, Regimental Letters Sent (NARA).
[28] A. B. Gray/E. D. Blake: September 18, 1861 (OR). "I have learned from Mr. Griswold, who has been down on duty connected with our work, that they have actually more hands at Fort Pillow than needed. He learns this from an officer stationed at Fort Pillow. They have about 2,300 now there and more coming in daily. If you could give me an order on the commanding officer at Fort Pillow for 500 hands to work at Island No. 10 for ten days, we can be ready for any number of troops and armament

when it may be deemed expedient to occupy the forts." A. B. Gray/E. D. Blake: October 16, 1861 (OR).

[29] Lewis P. Williamson/Leonidas Polk: August 27, 1861 in RG109/CSR (NARA).

[30] James A. Rogers/Gen. Polk: November 2, 1861 (MC).

[31] Sayers, "Fort Pillow: What the Federal Government Didn't Tell;" CWD.

[32] B.R. Johnson, "List of fortifications in the State of Tennessee, as far as reported to the Chief Engineer, September 15, 1861," (OR).

[33] Abstract from return, September 30, 1861, of the troops, Division No. 1, commanded by Maj. Gen. Leonidas Polk (OR).

[34] Sam Tate/Leonidas Polk: November 12, 1861 (OR)

[35] A. S. Johnston/S. Cooper: October 4, 1861 (OR); Sam Tate/Sidney Johnston: November 4, 1861 (OR); Sam Tate/Leonidas Polk: November 6, 1861 (OR).

[36] Sam Tate/Leonidas Polk: November 6, 1861 (OR).

[37] Lewis P. Williamson/Leonidas Polk: October 18 and 24, 1861 in RG109/CSR (NARA).

[38] E.D. Blue/Isaac N. Brown: November 1, 1861 (OR).

[39] Stevenson, *Thirteen Months in the Rebel Army.*

[40] Isham G. Harris/Albert Sydney Johnston: November 17, 1861 (OR)

[41] Pillow/Pettus: November 17, 1861 (OR); A.S. Johnston/J.P. Benjamin: November 18, 1861 (OR).

[42] A.S. Johnston/J.P. Benjamin: November 27, 1861 (OR).

[43] D.M. Frost/E.C. Cabell: December 9, 1861 (OR).

[44] Montgomery Lynch/Leonidas Polk: December 1, 1861 (OR).

[45] Williamson closed by saying that his "feeble efforts" – he had been ill with malaria ever since coming to Fort Pillow -- had been "cheerfully & gratuitously rendered" to provide for the "protection of our beloved Southern Confederacy." (Lewis P. Williamson/Leonidas Polk: November 9 and December 14, 1861 in RG109/CSR (NARA); William H. Carroll/S. Cooper: January 1, 1862 (OR); Organization of the First Division, Western Department, commanded by Maj. Gen. Leonidas Polk, C. S. Army, January, 1862.(OR).)

[46] Tilly, *Aspects of Social and Economic Life in West Tennessee Before the Civil War*, p. 7.

[47] Barry, *Rising Tide,* p. 40.

[48] Welsh, *Medical Histories of Confederate Generals*, pp. 18-19.

[49] G.T. Beauregard/"Memorandum": February 7, 1862 (OR). "Columbus must either be left to be defended to the last extremity by its proper garrison, assisted by Hollins' fleet of gunboats, and provided with provisions and ammunition for several months, or abandoned altogether, its armament and garrison being transferred, if practicable, to Fort Pillow, which, I am informed, is a naturally and artificially strong position, about 100 miles above Memphis." (G.S. Beauregard/A.S. Johnston: February 12, 1862 (OR).)

[50] Unidentified sailor/John Marsh: February 8, 1844; Andrew Hull Foote/John Marsh: May 10, 1846 in Marsh, *Temperance Recollections,* p. 141.
[51] G.T. Beauregard/Leonidas Polk: February 26, 1862 (OR).
[52] A. M. Rafter/James A. Rogers: February 11, 1862 (MC).
[53] Maness, "Fort Pillow Under Confederate Control."
[54] Anonymous [Beauregard?]: Memorandum: March 3, 1862 (OR). The memorandum refers to 22 guns, but Captain Lynch reported only twenty. "We have at this post the following ordnance stores: 604 32-pounder cartridges, 3,300 pounds cannon powder, 400 quill cannon primers, 200 friction tubes, 32 bridge barrels, 150 port-fires, 146 canister, 164. balls, 104 Read balls, 174 shells for 32-pounders, 4,560 32-pounder balls. Guns: Six 32-pounder rifle guns, and ten smooth-bore 32-pounders on river and four 32-pounders on back line, all mounted. Quartermaster's stores: 170 second-hand tents, without ropes. Amount of rations at Fort Pillow: 10,000 rations of rice, 10,000 rations of beans, 10,000 rations of molasses, 30,000 rations of salt, 15,000 rations of flour, 10,000 rations of candles, 4,000 rations of meal, 30,000 rations of vinegar, 40,000 rations of soap, 60,000 rations of coffee, 30,000 rations of sugar, 6,000 rations of bacon." (Montgomery Lynch/Leonidas Polk: March 3, 1862.
[55] Montgomery Lynch/Leonidas Polk: March 4, 1862 (OR).
[56] Leonidas Polk/J.P. McGown: March 7, 1862 (OR).
[57] J.M. Withers/G.T. Beauregard: March 10, 1862 (OR); G.T. Beauregard/J.M. Withers: March 11, 1862 in Hopping, *Life of Andrew Hull Foote,* p. 364. .
[58] Braxton Bragg/Thomas Jordan: March 18, 1862 (OR).
[59] G.T. Beauregard/J.P. McCown: March 21, 1862 (OR); Leonidas Polk/J.P. McCown: March 21, 1862 (OR).
[60] Anonymous, "Journal of the War," *Debow's review, Agricultural, commercial, industrial progress and resources.* June 1866, p. 650.
[61] Lyons/Horsler: March 14, 1862 in Lyons, Mark. Letters to Amelia Horsler, 1861 Feb. - 1865 Apr. 10. ALAV86-A952. Alabama State Archives.
[62] The New York *Herald,* December 4, 1861.
[63] Lyons/Horsler: March 8, 1862 in Lyons, Mark. Letters to Amelia Horsler, 1861 Feb. - 1865 Apr. 10. ALAV86-A952. Alabama State Archives.
[64] Charles S. Stewart (22nd Alabama Volunteers)/Julia Stewart: March 13, 1862.
[65] Lyons/Horsler: March 18, 1862 in Lyons, Mark. Letters to Amelia Horsler, 1861 Feb. - 1865 Apr. 10. ALAV86-A952. Alabama State Archives.
[66] Charles S. Stewart (22nd Alabama Volunteers)/Julia Stewart: March 13, 1862.
[67] A.P. Stewart/Thomas Jordan: March 21, 1862 (OR).

[68] Thomas Jordan/A.P. Stewart: March 21, 1862 in Hopping, *Life of Andrew Hull Foote,* p. 364.
[69] Pratt, *The Civil War on Western Waters,* p. 25; The New York *Herald,* December 4, 1861; Coombe, *Thunder Along the Mississippi,* pp. 85-94.
[70] G.T. Beauregard/Jefferson Davis: June 22, 1862 (OR).
[71] *Confederate Military History,* 5/422; The New York *Herald,* April 24, 1862; The Charleston *Mercury,* November 13, 1862.
[72] A.S. Johnston/General Orders: March 29, 1862 (OR).
[73] The Charleston *Mercury,* April 7, 1862.
[74] Beckham, "Where Was I And What I Saw During The Late War."
[75] Beckham, "Where Was I And What I Saw During The Late War."
[76] J.B. Villepigue/T. Jordan: April 6, 1862 (OR).
[77] S. Kellogg/W. D. Porter: April 8, 1862 in NFWW.
[78] Maness, "Fort Pillow Under Confederate Control."
[79] Sterling Price/Earl Van Dorn: April 12, 1862 (OR).
[80] Beckham, "Where Was I And What I Saw During The Late War."
[81] Lyons/Horsler: April 15, 1862.
[82] Captain Huger in John Adams/Van Dorn: April 13, 1862 (OR).
[83] Yost, *A Brief History of the U.S. Gunboat Cairo of the Mississippi Squadron. Jan. – Dec. 1862.*
[84] Pratt, *Civil War on Western Waters,* p. 93; J. Guthrie/C.B. Lasselle: April 21, 1862 in Indiana State Library. Going up from Fort Pillow, the Miss. Bends far to the west, presenting a point of land covered with timber, behind which the enemy's gun & mortar boats lay & throw shot & shell into the fort." (Lewis P. Williamson/Samuel H. Lockett: April 22, 1862, RG109/CSR (NARA).
[85] Lyons/Horsler: April 15, 1862.
[86] Brooklyn Daily *Eagle,* April 4, 1862; J. Guthrie/C.B. Lasselle: April 21, 1862 in Indiana State Library.
[87] Lyons/Horsler: April 15, 1862.
[88] The Brooklyn *Daily Eagle,* May 2 and 3, 1862. "I have to-day, as well as previously, informed the Secretary of the Navy of the state of things here, and from the most reliable authority I can command the rebels have at least 6,000 men in their fortifications and eleven gunboats."(A.H. Foote/M.C. Meigs: April 23, 1862 (OR); Abstracts from field return of the Army of the Mississippi, commanded by General G. T. Beauregard, April 15 and April 30, 1862 (OR).)
[89] Yost, *A Brief History of the U.S. Gunboat* Cairo.
[90] J.B. Villepigue/Bragg: April 14, 1862 (OR).
[91][91] Beauregard/Rust: April 14, 1862 in Hopping, *Life of Andrew Hull Foote,* p. 365.
[92] The Brooklyn *Daily Eagle,* April 23, 1862.
[93] My cave life in Vicksburg. With letters of trial and travel. By a lady. [Loughborough, Mary Ann Webster, Mrs.] 1836-1887. 196 p. map. 19 cm. New York [etc.] D. Appleton and company, 1864. p. 153.
[94] The Brooklyn *Daily Eagle,* May1 and 8, 1862.
[95] Thomas A. Scott/J.C. Kelton: April 14, 1862 (OR).

[96] Report of Major General Pope in United States. Congress. Joint Committee on the Conduct of the War. Supplemental report of the joint committee on the conduct of the war, in two volumes. Supplemental to Senate report no. 142, 38th Congress, 2d session. Washington, 1866.
[97] Hurlbut in Jordan and Pryor, *The Campaigns of Nathan Bedford Forrest*, p. 426.
[98] J.T. Headley. Farragut and our naval commanders. A companion volume to Headley's "Grant and Sherman" Comprising the early life and public services of the prominent naval commanders who, with Grant and Sherman and their generals, brought to a triumphant close the great rebellion of 1861-1865. New York, 1867. P. 179; John S. Packard Diary: April 18, 1862 in Vigo County Public Library (MC).
[99] Thomas A. Scott/Stanton: April 14, 1862 (OR).
[100] Report of Major General Pope in United States. Congress. Joint Committee on the Conduct of the War. Supplemental report of the joint committee on the conduct of the war, in two volumes. Supplemental to Senate report no. 142, 38th Congress, 2d session. Washington, 1866.
[101] Knox, Thomas W. Camp-fire and cotton-field: Southern adventure in time of war. Life with the Union armies, and residence on a Louisiana plantation. New York, 1865, p. 171.
[102] The Brooklyn *Daily Eagle*, May 3 and 5, 1862.
[103] Halleck/Foote: April 15, 1862 (OR).
[104] The Brooklyn *Daily Eagle*, April 25, 1862.
[105] Foote/"Brothers": May 5, 1862 in Pearce Civil War Collection, Navarro College, Corsicana, Texas.
[106] Hopping, Life of Andrew Hull Foote, pp. 297-298.
[107] The Brooklyn *Daily Eagle*, May 5 and 8, 1862.
[108] J. Guthrie/C.B. Lasselle: April 21, 1862 in Indiana State Library.
[109] The Brooklyn *Daily Eagle*, May 22, 1862.
[110] Browne 1865 in http://entomology.unl.edu/history_bug/civilwar/gallnippers.htm
[111] The Brooklyn *Daily Eagle*, May 7 and 8, 1862.
[112] Yost, *A Brief History of the U.S. Gunboat* Cairo.
[113] The Brooklyn *Daily Eagle*, May 7 and 10, 1862.
[114] A.H. Foote in Hoppin, *Life of Andrew Hull Foote*, p. 312.
[115] The Brooklyn *Daily Eagle*, May 16, 1862.
[116] The Twentieth Century Biographical Dictionary of Notable Americans, 4/140.
[117] J.T. Headley. *Farragut and our naval commanders. A companion volume to Headley's "Grant and Sherman" Comprising the early life and public services of the prominent naval commanders who, with Grant and Sherman and their generals, brought to a triumphant close the great rebellion of 1861-1865.* New York, 1867. p. 179.
[118] http://www.navyhistory.com/TB/Davis.html
[119] The Brooklyn *Daily Eagle*, May 5 and 12, 1862.
[120] Hopping, *Life of Andrew Hull Foote*, p. 564; CWD.

[121] The Brooklyn *Daily Eagle,* May 3 and 5, 1862.
[122] W.W. MacKall/Thomas Jordan: March 31, 1862 (OR).
[123] The Charleston *Mercury,* April 7, 1862.
[124] Twain, Mark. *Author's National Edition: The Writings of Mark Twain.* Volume 9. *Life on the Mississippi.* New York, 1903. Twain, *Life on the Mississippi,* p. 362.
[125] M. Lovell: May 22, 1862 (OR).
[126] The *General Bragg, General Price, General Van Dorn, General Beauregard, General M. Jeff. Thompson,* the *Colonel Lovell,* and the *Little Rebel.*
[127] The Brooklyn *Daily Eagle,* April 25 and May 5, 1862.
[128] Lyons/Horsler: April 17, 1862; Certainly the garrison was encouraged in this hope on the morning of the 17th when Pope's infantry departed for Pittsburg landing. (Thomas A. Scott/Stanton: April 19, 1862 (OR).)
[129] The Brooklyn *Daily Eagle,* May 7, 1862.
[130] Jarrette Law/Mrs. Law: April 28, 1862 from Univ. of Texas, Austin, archives call #2e313 (MC).
[131] The Brooklyn *Daily Eagle,* May 3, 5, 7, 8 and 12,1862.
[132] Lyons/Horsler: May 24, 1862.
[133] Maness, "Fort Pillow Under Confederate Control."
[134] The Brooklyn *Daily Eagle,* May 3 and 5, 1862.
[135] Lyons/Horsler: March 18 and April 17, 1862.
[136] M. Jeff Thompson/G.T. Beauregard: May 4 and 10, 1862 (OR).
[137] Roxbury [Massachusetts] *Gazette,* June 5, 1862.
[138] J.E. Montgomery/Beauregard: May 12, 1862 (OR); The Brooklyn *Eagle,* May 5, 1862.
[139] M. Jeff Thompson/Beauregard: May 10, 1862 (OR). In Montgomery's initial report he mistook the *Cincinnati* for the *Carondelet.* (J.E. Montgomery/Beauregard: May 12, 1862 (OR).
[140] The Brooklyn *Daily Eagle,* May 12 and 19, 1862.
[141] J.E. Montgomery/Beauregard: May 12, 1862 (OR).
[142] M. Jeff Thompson/Beauregard: May 10, 1862 (OR).
[143] Knox, Thomas W. Camp-fire and cotton-field: Southern adventure in time of war. Life with the Union armies, and residence on a Louisiana plantation. New York,1865, p. 172.
[144] Lyons/Horsler: May 13, 1862.
[145] J.E. Montgomery/Beauregard: May 12, 1862 (OR).
[146] M. Jeff Thompson/Beauregard: May 10, 1862 (OR).
[147] The Brooklyn *Daily Eagle,* May 19, 1862.
[148] Lyons/Horsler: May 10, 1862.
[149] J.E. Montgomery/Beauregard: May 12, 1862 (OR).
[150] Brooklyn *Daily Eagle,* May 12, 19, 22, 1862.
[151] Halleck/Foote: May 13, 1862 (OR).
[152] Brooklyn *Daily Eagle,* May 19 and 22, 1862.
[153] Willoughby, Gunboats & Gumbo.
[154] Halleck/Stanton: May 19, 1862 (OR)
[155] I.F. Quinby/J.C. Kelton: May 19, 1862 (OR).
[156] Lyons/Horsler: May 13 and 18, 1862.

[157] The Brooklyn *Daily Eagle,* May 12, 1862.
[158] Lyons/Horsler: May 24, 1862.
[159] Roxbury [Massachusetts] *Gazette,* June 5, 1862.
[160] Villepigue/C.H. Davis: May 20, 1862 (OR); C.H. Davis/Villepigue: May 21, 1862 (OR); Villepigue/C.H. Davis: May 21, 1862 (OR); Villepigue/Beauregard: May 22, 1862 (OR).
[161] The Charleston *Mercury,* May 23, 1862; Hopping, *Life of Andrew Hull Foote,* pp. 372-372.
[162] M. J. Thompson/E. Van Dorn: May 23, 1862 (OR).
[163] G. Fitch/John Pope: June 5, 1862 in RG94/E729A/Box 116 (NARA).
[164] Pratt, Civil War on Western Waters, pp. 97-98, 100.
[165] Charles Ellet Jr./C. H. Davis: May 28, 1862 (MC).
[166] The New York *Herald,* June 11, 1862.
[167] The Brooklyn *Daily Eagle,* May 7, 1862.
[168] Charles Ellet/Stanton: May 26, 1862 (OR).
[169] G.N. Fitch/John Pope: June 5, 1862 (OR). The *Herald* gave the captain's name as Schimmerhorn, but I could not find a Captain Schimmerhorn in the NPSSS. (The New York *Herald,* June 12, 1862.)
[170] Testimony of James Edward Montgomery (JCCW).
[171] Charles Ellet Jr./Stanton: June 4 and 16, 1862 (OR).
[172] Hopping, Life of Andrew Hull Foote, p. 373.
[173] G.T. Beauregard/Villepigue: May 28, 1862 (OR).
[174] Testimony of James Edward Montgomery (JSCCW); James Montgomery/G.W. Randolph: July 1, 1862.
[175] The Brooklyn *Daily Eagle,* May 29, 1862.
[176] The following suggests his volatility. "After the destruction of the fleet," Blount wrote, "I boarded the last train, and joined General Villepigue at Grenanda, Mississippi. I had a disagreement with one of the officers on General Villepigue's staff, a man named Simpson. He insulted me at table in the presence of General Villepigue. I took two revolvers and said we would shoot it out. But no! He refused to fight a duel with pistols, and I called him a low-down, dastardly coward. I called him everything. He ran like a baby and told general Villepigue about it. General Villepigue called me to him and asked if I had said it. I told him I had," whereupon Villepigue removed Blount from his staff. But not long afterward Villepigue regretted his decision. "Simpson was a dog," Blount recalled, still seething about it years later. "He went to New Orleans and turned Republican. They made him a justice of the peace. In a dispute between a white man, LaBlanc, and some negroes, he decided in favor of the negroes. LaBlanc shot and killed him." (Blount, "Captain Thomas Blount and His Memoirs," *Southwestern Historical Quarterly*, July, 1935.)
[177] Lyons/Horsler: June 7, 1862.
[178] Sessel, Edwin H./"Cousin": August 14, 1862 in "Our Evacuation of Fort Pillow." *Confederate Veteran*. January, 1898.
[179] The New York *Herald,* June 12, 1862.

[180] William Harper/Lydia Harper: May 29, 1862 in William Henry Smith Memorial Library (MC).
[181] The New York *Herald,* June 12, 1862.
[182] Cincinnati *Gazette,* June 5, 1862 (MC).
[183] G.N. Fitch/John Pope: June 5, 1862 (OR).
[184] The New York *Herald,* June 12, 1862.
[185] G.N. Fitch/John Pope: June 5, 1862 (OR).
[186] The New York *Herald,* June 12, 1862; Yost, *A Brief History of the U.S. Gunboat* Cairo.
[187] Knox, *Camp-fire and cotton-field,* p. 173.
[188] Cincinnati *Gazette,* June 5, 1862 (MC).
[189] The New York *Herald,* June 12, 1862.
[190] Moore, Frank. *Anecdotes, poetry, and incidents of the war: North and South,* pp. 14-15.
[191] New York *Herald*: June 12, 1862.
[192] Colonel Lake/Editor, The *Guardian*: November 22, 1862 in http://genweb.net/27th-Iowa/jedlake/nov221862.html
[193] G. Fitch/John Pope: June 5, 1862 in RG94/E729A/Box 116 (NARA).
[194] The New York *Herald,* March 22, 1862.
[195] Bailey, "The 'Bogus' Memphis *Union Appeal.*"
[196] Thomas H. Rosser/[Daniel] Ruggles: June 1, 1862 (OR).
[197] M. Jeff Thompson/Daniel Ruggles: June 3, 1862 (OR).
[198] Thomas Rosser/Daniel Ruggers: June 3, 1862 (OR).
[199] Brooklyn *Daily Eagle,* May 1, 1862.
[200] Thomas Rosser/Daniel Ruggers: June 3, 1862 (OR)
[201] Lyons/Horsler: June 7, 1862.
[202] George William Brent [Beauregard]: General orders No. 67 (OR).
[203] Confederate Military History, 5/422.
[204] Hopping, *Life of Andrew Hull Foote,* p. 374.
[205] Memphis *Avalanche,* June 6, 1862.
[206] Villepigue in L.D. McKissick/Ruggles: June 3, 1862 (OR).
[207] Testimony of James Montgomery (JCCCW).
[208] Charles Ellet, Jr./Stanton: June 11, 1862 (OR).
[209] Twain, Mark. *Author's National Edition: The Writings of Mark Twain.* Volume 9. *Life on the Mississippi.* New York, 1903. Twain, *Life on the Mississippi,* p. 233.
[210] Testimony of James Mon tgomery (JCCCW).
[211] Charles Ellet, Jr./Stanton: June 11, 1862 (OR); Ezra Green in http://www.brownwaternavy.com/diaries/e_greene14.htm
[212] Charles Ellet, Jr./Stanton: June 11, 1862 (OR).
[213] Testimony of James Montgomery (JCCCW).
[214] Charles Ellet, Jr./Stanton: June 11, 1862 (OR).
[215] Testimony of James Montgomery (JCCCW).
[216] M. Jeff Thompson/Beauregard: June 7, 1862 (OR).
[217] Ezra Green in http://www.brownwaternavy.com/diaries/e_greene14.htm (Italics mine).

[218] Sink, *Memoirs,* Indiana State Library.
[219] Charles H. Ellet/Stanton: June 16, 1862 (OR).
[220] Donhardt, "On the road to Memphis."
[221] Chales H. Davis/Welles: June 29, 1862 (OR).
[222] Charles Ellet, Jr./Stanton: June 5, 1862 (OR).
[223] Britton, *The Aftermath of the Civil War,* p. 113.
[224] http://www.civilwarartillery.com/manufacturers.htm
[225] The Brooklyn *Daily Eagle,* June 6, 1862.
[226] Testimony of Captain James Marshall, April 25, 1864, *Trade Regulations, & c.*, Senate Report 38-S, 4/142, part 3, Serial Set 1214, 35..
[227] Egbert Thompson/Charles H. Davis: June 9, 11 and 12, 1862, NA, M625/48, p. 722.
[228] N.C. Bryant/C.H. Davis: July 9, 1862 (OR).
[229] Gideon Welles/C. H. Davis: April 30, 1862 (NFWW).
[230] A. Winslow/C.H. Davis: July 7, 1862 (NFWW).
[231] C.H. Davis/N.C. Bryant: June 12 and 13, 1862 (OR).
[232] Willoughby, "Gunboats & Gumbo."
[233] C.H. Davis/Gideon Welles: June 29, 1862 (OR).
[234] Yost, *A Brief History of the U.S. Gunboat* Cairo.
[235] Willoughby, "Gunboats & Gumbo."
[236] C.H. Davis/A.M. Pennock: July 2, 1862 (OR).
[237] N.C. Bryant/C.H. Davis: July 9, 1862 (OR).
[238] C.H. Davis/N.C. Bryant: July 13, 1862 (OR).
[239] Willoughby, "Colonel Dawson & the Shadow War."
[240] Walker, Jeff. "Early History of McNairy County" *McNairy County Independent,* November 23, 1923.
[241] Willoughby, "Home-made Yankees."
[242] Montgomery, *Reminiscences Of A Mississippian In Peace And War,* p. 45.
[243] Johnson, "Civil War Recollection."
[244] TCW 1:96.
[245] Lauchlan Donaldson (TCWVQ).
[246] Brown, Andrew. "Sol Street: Confederate Partisan Leader." *The Journal of Mississippi History.* 21/3: July 1959.
[247] *Tennesseeans in the Civil War.*
[248] http://fp1.centurytel.net/Guerillas/burt_hays.htm
[249] http://fp1.centurytel.net/Guerillas/elias_thrasher.htm
[250] John Crawford in Rawick, ed., *The American Slave,* (Supplement/Series 2), 4(Texas):982-983.
[251] Nancy Stewart ([McNairy] County, Tennessee) in AM/ALH.
[252] Weatherred, "The Wartime Diary of John Weatherred of Bennett's Regiment or 9th Tennessee Cavalry, John Hunt Morgan's Command," http://www.jackmasters.net/we1863.html
[253] Samuel Gilliam (TCWVQ).
[254] Carroll, *Autobiography and Reminiscences,* pp. 63-64.
[255] Absolom A. Harrison (USA)/Susan Allstun Harrison: May 10, 1862.
[256] Sherman/R.M. Sawyer: January 31, 1864 in Moore, ed., *The Rebellion Record,* 8/352-353.

[257] Pratt, *Civil War on Western Waters*, p. 187
[258] Mays, *Autobiographical Sketch of the Life of William Tapley Mays*, Courtesy of Lois Mays Rizzo and Bob Mays.
[259] Christopher Wood Robertson (TCWVQ).
[260] Carroll, *Autobiography and Reminiscences*, p. 60.
[261] Willoughby, "Gunboats & Gumbo."
[262] Watkins, *Diary* (MC).
[263] Willoughby, "Gunboats & Gumbo."
[264] Watkins, *Diary* (MC).
[265] ___, *Hardeman County Historical Sketches*, p. 22.
[266] William C. Lord/Editor, Versailles *Dispatch*: November 15, 1862 in Versailles *Dispatch,* November 27, 1862 (MC).
[267] Anonymous, History of Rush County, Indiana, pp. 466-467.
[268] Goodspeed, ed., History of Shelby County, Indiana, p. 327.
[269] Thornbrough, Indiana in the Civil War Era, pp. 200-201; Harding, ed., History of Decatur County, pp. 407, 442-443.
[270] Pension file of Addison Sleeth; Addison Sleeth in Mainfort and Coats, eds., ""Soldiering at Fort Pillow: 1862-1864.""
[271] G.T. Bearregard/Bragg: September 2, 1862 (OR).
[272] Sherman/Rawlins: September 6, 1862 (OR).
[273] ___/Price: September 16, 1862 (OR).
[274] The Brooklyn *Daily Eagle,* June 16, 1862.
[275] Sherman/E.A. Carr: October 18, 1862 (OR).
[276] Willoughby, "Gunboats & Gumbo."
[277] Cupples, "Rebel to the Core."
[278] Thomas Frank Gailer in Silver, ed., *Mississippi in the Confederacy*, p. 185.
[279] The Charleston *Mercury,* August 18, 1862.
[280] Sherman/Rawlins [Grant]: July 30, 1862 (OR).
[281] (J.C.C./ New York *Jewish Messenger*: September 4, 1862.)
[282] Georgia Erwin File, RG 217 (Court of Claims), NA, Entry 991, Pt. II, RG 393 (MC).
[283] Testimony of Stephen Hurlbut (JCCCW).
[284] Lash, *Stephen A. Hurlbut*, p. 58.
[285] New York *Times,* September 19, 1861 in Lash, *Stephen A. Hurlbut*, p. 139nn.
[286] Testimony of W.S. Hillyer in Records of the Office of the Inspector General: Proceedings and Report of Court of Inquiry on Sale of Cotton and Produce at St. Louis, Missouri, 1863. RG159/Entry 27, volume 2, p. 550-551.
[287] E.H. Wolfe/James O. Pierce: September 12, 1862 (OR).
[288] F.A. Starring/Grenville Dodge: September 27, 1862 (OR).
[289] Sherman/C.C. Walcutt: September 24, 1862 (OR).
[290] C.H. Davis/J.A. Winslow: September 27, 1862 (OR); C.H. Davis/Egbert Thompson, September 29, 1862 (OR).
[291] C.H. Davis/John A. Winslow: September 22, 1862 (OR).

[292] Ross Griffin in Samuel B. and Hattie Lanier File, Court of Claims (NARA).
[293] W.T. Strickland/J.F. Quinby: October 2, 1862 (MC).
[294] Rushville (Indiana) *Jacksonian*, September 12, 1862 (MC).
[295] Cimprich, *Slavery's End in Tennessee*, p. 33.
[296] Andrew Johnson in Moore, ed., *The Rebellion Record*, 8/340-341.
[297] Watkins, Diary (MC).
[298] Captain Griffiths in File of William Conner, Southern Claims Commission. Italics mine.
[299] Brayman/Hurlbut: February 15, 1863 (NARA).
[300] One Mississippian pleaded that in order to procure necessities in Memphis he had to take the Oath, but since he lived in Mississippi, where, if it ever got around that he had taken it, he would be killed, he took the oath under an assumed name, and was eventually found out. Hurlbut was unmoved when he appealed his imprisonment at Irving Prison. "A man who has broken his word once & made a false personation taken on oath in a false name is not to be trusted." H.W. Griffith/Hurlbut (and nn.): March 21, 1863 (NARA).
[301] Asboth/"AAG" [Henry Binmore]: April 21, 1863 in RG94/E729A/Box 2 (NARA).
[302] W.C.Stanbery (32nd Iowa Infantry/E.H. Wolfe: April 23, 1863 in RG94/E729A/Box 3 (NARA).
[303] Frisby, "'Remember me to everybody:' The Civil War Letters of Samuel Henry Eells, Twelfth Michigan Infantry." Unpublished ms.
[304] Britton, *The Aftermath of the Civil War*, p. 179.
[305] Willoughby, Gunboats & Gumbo.
[306] F.A. Starring/Grenville Dodge: September 27, 1862 (OR).
[307] Addison Sleeth in Mainfort and Coats, eds., "Soldiering at Fort Pillow: 1862-1864."
[308] Claim of Carter Whitson in RG92/817/Box 726/218-1207 (NARA).
[309] Claim of Hiram Partee in RG92/794/Box 71/73 (NARA).
[310] Sleeth was told there were three hundred, but the evidence suggests it was closer to one hundred.
[311] Addison Sleeth in Mainfort and Coats, eds., "Soldiering at Fort Pillow: 1862-1864."
[312] Colonel Lake/Editor, The *Guardian*: November 22, 1862 in http://genweb.net/27th-Iowa/jedlake/nov221862.html
[313] Addison Sleeth in Mainfort and Coats, eds., "Soldiering at Fort Pillow: 1862-1864."
[314] J.C.C./ New York *Jewish Messenger*: September 4, 1862.
[315] Frisby, "'Remember me to everybody:' The Civil War Letters of Samuel Henry Eells, Twelfth Michigan Infantry." Unpublished ms.
[316] J.C.C./ New York *Jewish Messenger*: September 4, 1862.
[317] William Barber (Co. H, 21st Ohio Infantry)/Family: May 30, 1862.
[318] Britton, *The Aftermath of the Civil War*, p. 114.
[319] John Scott/Special Order Number 49: March 25, 1863 in 32nd Regiment Iowa Infantry, Regimental Orders Issued 1862-1865 (NARA).

[320] [Illegible]/Hurlbut[?]: ca January 11, 1863 in 16th Army Corps (Letters Received) RG98, Part 2, Entry 391, Box 7 (NARA); Special Order No. 34, May 15, 1863; NA, 52nd Regiment, Indiana Infantry Regimental Orders Issued
[321] Willoughby, "Colonel Dawson & the Shadow War."
[322] Co. C, 2nd Illinois Cavalry: Morning Report for October, 1863 in M594 (NARA).
[323] Rushville *Jacksonian*, December 31, 1862.
[324] Addison Sleeth in Mainfort and Coats, eds., *Soldiering at Fort Pillow, 1862-1864.* Emphases mine.
[325] W.T. Strickland/J. Lovell: November 27, 1862 in RG93, District of Columbus (MC).
[326] Hurlbut/T.A. Daniels: December 10, 1862 in RG393, District of Columbus (NARA).
[327] Jefferson C. Davis/Sherman: December 12, 1862 in RG94/E729A/Box 2 (NARA).
[328] Willoughby, "Gunboats & Gumbo."
[329] Willoughby, "Colonel Dawson & the Shadow War."
[330] Chalmers, "Lieutenant General Nathan Bedford Forrest And His Campaigns," *Southern Historical Society Papers,* October, 1879.
[331] J.M. Tuttle/Hurlbut: January 3, 1863 in 16th Army Corps (Letters Received) RG98, Part 2, Entry 391, Box 7 (NARA).
[332] Willoughby, "Gunboats & Gumbo."
[333] Addison Sleeth in Mainfort and Coats, eds., "Soldiering at Fort Pillow: 1862-1864."
[334] Colonel Lake/Editor, The *Guardian*: November 22, 1862 in http://genweb.net/27th-Iowa/jedlake/nov221862.html
[335] Addison Sleeth in Mainfort and Coats, eds., "Soldiering at Fort Pillow, 1862-1864."
[336] E.H. Wolfe/Special Order No. 34: December 26, 1862 in 52nd Regiment Indiana Infantry, Regimental Orders Issued (NARA).
[337] Ryan, *Reminscences.*
[338] Watkins, *Dairy* (MC).
[339] J.C.C./ New York *Jewish Messenger*: April 10, 1863.
[340] Investigation into Cotton Speculation and Corruption along the Mississippi. Testimony of Stephen A. Hurlbut: May 8, 1863 (NARA).
[341] Indianapolis *State Journal*, September 27, 1862 (MC).
[342] Addison Sleeth in Mainfort and Coats, eds., ""Soldiering at Fort Pillow: 1862-1864.""
[343] My depiction of the orientation of these encampments is based on a map drawn by William D. Power of the 32nd Iowa which was obtained by Robert Mainfort and exhibited at Fort Pillow, from which it was later stolen. My copy is a computer-enhanced version of a color print Mainfort kindly provided me.
[344] Ross Griffin in Samuel B. and Hattie Lanier File, Court of Claims (NARA).

[345] Richard W. Meade/David D. Porter: November 1, 1862 (OR).
[346] Willoughby, "Gunboats & Gumbo."
[347] Colonel G.N. Fitch in Willoughby, "Gunboats & Gumbo."
[348] Thomas A. Davies/Halleck: December 27, 1862 (OR); Clinton B. Fisk/Samuel R. Curtis: December 27, 1862 (OR).
[349] Edward H. Mix/Assistant Adjutant General: January 20, 1863 in Regimental Record Books, 32nd Regiment Iowa Infantry, Regimental Letters Sent 1862-1865 (NARA).
[350] Sage, *A History of Iowa,* pp. 147-148.
[351] Aptheker, *To Be Free,* p. 92.
[352] Wubben, *Civil War Iowa,* pp. 1, 52, 77, 82, 87, 92, 95, 97-98, 102-103.
[353] Thomas A. Davies/E.A. Carr: January 12, 1863 (OR).
[354] And the same regiment in which Harry Truman would serve in World War I.
[355] Charles Aldrich/J. Edgington: April 2, 1863 Regimental Record Books, 32nd Regiment Iowa Infantry, Regimental Letters Sent: 1862-1865 (NARA).
[356] Aldrich, "Incidents."
[357] Scott, ed., *Story of the Thirty Second Iowa Infantry Volunteers,* pp. 83-84. John Lewis Waller began his legal and political career in Iowa, but moved to Topeka in 1878 after hearing of Pap Singleton's efforts to establish black settlements in Kansas. Within four years he had started his newspaper Western Recorder in Lawrence, and in 1888 he became one of the first black Republican members the electoral college. Appointed by President Benjamin Harrison to serve as Consul to Madagascar. Waller was accused of giving military information to local people in an attempt to prevent a French takeover. He was sentenced to twenty years in a French prison, buthe was released after President Grover Cleveland demanded he be set free. Returning to the United States, Waller organized a black Kansas regiment for service in World War I.
[358] Thomas A. Davis/Captain Ebert: December 27, 1862 and Thomas A. Davis/Commanding Officer, *New Era*: December 27, 1862 in District of Columbus, Kentucky, Volume 93, Letters Sent 1862-1864 (NARA).
[359] John Ritland in Mainfort, Unpublished and untitled ms. (MC).
[360] James Jenkinson/Mrs. H. Green: February 3, 1863 in Orrin Elmore. Empasis mine. Stanley papers, University of Oregon Library. Lieutenant-Colonel Mix wrote the following memorial for one of these victims: "It is with feelings of keen regret that the death of Private James L. Fry, of Company "B" 32nd Iowa Infantry is announced to this command. His case was a peculiar one. He had a large circle of relatives, but without exception, they were arrayed in arms against the holy cause in which his young life became a willing Sacrifice. He had left his early house where only a life of ease and comfort was before him, to struggle unaided as a pioneer in the free atmosphere of North Western Iowa. When the rights which he came North to enjoy were assailed he entered the ranks of the patriot Army willing and anxious to give anything to our Sacred Cause.

He has met a Soldiers death, leaving none but Soldiers behind to drop a tear at his lowly grave or keep abright his memory. Let us emulate his noble Self Sacrifice and profit by his patriotic example." Edward H. Mix/Special Order Number 37 in 32 Iowa Infantry, Regimental Orders Issued 1862-1865 (NARA).

[361] Aldrich, pp. 82-83; Scott, pp. 100-101.

[362] Alexander Cissell in Samuel B. & Hattie Lanier File, RG124 (Court of Claims), (NARA).

[363] John Scott/H.Z. Curtis: April 29, 1863 in Regimental Record Books, 32nd Regiment Iowa Infantry, Regimental Letters Sent 1862-1865 (NARA).

[364] Charles Aldrich/Commanding Officer of 32nd Iowa Infantry: May 12, 1863 in Regimental Record Books, 32nd Regiment Iowa Infantry, Regimental Letters Sent 1862-1865 (NARA).

[365] John Scott/[Asboth]: May 13, 1863 in Regimental Record Books, 32nd Regiment Iowa Infantry, Regimental Letters Sent 1862-1865 (NARA).

[366] E.H. Wolfe/Special Order Number 33: December 23, 1862 in 52nd Regiment Indiana Infantry, Regimental Orders Issued (NARA).

[367] John Scott/Samuel R. Curtis: January 1, 1863 (OR).

[368] Edward H. Mix/L.S. Coffin: January 13, 1863 in Regimental Record Books, 32nd Regiment Iowa Infantry, Regimental Letters Sent 1862-1865 (NARA).

[369] Samuel Curtis: January 5, 1863 (OR).

[370] Scott, ed., *Story of the Thirty Second Iowa Infantry Volunteers*, pp. 86, 92 and 94; William K. Strong/Albert G. Brackett: February 26, 1863 (OR).

[371] An Indianan wrote home that it had become "the area's trading center." Rushville *Republican*, December 17, 1862 (MC).

[372] During his archaeological research at Fort Pillow, Robert Manfort unearthed shards of purple plates, stoneware jugs and ale bottles, pipe stems, shards of mirror, amber glass bottles, olive green wine and ale bottles, ration cans of sardines and evaporated milk, and in the moat where the Union slain were buried, four-holed iron and gilt brass Scoville buttons. Mainfort, *Archaeological Investigations*.

[373] Z.S. Main/Special Order Number 6: March 30, 1863 in 52nd Regiment Indiana Infantry, Regimental Orders Issued (NARA).

[374] E.H. Wolfe/Special Order No. 10: March 16, 1863 in 52nd Regiment Indiana Infantry, Regimental Orders Issued (NARA).

[375] E.H.Wolfe/W.H. Thurston: June 13, 1863 in RG94/E729A/Box 3 (NARA).

[376] Amos S. Collins/16th Army Corps: March 19, 1863 in 16th Army Corps, Volume 4, Register of Letters Received 1863 (NARA).

[377] Aldrich, "Incidents."

[378] Edward H. Mix/L.S. Coffin: January 13, 1863 in Regimental Record Books, 32nd Regiment Iowa Infantry, Regimental Letters Sent 1862-1865 (NARA).

[379] Samuel Lanier file in Court of Claims (NARA).

[380] "And after peace was made he made a warm personal friend of mine. At his death I was one of the pall-bearers and helped to place his remains in their last resting place. Peace to his ashes!" Carroll, *Autobiography and Reminiscences*, p. 27.
[381] Addison Sleeth in Mainfort and Coats, eds., *Soldiering at Fort Pillow, 1862-1864*
[382] Jewell, ed., *Jewell's Crescent City*.
[383] Thomas A. Davies/Halleck: December 25, 1862 (OR).
[384] www.altonhauntings.com
[385] Willoughby, "Gunboats & Gumbo."
[386] Ryan, *Reminscences*; The New York *Herald*, January 12, 1863. ; E.H. Wolfe/J. Lovell: January 9, 1863 in RG393, District of Columbus (NARA). Ryan recalled that they captured some 150 prisoners, but General Fisk reported 47, including several officers. Wolfe sent 45 prisoners down but may have kept a couple at the Fort for interrogation. (Clinton B. Fisk/Samuel Curtis: January 9, 1863 (OR).)
[387] J. Lovell/E.H. Wolfe: January 13, 1863 in District of Columbus, Kentucky, Volume 93, Letters Sent 1862-1864 (NARA).
[388] Willoughby, "Colonel Dawson & the Shadow War."
[389] E.H. Wolfe/W.H. Thurston: January 12, 1864 in Regimental Papers, 178th Regiment New York Infantry (NARA).
[390] Thomas M. Ninient/Hurlbut: January 22, 1863 in 178th Regiment New York Infantry, Regimental Orders Issued (NARA).
[391] J. Hough/E.H. Wolfe: January 16, 1864 in 52nd Regiment Indiana Infantry, Regimental Orders Issued (NARA).
[392] Grant/C.S. Hamilton: January 22, 1863 (OR).
[393] C.S. Hamilton/Grant: January 25, 1863 (OR).
[394] Asboth/Hurlbut: February 8, 1863 (OR); E.H. Wolfe/Special Order Number 20: April 1, 1863 in 52nd Regiment Indiana Infantry, Regimental Orders Issued (NARA).
[395] Willoughby, "Colonel Dawson & the Shadow War."
[396] Willoughby, "Gunboats & Gumbo."
[397] E.H. Wolfe/Asboth: March 11, 1863 RG393, District of Memphis (NARA).
[398] Court Martial of William Lieuellin [Llewelyn?], Joel Menassa, William Stephens, J.M. Burton, Sampson Ryon [Ryan], LL1048 (NARA).
[399] Scott, ed., *Story of the Thirty Second Iowa Infantry Volunteers*, pp. 104-105.
[400] Ryan, *Reminiscences*.
[401] Asboth/Hurlbut: March 2, 1863 (OR);"A record of events on the tri-monthly return of Feb. 28, 1863," District of Columbus, Department of Tennessee (16th Army Corps) (NARA); E.H. Wolfe/Asboth: February 28, 1863 in RG393, Records of the U.S. Army Continental Commands, Entry 991, District of Western Kentucky, Letters Received 1862-1865 (NARA).
[402] Asboth/E.H.Wolfe: March 3, 1863 in District of Columbus, Kentucky, Volume 93, Letters Sent 1862-1864 (NARA).

[403] "John Ritland Civil War History: Chapter One," at iowa-counties.com/civilwar/index.shtml.
[404] Courtmartial of Private William B. Goodman, Co. C, 52nd Indiana Infantry NN65 (NARA).
[405] Courtmartial of Manliff Malson of Co. F, 52nd Indiana Infantry NN65 (NA).
[406] E.H. Wolfe/Asboth: February 7, 1863 in RG393, District of Columbus (NARA).
[407] Courtmartial of Private James A. Raney, Co. C, 52nd Indiana Infantry NN65 (NARA).
[408] Asboth/Unknown: March 25, 1863 in RG393, District of Columbus (NARA).
[409] John Scott/Asboth: March 29, 1863 in Regimental Record Books, 32nd Regiment Iowa Infantry, Regimental Letters Sent 1862-1865 (NARA).
[410] E.H. Wolfe/John Scott: March 30, 1863 in 32nd Regiment Iowa Infantry, Regimental Orders Issued: 1862-1863 (NARA).
[411] Addison Sleeth in Mainfort and Coats, eds., *Soldiering at Fort Pillow, 1862-1864.*
[412] John Ritland in Mainfort, Unpublished and untitled ms. (MC).
[413] Court Martial of S. Calhoun, J.A. Hill and S.P. Sheldon, LL1048 (NARA).
[414] John Ritland in Mainfort, Unpublished and untitled ms. (MC).
[415] Ryan, *Reminiscences.*
[416] Court Martial of S. Calhoun, J.A. Hill and S.P. Sheldon, LL1048 (NARA); ; Asboth/John A. Rawlins: February 11, 1863 and G. Fitch/John Pope: June 5, 1862 in RG94/E729A/Box 119 (NARA).
[417] Will Kennedy/A. S. Kennedy: February 17, 1863 in Kennedy Manuscripts, Southern Historical Collection (SHA) (MC).
[418] Shiflitt, *Letters* at www.geocities.com/~jcrosswell/War/CW/hillory14.html I have substituted "they" for Saunders's "tha" and "could" for "cood in this transcription.
[419] Willoughby, "Colonel Dawson & the Shadow War."
[420] Moore, Frank, ed. *Anecdotes, poetry, and incidents of the war: North and South. 1860-1865.* New York, 1867.
[421] Willoughby, "Gunboats & Gumbo;" Asboth/Henry Binmore: May 22, 1863 in RG94/E729A/Box 3 (NARA). In late May, Wolfe was commanded to send Captain Moore and his men upriver to Columbus to testify against Cushman . (Asboth/E.H. Wolfe: May 25, 1863 in RG393 Records of U. S. Army Continental Commands, Entry 992, District of Western Kentucky, General Orders, 1862 Vol. 101/248A (MC).)
[422] Main, *The Third United States Cavalry,* p. 301.
[423] E.H. Wolfe/W.H. Thurston: June 12, 1863 in RG94/E729A/Box 3 (NARA).
[424] E.H. Wolfe/Special Orders Number 17: March 28, 1863 in 32nd Regiment Iowa Infantry, Special Orders, Company B: 1862-1863 (NARA).

[425] W. B. Church/ed.: May 25, 1863 in Mason City *Cerro Gordo Republican* (MC).
[426] F.P. Turnure/Mrs. H. Green: April 9, 1863 in University of Oregon Library, Orrin Elmore Stanley papers.
[427] Thomas O. Howard/Mrs. H. Green: April 4, 1863. University of Oregon Library. Orrin Elmore Stanley papers
[428] Thomas O. Howard [probably] to Mrs. H. Green, April 4, 1863; University of Oregon Library, Orrin Elmore Stanley papers.
[429] Asboth/E.H. Wolfe: May 25, 1863 in RG393 Records of U. S. Army Continental Commands, Entry 992, District of Western Kentucky, General Orders, 1862 Vol. 101/248A (MC).
[430] Thomas James/Hurlbut: May 9, 1863 in RG94/E729A/Box 3 (NARA).
[431] E.H. Wolfe/Thomas H. Harris: May 31, 1863 in RG94/E729A/Box 3 (NARA).
[432] John Scott/Assistant Adjutant General: April 3, 1863 in Regimental Record Books, 32nd Regiment Iowa Infantry, Regimental Letters Sent: 1862-1865 (NARA).
[433] John Scott/E.H. Wolfe: April 15, 1863 in Regimental Record Books, 32nd Regiment Iowa Infantry, Regimental Letters Sent 1862-1865 (NARA).
[434] E.H. Wolfe/Asboth: April 4 and 6, 1863 in RG393, District of Columbus (NARA).
[435] Ryan, *Reminscences.*
[436] Willoughby, "A Cold Blue Wind: Waring's Brigade sweeps through Dyer County in 1864."
[437] Addison Sleeth in Mainfort and Coats, eds., *Soldiering at Fort Pillow, 1862-1864.*
[438] NA, M594, 2nd Illinois Cavalry.
[439] Hiram McCorkle in Willoughby, "Gunboats & Gumbo."
[440] M.K. Lawler/E.D. Mason: April 17, 1863 (OR).
[441] Addison Sleeth in Mainfort and Coats, eds., *Soldiering at Fort Pillow, 1862-1864.*
[442] Scott, ed., *Story of the Thirty Second Iowa Infantry Volunteers,* p. 99.
[443] Sleeth.
[444] Britton, *The Aftermath of the Civil War,* pp. 169-170; Addison Sleeth in Mainfort and Coats, eds., *Soldiering at Fort Pillow, 1862-1864.*
[445] "Chris"/"Mr. Curtis": May 25, 1864 in TSLA.
[446] Scott, ed., *Story of the Thirty Second Iowa Infantry Volunteers,* p. 102.
[447] Report of Sick and Wounded, Fort Pillow, Tenn., September, 1863, James W. Martin, Surgeon, 52nd Regiment Indiana Volunteers; James W. Martin manuscript collection, Indiana Division, Indiana State Library (MC).
[448] " Freemon, "The Medical Challenge of Military Operations in the Mississippi Valley."
[449] Report of Sick and Wounded, Fort Pillow, Tenn., September, 1863, James W. Martin, Surgeon, 52nd Regiment Indiana Volunteers; James W. Martin manuscript collection, Indiana Division, Indiana State Library (MC).

[450] Hurlbut/Asboth: May 27,'1863 in 16th Army Corps Volume 2, Ledtters sent: 1863 (NARA).
[451] John Ryan recalled the second regiment as a Wisconsin regiment whose number he could not recall. He undoubtedly meant the 32nd Iowa Regiment. Ryan, *Reminiscences.*
[452] John Scott/Hurlbut:June 8, 1863 in 16th Army Corps, Volume 6, Register of Letters Received, 1863 (NARA).
[453] John Scott/Asboth: June 1, 1863 in Regimental Record Book, 32nd Regiment Iowa Infantry, Regimental Letters Sent 1862-1865 (NARA).
[454] Frisby, "'Remember me to everybody:' The Civil War Letters of Samuel Henry Eells, Twelfth Michigan Infantry." Unpublished ms.
[455] John Scott/Special Order Number 5: May 16, 1863 in in 32nd Regiment Iowa Infantry, Regimental Orders Issued 1862-1865 (NARA).
[456] Charges and specifications performed by Col. Edward H. Wolfe 52d Reg. Ind. Infty. Vol. Com'dg Post of Fort Pillow" (MC).
[457] E.H. Wolfe/Special Order Number 45: May 30, 1863 in 52nd Regiment Indiana Infantry, Regimental Orders Issued (NARA).
[458] *Report of the Adjutant General of the State of Indiana, Volume V. — 1861-1865*, Indianapolis, 1866; Asboth/Lorenzo Thomas: July 31, 1863 in Reg papers Vol. Orgs. Civil War 52nd Ind. Infty (MC).
[459] William P. Mellen/Peter casey: June 13, 1863 in RG94/E729A/Box 3 (NARA).
[460] E.H. Wolfe/W.H. Thurston: June 12, 1863 in RG94/E729A/Box 3 (NARA).
[461] Z.S. Main/W.H. Thurston: June 13, 1863 in RG94/E729A/Box 3 (NARA).
[462] Asboth/Henry Binmore: May 30, 1863 in RG94/E729A/Box 3 (NARA); E.H. Wolfe/Special Order Number 50 in 52nd Regiment Indiana Infantry, Regimental Orders Issued (NARA).
[463] Asboth/Special Orders Number 134: June 5, 1863 in RG393 Records of U. S. Army Continental Commands, Entry 992 District of Western Ky, General Orders, 1862,Vol. 101/248A (NARA).
[464] E.H. Wolfe/Special Order Numbers 46, 54 and 55: June 8, 1863 in 52 Regiment Indiana Infantry, Regimental Orders Issued (NARA).
[465] John Scott/[W.H.] Thurston: June 13, 1863 in RG94/E729A/Box 3 (NARA).
[466] L. Thomas/Stanton: October 5, 1865 (OR).
[467] John Scott/Henry Binmore: May 26, 1863 in Regimental Record Books, 32nd Regiment Iowa Infantry, Regimental Letters Sent 1862-1865 (NARA).
[468] Hurlbut/Schofield: June 3, 1863 in 16th Army Corps, Volume 2, Letters Sent 1863 (NARA).
[469] Asboth/Special Order Number 145: June 16, 1863 in RG393 Records of U. S. Army Continental Commands, Entry 992 District of Columbus Ky, General Orders, 1862, Vol. 101/248A (NARA); T.J. Harris [Asboth]/Special Order Number 161: July 2, 1863 in 52nd Regiment Indiana Infantry, Regimental Orders Issued (NARA).

[470] E.H. Wolfe: May 24, 1863 in 16th Army Corps, Volume 6, Register of Letters Received, 1863 (NARA).
[471] John Scott/W.H. Thurston: June 14, 1863 in RG94/E729A/Box 3 (NARA).
[472] Aldrich, "Incidents."
[473] Capt. A. B. Miller/ed.: June 22, 1863 in Mason City *Cerro Gordo Republican* (MC)
[474] Aldrich, "Incidents."
[475] http://www.globegazette.com
[476] Hurlbut/John A. Rawlins: June 26, 1863 (OR).
[477] E.H. Wolfe/Special Order Number 71: June 28, 1863 in 52nd Regiment Indiana Infantry, Regimental Orders Issued (NARA).
[478] Z.S. Main/General Order Number 12: July 22, 1863 in 52nd Regiment Indiana Infantry, Regimental Orders Issued (NARA).
[479] William S. Burns/Inspection Report: July 30, 1863 in RG393/1/4757/1: Letters Sent and Received: office of Inspector General, Department of Tennessee (NARA); E.H. Wolfe/George W. Fetterman: September 20, 1863 in 52nd Regiment Indiana Infantry, Regimental Letters Sent (NARA).
[480] E.H. Wolfe/General Order Number 7: July 30, 1863 in 52nd Regiment Indiana Infantry, Regimental Orders Issued
[481] Court Martial Records mm593; nn885, LL1096; nn65 folder 1 (NARA).
[482] Z.S. Main/Ross Griffin: July 5, 1863 in 52nd Regiment Indiana Infantry, Regimental Letters Sent (NARA).
[483] Addison Sleeth in Mainfort and Coats, eds., *Soldiering at Fort Pillow, 1862-1864.*
[484] Addison Sleeth in Mainfort and Coats, eds., *Soldiering at Fort Pillow, 1862-1864.*
[485] Court Martial of Thomas Koons, NN193 (NARA).
[486] E.H. Wolfe/General Order Number 6: July 13, 1863 in 52nd Regiment, Indiana Infantry, Regimental Orders Issued (NARA).
[487] Z.S. Main/General Order Number 11: July 2, 1863 in 52nd Regiment Indiana Infantry, Regimental Orders Issued (NARA).
[488] Courtmartial records: mm1103, mm1; nn273 folder 1; nn 193 (NARA).
[489] E.H. Wolfe/General Orders Number 3: August 19, 1863 in 52nd Regiment Indiana Infantry, Regimental Orders Issued (NARA).
[490] E.H. Wolfe/Asboth: July 13, 1864 in 16th Army Corps, Volume 6, Register of Letters Received, 1863 (NARA).
[491] Forrest C. Pogue Public History Institute, *The Civil War in the Jackson Purchase Region of Kentucky: A Survey of Historic Sites and Structures.*
[492] L.F. Micrillis/Henry Binmore [Asboth]: July 20, 1863 (OR).
[493] Fielding Hurst/Edward Hatch: July 20, 1863 (OR).
[494] Alley, *Memoirs.*
[495] J.C.C./ New York *Jewish Messenger*: July 16, 1863.
[496] E.H. Wolfe/W.L. Lathrop: July 8, 1863 in 52nd Regiment Indiana Infantry, Regimental Letters Sent (NARA).
[497] J.C.C./ New York *Jewish Messenger*: July 16, 1863.

[498] The 52nd was absent when, a few days later, the third killer was hanged from the same tree. Sleeth.
[499] E.H. Wolfe: July 27, 1863 in RG393, District of Columbus (NARA).
[500] Henry Binmore/B.H. Grierson: July 28, 1863 (OR); Hurlbut/Asboth: July 29, 1863 (OR).
[501] Jno Phillips/Henry Binmore: September 8, 1863 in RG94/E729A/Box 4 (NARA).
[502] E.H. Wolfe/General Orders Number 7 and Number 8: July 30, 1863 in 52nd Regiment Indiana Infantry, Regimental Orders Issued (NARA); Co. C, 2nd Illinois Cavalry Morning Report for July 1863. NA, RG94, Regimental Papers 2nd Illinois Cavalry (NARA).
[503] Willoughby, "Gunboats & Gumbo."
[504] E.H. Wolfe/Specioal Order Number 98: August 11, 1863 in 52nd Regiment Indiana Infantry, Regimental Orders Issued (NARA).
[505] Co. C, 2nd Illinois Cavalry Morning Report for November [misprinted] 1863 in RG94, Regimental Papers 2nd Illinois Cavalry (NARA).
[506] Addison Sleeth in Mainfort and Coats, eds., *Soldiering at Fort Pillow, 1862-1864.*
[507] David J. Temple and William H. Herron in Graf, *The Papers of Andrew Johnson,* 6/327 (MC).
[508] James V. Ledsinger/C. U. Collins: September 23, 1863 (MC).
[509] John Brownlow served in Company C of the 19th Tennessee Cavalry. Brownlow, "John Brownlow's First Published Memoirs" in Columbia, Tennessee *Daily Herald,* September 30, 1984.
[510] Willoughby, "Gunboats & Gumbo."
[511] Isaac hawkins/[Hurlbut]: September 20, 1863 in RG94/E729A/Box 4 (NARA).
[512] Asboth/Henry Binmore: August 9, 1863 (OR).
[513] NA, R6 24, Log of the *Fawn* (MC).
[514] Asboth/Special Orders Number 238: September 23, 1863 in District of Columbus, Kentucky, Volume 93, Letters Sent 1862-1864 (NARA).
[515] E.H. Wolfe/John Hough: September 28, 1863 (OR); E.H. Wolfe/Special Order Number 150: October 13, 1863 in 178th Regiment New York Infantry, Regimental Orders Issued (NARA).
[516] The New York *Herald,* October 5, 1863.
[517] Willoughby, "Gunboats & Gumbo."
[518] E.H. Wolfe/Henry Binmore: September 13, 1863 in 52nd Regiment Indiana Infantry, Regimental Letters Sent (NARA).
[519] William S. Burns/Inspection Report: September 30, 1863 in RG393/1/4757/1: Letters Sent and Received: office of Inspector General, Department of Tennessee (NARA).
[520] E.H. Wolfe/Special Order Number 149: October 13, 1863 in 178th Regiment New York Infantry, Regimental Orders Issued (NARA).
[521] Hurlbut/A.J. Smith: October 14, 1863 (OR).
[522] E.H. Wolfe/John Hough: October 21, 1863 (OR).

[523] E.H. Wolfe/Dement: October 29, 1863 in 52nd Regiment Indiana Infantry, Regimental Letters Sent (NARA).
[524] Willoughby, "Gunboats & Gumbo;" R6 94, Regimental Papers 2nd Illinois Cavalry (NARA).
[525] E.H. Wolfe/John Hough: November 20, 1863 in 52nd Regiment Indiana Infantry, Regimental Letters Sent (NARA).
[526] John D. Stevenson/Hurlbut: November 21, 1863 in RG94/E729A/Box 5 (NARA).
[527] Addison Sleeth in Mainfort and Coats, eds., *Soldiering at Fort Pillow, 1862-1864*; E.H. Wolfe/John Hough: November 22, 1863 (OR); George E. Waring/John Hough: November 23, 1863 (OR).
[528] George E. Waring/John Hough: November 24, 1863 (OR); John Hough/E.H. Wolfe: November 25, 1863 (OR).
[529] E.H. Wolfe/H.W. Brown: November 25, 1863 in 52nd Regiment Indiana Infantry, Regimental Letters Sent (NARA).
[530] E.H. Wolfe/John Hough: December 1, 1863 in 52nd Regiment Indiana Infantry, Regimental Letters Sent (NARA).
[531] E.H. Wolfe/Harris & Company: December 29, 1863 in 52nd Regiment Indiana Infantry, Regimental Letters Sent (NARA).
[532] E.H. Wolfe/Special Order Number 190: December 8, 1863 in 52nd Regiment Indiana Infantry, Regimental Letters Sent (NARA).
[533] Addison Sleeth in Mainfort and Coats, eds., *Soldiering at Fort Pillow, 1862-1864*.
[534] Willoughby, "Gunboats & Gumbo."
[535] Hancock, p. 290; Fielding Hurst/William H. Morgan: December 2, 1863 (OR).
[536] Fielding Hurst/B.H. Grierson: December 5, 1863 (OR).
[537] Forrest/Joseph E. Johnston: December 6, 1863 (OR).
[538] John D. Stevenson/Hurlbut: December 11, 1863 in RG94/E729A/Box 6 (NARA).
[539] Hurlbut/A.J. Smith: December 16, 1863 (OR).
[540] Chalmers, "Lieutenant General Nathan Bedford Forrest And His Campaigns," *Southern Historical Society Papers*, October, 1879.
[541] "The people were greatly troubled because of Grierson's Raid, and thought it beat everything done by Forrest and Morgan." H. T. REID, Brigadier-General, Commanding at [Lake] Providence, La. NFWW.
[542] Forrest/Joseph E. Johnston: December 18, 1863 (OR).
[543] E.H. Wolfe/Thomas H. Harris: July 27, 1863 in RG393, District of Columbus (NARA).
[544] Hurst, *Nathan Bedford Forrest*, p. 145.
[545] Chalmers, "Lieutenant General Nathan Bedford Forrest And His Campaigns," *Southern Historical Society Papers*, October, 1879.
[546] J.C. Jackson (Forrest's Escort)/General Thomas Jordan: June 4, 1867, Papers of Leroy Nutt/2285/Folder 8 (SHC/UNCCH).
[547] Hancock, pp. 296-297.
[548] Forrest/Hurlbut: December 30, 1863 in RG94/E729A/Box 6 (NARA).

[549] E.H. Wolfe/Special Orders Number 308: December 18, 1863 in 52nd Regiment Indiana Infantry, Regimental Letters Sent (NARA).
[550] Edward Wehler/John Hough: December 24, 1863 in 178 Regiment New York Infantry, Regimental Letters Sent (NARA).
[551] E.H. Wolfe/Special Order Number 198: December 29, 1863 in 178th Regiment New York Infantry, Regimental Letters Sent (NARA).
[552] Edward Wehler/Provost Marshall of Paducah: December 30, 1863 in 52nd Regiment Indiana Infantry, Regimental Letters Sent (NARA)
[553] Edward Wehler/Council of Administration of the 178th New York Volunteers: December 30, 1863 in 178th Regiment New York Infantry, Regimental Letters Sent (NARA).
[554] The New York *Herald,* January 6, 1864.
[555] Addison Sleeth in Mainfort and Coats, eds., *Soldiering at Fort Pillow, 1862-1864.*
[556] E.H. Wolfe/Special Order Number 200: December 31, 1863 in 178th Regiment New York Infantry, Regimental Letters Sent (NARA).
[557] For the sake of continuity, I have transposed Guffin's post-war, present-tense account to the past tense. (Guffin, Ross, *Putnam's Magazine,* April 1870, pp. 419-424.)
[558] Sherman/Hurlbut: January 11, 1864 in 16th Army Corps (Letters Received) RG98, Part 2, Entry 391, Box 7 in NARA.
[559] Sayers, Alethea, "Fort Pillow: What the Federal Goverbnment Didn't Tell," A Nation Divided online magazine.)
[560] E.H. Wolfe/Thomas H. Harris: January 2, 1864 in RG94/E729A/Box 7 in NARA.
[561] T.H. Harris/E.H. Wolfe: January 17, 1864 in 16th Army Corps, Volume 3, Letters Sent, 1863-1864 in NARA.
[562] Asboth/Special Orders Number 151: June 22, 1863 in RG 393 Records of U. S. Army Continental Commands, Entry 992 District of Western Ky, General Orders, 1862, Vol. 101/248A.
[563] E.H. Wolfe/Special Order Number 69: June 25, 1863 in 52nd Regiment Indiana Infantry, Regimental Orders Issued (RMC).
[564] E. H. Wolfe/Special Order Number 77 in 52nd Indiana Infantry, Regimental Orders Issued (RMC).
[565] W.R. Roberts/Charles Adams: August 6, 1863 in RG 393 Records of the U.S. Army Continental Commands Entry 991 District of Western Ky, Letters Received 1862-1865 (RMC).
[566] E. H. Wolfe/Special Order Number 112 I: August 31, 1863 in 52nd Indiana Infantry, Regimental Orders Issued (RMC).
[567] N.B. Buford/T.H. Harris: January 24, 1864 in 16th Army Corps (Letters Received) RG98, Part 2, Entry 391, Box 7 in NARA. For clarity's sake, I have juxtaposed the second and third clauses of this sentence.
[568] E.H. Wolfe/Special Orders Number 15: January 18, 1864 in 16th Army Corps, Volume 3, Letters Sent, 1863-1864 in NARA; Hurlbut/A.J. Smith: January 16, 1864 in District of Columbus, Kentucky, Volume 93, Letters Sent 1862-1864 in NARA.

[569] Addison Sleeth in Mainfort and Coats, eds., Soldiering at Fort Pillow, 1862-1864.
[570] E.H. Wolfe/Special Order Number 9: January 16, 1864 in 178th Regiment New York Infantry, Regimental Papers in NARA.
[571] Addison Sleeth in Mainfort and Coats, eds., Soldiering at Fort Pillow, 1862-1864; J. Hough/E.H. Wolfe: January 16, 1864 (OR). According to J.N. Lewis, the second garrison arrived at Fort Pillow on the 22nd, not, as Harris and Hurlbut testified, on the 25th. J. N. Lewis/T.H. Harris: 1/22/1864 in 16th Army Corps (Letters Received) RG98, Part 2, Entry 391, Box 7 in NARA.

ACKNOWLEDGMENTS

Many of the same people who assisted me with *River Run Red* deserve recognition here as well, for much of what they kindly contributed overlapped both books, and everything they shared with me contributed to my perspective on both the massacre and all that led up to it. The following is a list of contributors by state.

Alabama I am especially indebted to Derek Frisby for his generous and collegial assistance as we reviewed together some of the material on which this book is based. Also thanks to the Alabama Department of Archives and History for the letters of Charles S. Stewart and Mark Lyons.

Arkansas My special thanks to Dr. Robert C. Mainfort, Professor of Anthropology at the University of Arkansas and Sponsored Research Administrator and Series Editor with the Arkansas Archeological Survey for sharing his extraordinary collection of material relating to the history of Fort Pillow. Thanks also to Special Collections, University of Arkansas Libraries at Fayetteville. **California:** Michele Sensano of the Fresno Historical Society for material relating to Tyree Bell; Stanford University Library; Los Angeles Public Library. **Delaware:** Professor Thomas J. Reed of the Widener University School of Law for help researching the 20th Tennessee Cavalry. **District of Columbia:** My special thanks to my nephew Sam Heldman, my honorary niece Hilary Ball, and my learned grandnephew Julius for putting up with me during the many weeks I spent at the National Archives. At the Archives, I am especially indebted to Michael Musick, former head of the National Archives Department of Old Military and Civil Records, and to Rebecca Livingston for her assistance reviewing naval records. I also wish to thank Joellen El Bashir, Curator of Manuscripts at the Moorland-Spingarn Research Center at Howard University. **Illinois:** Emily Victorson, The Research Center Chicago Historical Society and the staff of the Manuscripts Department of the Illinois State Historical Library in Springfield. **Indiana:** Susan Truax for her research on my behalf at the Indiana State Library. **Kansas:** The staff of the Kansas History Center in Topeka. **Kentucky:** Joe Williams of Radcliff for information relating to his ancestor Peter Williams, ex-slave from Savannah, Tennessee and Fort Pillow survivor from the 6th USCHA; Shelia E. Heflin of the Daviess County Public Library for editions of the Owensboro *Monitor*; Ray Parrish of Scottsville; University of Kentucky Special Collections and Archives. **Louisiana:** April Ayto of the Hill Memorial Library of Louisiana State University for the papers of Aaron Charter Harper, John Forman, George Baylor, and Samuel Wragg. **Massachusetts :** My old friend Mario Valdez for reviewing the coverage of Fort Pillow in the African American press. **Michigan:** Evelyn Leasher, Public Services Librarian, Clarke Historical Library, Central Michigan University, for John Ryan's Reminiscences; the staff of Carolyn E. Hart, Curatorial Assistant at the William L. Clements Library and the staff of the Michigan Historical Collections of the Bentley Historical Library at the University of Michigan at Ann Arbor. **Mississippi:** The staff of the Archives and Library Division of the Mississippi Department of Archives & History at Jackson; Andrew Gladman of the J.D. Williams Library at the University of Mississippi for the

papers of Lionel Baxter, and the Dean and Juanita Brown collections; Bobs M. Tusa of the McCain Library and Archives of the University of Southern Mississippi for the letters of W.L. Chatham and Captain John P. Worthing; Margaret Hardee Roseborough for her assistance in locating the original diary of Dewitt Clinton Fort; The McCain Library and Archives of the University of Southern Mississippi for the letters of W.L. Chatham and Captain John P. Worthing; Jeff Giambrone of Bolton for his book on the 38th Mississippi Cavalry. **Missouri:** C.W. and Betty Browning for their assistance in tracing the lives of the McCulloch family; George and Linda McCollum of Sedalia for their assistance in contacting the descendants of the fighting McCulloch cousins McCulloch; C.W. Browning and his wife Betty McCulloch, the colonel's distant cousin, for providing me with biographical material about the two Bobs; Muriel Brewer of the Cooper County Historical Society; Gerald Early, Merle Kling Professor of Modern Letters and Director of the African and Afro-American Studies Program at Washington University in St. Louis; Dr. Glen E. Holt, Executive Director of the St. Louis Public Library; James Joplin of Springfield; Terrell Dempsey of Hannibal; the staff of the G-3 Curtis Laws Wilson Library at the University of Missouri at Rolla; Dr. John A. Wright of University City; Roger Baker of Cole County, Missouri for his assistance researching the 2nd Missouri Cavalry; Tom Pearson of the St. Louis Public Library for various issues of Missouri publications relating to Fort Pillow and the 2nd Missouri Cavalry, including the *Pioneer Times*, the *Prairie Gleaner*, and various St. Louis newspapers; the Western Historical Manuscript Collection at the University of Missouri at Columbia. **North Carolina:** Southern History Collection at the University of North Carolina at Chapel Hill for a mountain of unpublished material; Janie C. Morris of Duke University for the letters of General Mosby Monroe Parsons, Hubert Saunders, and William Wylie. **Nevada:** Stan Armstrong for sharing with me his documentary on Fort Pillow. **New Jersey:** Richard L. Fuchs, Esquire of Cranbury, the author of *Unerring Fire* (1994), the first serious 20th century book on the Fort Pillow massacre.
New York: My brother, the historian Geoffrey C. Ward, for many commiserations and much sound advice; Richard Snow, Editor of *American heritage*; the Chatauqua County Historical Society in Westfield.
Ohio: The staff of the Jerome Library at Bowling Green State University; the staff of the Oberlin College Archives. **Oklahoma** Peggy Truesdell of Tulsa for the memoir of William L. Ridgeway of the 20th Tennessee Cavalry (CSA). **Pennsylvania:** The U.S. Army Military History Institute for the letters of Jonas D. Elliott and John P. Brownlow. **Rhode Island:** Peter Harrington, curator of the Anne S.K. Brown Military Collection at Brown University. **Tennessee:** Special thanks to my cousin Marilyn Tomlinson and her sons Jon and Andrew for their generosity and hospitality during my weeks researching the Fort Pillow story in Memphis and Nashville. Thanks also to my excellent researchers Jim Havron (Nashville) and Debra Burrell (Memphis); Fred Montgomery; Bonnie Brooks of the Benton County Education Association; Debra Burrell for her research on my behalf in various Memphis archives and collections; Earl Willoughby for his advice and for sharing his excellent articles on the Civil War history of West Tennessee; Ed Frank of the Mississippi Wilderness Collection at Memphis

State University for his assistance and sound advice; Jennifer Goforth of the Fort Pillow State Park Interpretive Center; Edward F. Williams, III of Memphis for directing me to the story of Forrest's black servants; Jere Cox at the Gordon Browning Museum of the Carroll County Historical Society for the letters of Captain John A. Crutchfield and miscellaneous documents and articles relating to the Civil War in West Tennessee; the staff of the Memphis and Shelby County Room of the Memphis and Shelby County Public Library for miscellaneous clippings regarding Nathan Bedford Forrest and Fort Pillow, especially articles from the Memphis *Commercial Appeal* and *Bulletin*; genealogist Arthur L. Webb of Memphis; Virginia Morton for directing me to the journal of Dewitt Clinton Fort; Marilyn Tillman and the staff of the Lauderdale County Library; the staff of the Lauderdale County courthouse; the staff of the Fort Pillow State Historic Park; Ralph Babin of La Place for information about the Bowles men who served under Forrest; Mayor Russell Bailey of Covington; Rebel C. Forrester, Obion County Historian in Union City; Natalie Huntley of the Dyer County Historical Society; Charles yates of Gibson County; Rick Tuck; Milton Webb; Dr. Calvin Dickinson and the staff of the Putnam County Main Library at Cookeville; the staff of the McIver's Grant Public Library in Dyersburg; the staff of the Giles County Historical Society in Pulaski; Dr. James Jones of the Tennessee Historical Commission in Nashville; Ken Feith of the Nashville Metropolitan Archives of Nashville and Davidson County; R.M. Price of the 20th Tennessee Cavalry web page; Richard Saunders, Curator of Special Collections, Paul Meek Library, University of Tennessee at Martin; the staff of the Special Collections at the Jean and Alexander Heard Library at Vanderbilt University in Nashville; Benny Smith; Gary Overall for permission to quote from his ancestor Isaac Overall's letters; Marie Kleeberg for information about the 8th Tennessee Cavalry. **Texas:** Peggy Fox, Director, Research Center, the Harold B. Simpson Hill College History Complex of Hillsboro, Texas for A.J. Grantham's reminiscences; and Laura Garcia, Supervisor, Local History Department, Corpus Christi Public Library; Julie Holcomb, Archivist at the Navarro College Library and Learning Resource Center at Navarro College for letters by Nathan Bedford Forrest defending his actions at Fort Pillow; Peggy Scott Holley for sharing with me her research into the treatment of Tennessee Unionists in Confederate prisons; Troy Groves for his marvelous website devoted to Terry's Texas Rangers, A.K.A. the 8th Texas Cavalry; Dr. B.D. Patterson of Hillsboro; Gary P. Whitfield of Fort Worth. **Virginia:** Aaron Crawford, researcher, at the University libraries of Virginia Tech; Thomas P. and Beth Lowry of the Index Project, Inc. **Washington:** John Thorne and Gordon Lingley for their faithful transcriptions of the voluminous materials I brought back from my researches; Jacqueline E.A. Lawson of Diversitudes and the Black Genealogy Research Group of Seattle for her researches on my behalf; Quintard Taylor, the Bullitt Professor of History at the University of Washington, for his friendship, sage advice and helpful introductions; the naval historian John W. Hinds for reviewing portions of my manuscript; and finally, but preeminently, my thanks to my wife Debbie for her love and encouragement.

SOURCES

KEY

CV	*Confederate Veteran*
CWH	*Civil War History*
RMC	Robert Mainfort Collection
SHSP	*Southern Historical Society Papers*
THQ	*Tennessee Historical Quarterly*
TSLA	Tennessee State Library and Archives (Nashville)
SHC/UNCCH	Southern History Collection University of North Carolina at Chapel Hill
SHSP	*Southern Historical Society Papers*
WTHSP	*West Tennessee Historical Society Papers*

PUBLISHED SOURCES

American Missionary Association. *History of the American Missionary Association: Its Churches and Educational Institutions among the Freedmen, Indians, and Chinese, with Illustrative Facts and Anecdotes.* New York, 1874.

American Missionary Association. *Twenty-Fifth Annual Report of the American Missionary Association.* New York, 1871.

Anonymous. *Army of the Cumberland.* Philadelphia, 1863.

Anonymous. *Christian Reconstruction: The American Missionary Association and Southern Blacks, 1861-1890.* Athens (GA), 1986.

Anonymous. *History of Rush County, Indiana.* (Reprint of 1888 edition.) Knightstown (IN), 1966. Anonymous. *History of Tennessee: From the Earliest Time to the Present; Together With an Historical and a Biographical Sketch of Lauderdale, Tipton, Haywood, and Crockett Counties; Besides a Valuable Fund of Notes, Reminiscences, Etc., Etc.* Reprint of 1886 edition. Greenville (SC), 1997.

Anonymous. *Old Times in West Tennessee.* Memphis, 1873.

Aptheker, Herbert. *To Be Free.* New York, 1991.

Ash, Stephen V., ed. *Secessionists and Other Scoundrels: Selections from Parson Brownlow's Book.* Baton Rouge, 1999.

Bailey, Fred Arthur. *Class and Tennessee's Confederate Generation.* Chapel Hill, 1987.

Baker, Pansy N. and Charlotte S. Reynolds. *Weakley Remembered.* Three volumes. Bradford (TN), 1982.

Basler, Roy P. *The Collected Works of Abraham Lincoln.* 8 vols. and Index. New Brunswick [NJ], 1953. [CWAL]

Bears, Edwin C., *Forrest at Brice's Cross Roads and in North Mississippi in 1864.* Dayton [OH], 1991.

Bedford County (Tennessee). Deed Book: January 15, 1833.

Berlin, Ira et al, eds. *Free At Last: A Documentary History of Slavery, Freedom, and the Civil War.* New York, 1992.

Berlin, Ira, ed. *The Wartime Genesis of Free Labor: The Upper South,* Series I, Volume II of *Freedom: A Documentary History of Emancipation: 1861-1867.* Cambridge, 1993.

Berlin, Ira. *Slaves without Masters: The Free Negro in the Antebellum South.* New York, 1974.
Berry, Thomas F. *Four Years with Morgan and Forrest.* Oklahoma City, 1914.
Berwanger, Eugene H. *The Frontier Against Slavery: Western Anti-Negro Prejudice and the Slavery Extension Controversy.* Chicago, 1971.
Billings, John D. *Hardtack & Coffee: The Unwritten Story of Army Life.* Reprint of 1887 edition. Lincoln (NB), 1993.
Blight, David W. *Race and Reunion: The Civil War in American Memory.* Cambridge (MA), 2001.
Blount, T.W. "Captain Thomas Blount and His Memoirs." *Southwestern Historical Quarterly.* July, 1935.
Boles, John B. *Masters and Slaves in the House of the Lord: Race and Religion in the American South, 1740-1870.* Lexington, 1988.
Botkin, B.A., ed. *Lay my Burden Down: A Folk History of Slavery.* Chicago, 1969.
Britton, Wiley. *The Aftermath of the Civil War Based on Investigation of War Claims.* Kansas City (MO), 1924.
Brockett, L.P. and Mary C. Vaughan. *Woman's work in the Civil War: A Record of Heroism, Patriotism and Patience.* Boston, 1867.
Brooksher, William R. & David K. Snider. *Glory at a Gallop: Tales of the Confederate Cavalry.* McLean (VA), 1993.
Brown, Barbara W. and James M. Rose, editors. *Black Roots in Southeastern Connecticut, 1650-1900.* Detroit, 1980.
Brown, Tully. *Nathan Bedford Forrest: Lecture Delivered at Vendome Theatre, Nashville, Tennessee, January 26, 1905.* Unpublished ms. (TSLA).
Buckley, Gail. *American Patriots: the Story of Blacks in the Military from the Revolution to Desert Storm.* New York, 2001.
Caldwell, Merrill S. "A Brief History of Slavery in Boone County, Kentucky." Unpublished paper delivered to the Boone County Historical Society at Florence, Kentucky, June 21, 1957.
Campbell, Given. Papers. Wilson Library, University of North Carolina at Chapel Hill.
Casstevens, Francis H. *Edward A. Wild and the African Brigade in the Civil War.* Jefferson (NC), 2003.
Catteral, Helen Tunnicliff, ed. *Judicial Cases concerning American Slavery and the negroSlavery.* Volume 4. Washington, 1926-1937.
Cimprich, John. *Slavery's End in Tennessee.* Tuscaloosa (AL), 1985
Civil War Centennial Commission [Nashville]. *Tennesseeans in the Civil War: A Military History of Confederate and Union Units with Available Rosters of Personnel.* Two volumes. Nashville, 1964.
Clayton, W.W. *History of Davidson County, Tennessee with Illustrations and Biographical Sketches of its Prominent Men and Pioneers.* Reprint of 1897 edition. Nashville, 1971.
Coombe, Jack D. *Thunder Along the Mississippi: The River Battles that Split the Confederacy.* New York, 1998.
Cornish, Dudley Taylor. *The Sable Arm: Negro Troops in the Union Army, 1861-1865.* New York, 1966.
Crawford, Charles W. *Weakley County.* Memphis, 1983.
Crutchfield, James A. *Williamson County: A Pictorial History.* Nashville, 1980.

Culp, FM and Mrs. R.E. Ross. *Gibson County Past & Present.* Trenton (TN), 1961.
Currotto, William F. *Wizard of the Saddle.* Memphis, 1996.
Curry, Richard O., ed. *The Abolitionist.* New York, 1965.
Daniel, Larry J. *Soldiering in the Army of Tennessee: A Portrait of Life in a Confederate Army.* Chapel Hill, 1991.
Davis, William C. *The Cause Lost: Myths and Realities of the Confederacy.* Lawrence (KS), 1996.
Davis, William C., ed. *The Confederate General.* Volume One. Washington (DC), 1991.
Deaderick, Barron. *Forrest: "Wizard of the Saddle."* Memphis, 1960.
Dew, Charles B. *Apostles of Disunion: Southern Secession Commissioners and the Causes of the Civil War.* Charlottesville (VA), 2001.
Dinkins, James. *Furl That Banner: Personal Recollections and Experiences in the Confederate Army.* Cincinnati, 1897.
DuBois, W. E. B. *Black Reconstruction in America 1860-1880.* New York, 1935.
Dunnavant, Robert, Jr. *The Railroad War: N.B. Forrest's 1864 Raid Through Northern Alabama and Middle Tennessee.* Athens (AL), 1994.
Dyer Heritage Committee. *A History of the Dyer, Tennessee Community: The People and their Work.* Dyer (TN), 1986.
Dyer, G.W. and J.T. Moore, eds., *The Tennessee Civil War Veterans Questionnaires* [1915-1922]. Five Volumes. Easley (SC), 1985.
Eddy, Colonel A.R., *History of Forts Pickering and Pillow, Tennessee,* Adjutant General's Office. NARA.
Eden, Horatio. Memoir. TSLA.
Eisenschiml, Auto and Ralph Newman. *Eyewitness: The Civil War as We Lived it: The American Iliad.* New York, 1956.
Elkins, Stanley M. *Slavery: A Problem in American Institutional and Intellectual Life.* Chicago, 1967.
Evans, Clement A., comp. *Confederate Military History; a Library of Confederate States History, in Twelve Volumes, Written by Distinguished Men of the South.* (Reprint of the 1899 edition .) New York, 1962.
Ewell, Leighton. *History of Coffee County Tennessee.* Manchester (TN), 1936.
Fehrenbacher, Don E. *The Slaveholding Republic: An account of the United States Government's Relations to Slavery.* New York, 2001.
Fitzgerald, Ross. *A Visit to the Cities and Camps of the Confederate States.* London, 1865.
Fletcher, Samuel. *The History of Company A, Second Illinois Cavalry.* Chicago, 1912.
Forrester, Rebel C. *Glory and Tears: Obion County, Tennessee 1860-1870.* Union City (TN), 1970.
Franklin, John Hope, ed. *The Diary of James T. Ayers: Civil War Recruiter.* Springfield (IL), 1947.
Freehling, William W. *The South vs. the South: How Anti-confederate Southerners Shaped the Course of the Civil War.* New York, 2001.
Freehling, William W. & Craig M. Simpson, eds. *Secession Debated: Georgia's Showdown in 1860.* New York, 1992.
Gallagher, Gary W. & Alan T. Nolan, eds. *The Myth of the Lost Cause and the Civil War History.* Bloomington (IN), 2000.

Garrison, Webb. *Civil War Curiosities: Strange Stories, Oddities, Events, and Coincidences.* Nashville, 1994.
Gauss, John. *Black Flag! Black Flag!: The Battle at Fort Pillow.* Lanham (MD), 2003.
Genovese, Eugene D. *The Political Economy of Slavery: Studies in the Economy and Society of the Slave South.* New York, 1967.
Genovese, Eugene. *Roll, Jordan, Roll: the World the Slaves Made.* New York, 1976.
Genweb Homepage
Gillette, William. *Retreat from Reconstruction., 1869-1879.* Baton Rouge, 1979.
Gladstone, William A. *United States Colored Troops: 1863-1867.* Gettysburg, 1990.
Glatthaar, Joseph T. *Forged in Battle: The Civil War Alliance of Black Soldiers and White officers.* New York, 1990.
Glatthaar, Joseph T. *The March to the Sea and Beyond.* Baton Rouge, 1995.
Goldhurst, Richard. *Many Are the Hearts: The Agony and triumph of Ulysses S. Grant.* New York, 1975.
Goodspeed Publishing Co., *Lauderdale County History.* Chicago, 1887.
Goodspeed Publishing Company, *History of Knox & Davies Counties, Indiana.* Chicago, 1886.
Goodspeed Publishing Company. *History of Knox & Davies Counties, Indiana.* Chicago, 1886.
Goodspeed Publishing Company. *Lauderdale County History.* Chicago, 1887.
Goodstein, Anita Shafer. *Nashville, 1780-1860: From Frontier to City.* Gainesville, 1989.
Graf, Leroy P. and Haskins, Ralph W Haskins, eds. *The Papers of Andrew Johnson.* Volume 6. Knoxville, 1983.
Green, Nathaniel E. *The Silent Believers.* Louisville, 1972.
Grigsby, Melvin. *The Smoked Yank.* Sioux Falls (SD), 1888.
Grimsley, Mark. *The Hard Hand of War: Union Military Policy Toward Southern Civilians, 1861-1865.* New York, 1995.
Hamer, Philip M. *Tennessee: A History: 1673-1932.* Volume One. New York, 1933.
Hardeman County Historical Commission. *Hardeman County Historical Sketches.* Dallas, 1979.
Harding, Lewis A., ed. *History of Decatur County, Indiana.* Indianapolis, 1915. RMC.
Henry County Historical Society. *Pen Sketches: Henry County, Tennessee.* Paris, 1976.
Henry, Robert Selph, *"First With the Most" Forrest,* Indianapolis, 1944.
Henry, Robert Selph. *As They Saw Forrest: Some recollections and comments of contemporaries.* Wilmington (NC), 1987.
Henry, Robert Selph. *The Story of the Confederacy.* Reprint of 1931 edition. New York, 1964.
Higginson, Thomas Wentworth. *Army Life in a Black Regiment.* Boston, 1870.
Hinton, Thomas C. Letter. *The Christian Recorder.* May 21, 1864.
Hirshson, Stanley P. *Farewell to the Bloody Shirt: Northern Republicans and the Southern Negro 1877-1893.* Chicago, 1968.

Hopping, James Mason. *Life of Andrew Hull Foote, Rear Admiral United States Navy*. New York, 1874. RMC.
Howard, Goldena Roland. *Ralls County*. New London (MO), 1980.
Howlett, R.E. *Dr. R.E. Howlett in the Civil War: Record of the Service in the Confederate Army of Dr. R E. Howlett, Otterville, Mo., as dictated by him to George Zollinger, September 2nd, 1916*. Unpublished ms. Western Historical Manuscript Collection, University of Missouri/State Historical Society of Missouri. C699.
Hubbard, John Milton. *Notes of a Private*. St. Louis, 1913.
Hurst, Jack. *Nathan Bedford Forrest: A Biography*. New York, 1993.
Ingersoll, Lurton Dunham. *Iowa and the Rebellion: A History of the Troops Furnished by the State of Iowa to the Volunteer Armies of the Union, Which conquered the Great Southern Rebellion of 1861-5*. Philadelphia, 1867. RMC.
Ingmire, Frances T. *Confederate POWs: Soldiers & Sailors Who Died in Federal Prisons & Military Hospitals in the North*. Washington (DC), 1915).
Jacobs, Lee. *The Gray Riders: Stories from the Confederate Cavalry*. Shippensburg (PA), 1999.
Jewell, Edwin Lewis, ed. *New Orleans, including biographical sketches of its distinguished citizens, together with a map and general strangers' guide*. New Orleans, 1873.
Johnson, Adam Rankin. *The Partisan Rangers of the Confederate States Army*. Reprint of the 1904 edition. Austin, 1995.
Joint Committee on the Conduct of the War [Wade], *Report of the Joint committee on the conduct of the war at the second session Thirty-eighth Congress*. Washington (DC), 1865.
Jordan, Thomas and J.P. Pryor. *The Campaigns of Lieut.-Gen. N.B. Forrest, and of Forrest's Cavalry*, Reprint, 1868 edition. New York, 1996.
Josyph, Peter, ed. *The Wounded River: The Civil War Letters of John Nance Lauderdale, M.D.* East Lansing (MI), 1993.
Kane, Joseph Nathan. *The American Counties: Origins of names, dates of creation and organization, area, population, historical data, and published sources*. Third edition. Metuchen (NJ), 1972.
Kaplan, Justin. *Mr. Clemens and Mark Twain*. New York, 1966.
Kirke, Edmund. *Down in Tennessee*. Reprint of 1864 edition. Westport (Connecticut), 1970.
Kirkland, Frazar. *The Pictorial Book of Anecdotes and Incidents of the War of the Rebellion, Civil, Military, Naval and Domestic: Embracing the Most Brilliant and Remarkable Anecdotal Events of the Great Conflict in the United States*. Hartford, 1866.
Lamon, Lester C. *Blacks in Tennessee: 1791-1970*. Knocksville, 1993.
Lauderdale County. Will Books.
Lee, George R. *Slavery North of St. Louis*. TC
Lee-Davis UDC Historical Society. *Families and History of Gibson County, Tennessee to 1989*. Milan, TN, 1989.
Lindsley, John B. *Military Annals of Tennessee: Confederate -- First Series*. Nashville, 1886.
Lonn, Ella. *Desertion During the Civil War*. New York, 1928.
Lovett, Bobby L. and Linda T. Wynn, eds. *Profiles of African Americans in Tennessee*. Nashville, 1996.

Lovett, Bobby L., ed. *The Afro-American History of Nashville, Tennessee: 1870-1930*. Nashville, 1981.
Lowry, Thomas, M.D. *The Story the Soldiers Wouldn't Tell: Sex in the Civil War*. Mechanicsburg (PA), 1994.
Macaluso, Gregory J. *The Fort Pillow Massacre: The Reason Why*. New York, 1989.
Magness, Perre. *Past Times: Stories of Early Memphis*. Memphis, 1994.
Main, Edward M. *The Story of the Marches, Battles and Incidents of the Third United States Cavalry: A Fighting Regiment in the War of the Rebellion, 1861-5*. New Orleans, 1908.
Mainfort, Robert C. *Archaeological Investigations at Fort Pillow State Historic Area: 1976-1978*. Nashville, 1980.
Maness, Lonnie E. *An Untutored Genius: The Military Career of General Nathan Bedford Forrrest*. Oxford (MS), 1990.
Marrs, Elijah p. *Life and History of Elijah P. Marrs*. Louisville, 1885.
Marshall, E.H. *History of Obion County*. Union City (TN), 1941.
Maslowski, Peter. *Treason Must Be Make Odious: Military Occupation and Wartime Reconstruction in Nasville, Tennessee, 1862-65*. Millwood (New York), 1978
Mathes, J. Harvey *The Old Guard in Gray*. Memphis, 1899.
Mathes, J. Harvey. *General Forrest*. New York, 1902.
McKay, John. "Final Report of the American Freedman's Inquiry Commission: June 22, 1864." Records of the U.S. Senate, 38th Congress, NARA.
McLeary, Andrew C. *Humorous Incidents of the Civil War*. Privately published, ca. 1902.
McPherson, James M. *The Abolitionist Legacy from Reconstruction to the NAACP*. Princeton, 1975.
McPherson, James M. *The Battle Cry of Freedom: The Civil War Era*. New York, 1988.
McPherson, James M. *The Negro's Civil War: How American Negroes Felt and Acted During the War for the Union*. New York, 1965.
Miles, Jim. *A River Unvexed: A History and Tour Guide of the Campaign for the Mississippi River*. Nashville, 1994.
Montgomery, Frank Alexander. *Reminiscences Of A Mississippian In Peace And War*. Cincinnati, 1901.
Moore, Frank, ed. *The Rebellion Record: A Diary of American Events with Documents, Narratives, Illustrative Incidents, Poetry, Etc*. Volume 8. New York, 1865.
Moore, Frank. *Anecdotes, poetry, and incidents of the war: North and South. 1860-1865: Collected and arranged by Frank Moore*. New York, 1867.
Moore, Kenneth. "Fort Pillow, Forrest, and the United States Colored Troops in 1864." THQ. 1995.
Morgan, Mrs. Irby. *How It Was; Four Years Among The Rebels*: Nashville, 1892. UNCCH
Morison, Samuel Eliot. *The Oxford History of the American People*. New York, 1965.
Morton, John Watson. *The Artillery of Nathan Bedford Forrest's Cavalry*. Reprint of 1909 edition. Marietta (GA), 1995.

National Historical Company. *History of Howard and Cooper Counties, Missouri.* St. Louis, 1883.
Ndilei, David. *Extinguish the Flames of Racial Prejudice.* Yellville (AK), 1996.
Nevin, David. *Sherman's March: Atlanta to the Sea.* New York, 1986.
Nicolay, John G. and John Hay. *Abraham Lincoln: A History.* Ten volumes. New York, 1890.
Patterson, Caleb Perry. *The Negro in Tennessee: 1790-1865.* Reprint of 1941 edition. Spartanburg (S.C.), 1974.
Payne, W.O. *History of Story County, Iowa.* Chicago, 1911.
Peters, Kate Johnson, ed. *Lauderdale County from Earliest Times: An Intimate and informal account of the towns and communities, its families and famous individuals.* Ripley (TN), 1957.
Phillips, Margaret I. *The Governors of Tennessee.* Gretna (**TC**), 1998.
Pratt, Fletcher. *The Civil War on Western Waters.* New York, 1956.
Quarles, Benjamin. *The Negro in the Civil War.* New York, 1989.
Rawlins, Richard, ed. *Black Southerners in Gray: Essays on Afro-Americans in Confederate Armies.* Murfressboro, 1994.
Rennolds, Edwin H. *A History of the Henry County Commands.* Reprint of 1904 edition. Kennesaw [GA], 1961.
Robbins, Faye Wellborn. *World-within-a-World: Black Nashville, 1880-1915.* Ann Arbor, 1980.
Ross, Fitzgerald. *A Visit to the Cities and Camps of the Confederate States.* London, 1865.
Russ, Lee H. "Firing a Captured Cannon at Fort Pillow." *Confederate Veteran.* June, 1904.
Sage, Leland L. *A History of Iowa.* Ames (IO), 1974. RMC.
Samuel W. Scott and Samuel P. Angel, *History of the Thirteenth Regiment, Tennessee Volunteer Cavalry, U.S.A.* (Philadelphia, 1903).
Scharf, J. Thomas. *History of the Confederate States Navy.* New York, 1996.
Scott, John, ed. *Story of the Thirty Second Iowa Infantry Volunteers.* Nevada (Iowa), 1896.
Sheppard, Eric William. *Bedford Forrest: The Confederacy's Greatest Cavalryman.* New York, 1930.
Sherman, William T. *Memoirs of William T. Sherman.* Volume 2. New York, 1875.
Sherril, Charles A. ed.. *Tennessee's Confederate Widows and Their Families.* Cleveland (Tennessee),1992.
Sifakis, Stewart. *Who Was Who in the Civil War.* New York, 1988.
Silver, James W., ed. *Mississippi in the Confederacy as Seen in Retrospect.* Baton Rouge, 1961.
Simon, John Y., ed. *The Papers of Ulysses S. Grant: Volume 10: January 1-May 31, 1864.* Carbondale (Illinois), 1998.
Starr, Stephen Z.. *The Union Cavalry in the Civil War: The War in the West 1861 – 1865.* Volume III. Baton Rouge, 1985.
State of Louisiana, "Constitutional convention, 1864." New Orleans, 1864.
Stearns, Charles. *The Black Man of the South, and the Rebels.* Reprint of 1872 edition. New York, 1969.
Stevenson, William G. *Thirteen Months in the Rebel Army.* New York, 1862.

Tap, Bruce. *Over Lincoln's shoulder: the Committee on the Conduct of the War.* Lawrence (KS), 1998.
Tennessee Department of Conservation. *Master Plan Report: Fort Pillow: State Historic Area.* Nashville, 1975.
Tennessee, State of. Civil War (Federal) Collection (TSLA).
Thornbrough, Emma Lou. *Indiana in the Civil War Era.* (*The History of Indiana, Volume 3*). Indianapolis, 1965.
Trudeau, Noah Andre. *Like Men of War: Black Troops in the Civil War, 1862-1865.* Boston, 1998.
Turner, William Bruce. *History of Maury County Tennessee.* Nashville, 1955.
U.S. Congress, *Journal of the Senate of the United States of America, 1789-1873*, June 2, 1864.
United Daughters of the Confederacy [Missouri Division]. *Reminiscences of the women of Missouri during the sixties, gathered, compiled and published by Missouri division, United daughters of the confederacy.* Jefferson City (MO), 1913.
United Daughters of the Confederacy [Nashville Division]. *Tennessee C.S.A.* Nashville, 1998.
United States Army. *Proceedings of a Military Commission Convened at St. Louis, Mo. [October 16, 1864], by virtue of [Special Orders 287].* Special Collections Division, University of Arkansas Libraries
United States Congress. *Journal of the House of Representatives of the United States, 1789-1873.* Washington, 1873.
United States Congress. *Journal of the Senate of the United States of America, 1789-1873.* Washington, 1873.
United States Congress. *Ku Klux Conspiracy: Report of the Joint Select Committee to Inquire into the Condition of Affairs in the Late Insurrectionary States.* Washington, 1872.
United States. Census for 1850, 1860, 1870.
Walvin, James. *Questioning Slavery.* London, 1996.
Ward, Geoffrey C. with Ric Burns & Ken Burns. *The Civil War: An Illustrated History.* New York, 1990.
Warner, Ezra J. *Generals in Blue: Lives of the Union Commanders.* New Orleans, 1964.
Welsh, Jack D. *Medical Histories of Confederate Generals.* Kent (OH), 1995.
Wharton, Vernon Lane. *The Negro in Mississippi: 1865-1890.* New York, 1965.
Wiley, Bell Irvin. *Southern Negroes: 1861-1865.* Reprint of 1938 edition. New haven, 1965.
Wiley, Bell Irvin. *The Plain People of the Confederacy.* Chicago, 1963.
Williams, Edward F. (III). *Confederate Victories at Fort Pillow.* Memphis, 1984.
Williams, Walter, ed. *A History of Northeast Missouri.* Chicago, 1913.
Wilson, Joseph T. *The Black Phalanx.* Hartford, 1888.
Woodward, C. Vann. *The Burden of Southern History.* New York, 1968.
Wright, Louise Wigfall. *A Southern Girl in '61: The War-Time Memories of a Confederate Senator's Daughter*: 1998 electronic edition of New York, 1905 edition. UNCCH.
Wright, Marcus J. *Tennessee in the War 1861-1865.* New York, 1908.
Wubben, Hubert H. *Civil War Iowa and the Copperhead Movement.* Ames [Iowa], 1980.

Wyeth, John Allan. *That Devil Forrest: Life of General Nathan Bedford Forrest.* New York, 1959.

PERIODICALS
Agnew, Samuel A. "Battle of Tishomingo Creek." *CV*. September 1900.
Aldrich, Charles. "Incidents Connected with the History of the Thirty-Second Iowa Infantry." *The Iowa Journal*. January, 1906.
Allen, W.B. with George Albright and C. D. Covington. *CV*. Letter. July, 1899.
Anderson, Charles W. "Col. Wiley M, Reed." *CV*. March, 1897.
Anglo African, April 23, 1864.
Anonymous. "Rebel Atrocities." *Harper's Weekly*. May 21, 1864
Anonymous. "Request for Information." *CV*. July, 1909.
Anonymous. "Reunion of Forrest's Escort," *CV*. March, 1894.
Anonymous. "The Last Roll: Gen. Tyree H. Bell." *CV*. October, 1902.
Anonymous. "Visit to Historic Ground." Memphis *Argus*. September 10, 1865. RMC.
Anonymous. "When Will Poppa Come?" *CV*. September, 1896.
Armstrong, William M. "Cahaba to Charleston: The Prison Odyssey of Lt. Edmund E. Ryan." *CWH*. June, 1962.
Atkinson, J.H., ed. "A Civil War Letter of Captain Elliott Fletcher, Jr." *Arkansas Historical Quarterly*. 1963 (22)1: 49-54.
Atlanta *Confederacy* in Charleston *Mercury*. May 6, 1864.
Bailey, Robert. "The 'Bogus' Memphis *Union Appeal*: A Union Newspaper in Occupied Confederate Territory. *WTHSP*, 1978.
Ballard, Elsie Miner. "James Dick Davis: (1810-1880) A Genealogical Sketch." *WTHSP*. 1975.
Beckham, Elihu C. "Where Was I And What I Saw During The Late War." Melbourne [Arkansas] *Times*, September 6, 1906.
Benton, Edward. Letter. New York *Herald*. April 24, 1864.
Blanton, J.C. "Forrest's Old Regiment." *CV*. 3/2, February, 1895.
Blount, T.W. "Captain Thomas Blount and His Memoirs." *Southwestern Historical Quarterly*. July, 1935. RMC.
"Boatman," "Letter from Pillow Battery (Camp of Southern Guards: July 14, 1861)." The Memphis *Avalanche*. July 16, 1861. RMC.
Bolivar [Tennessee] *Bulletin*. "Site of Fort Pillow in Mississippi River." *CV*. December, 1908.
Branch, Mary Polk. *Memoirs of a Southern Woman "within the Lines" and a Genealogical Record*. Chicago, 1912. UNC/CH.
Brewer, Thomas. "Storming Of Fort Pillow." *CV*. December, 1925.
Brown, Andrew. "Sol Street: Confederate Partisan Leader." *Journal of Mississippi History*. July, 1959.
Brownlow, John. "John Brownlow's First Published Memoirs." Columbia, Tennessee *Daily Herald*. September 30, 1984.
Burney, Tom. "Shannon's Scouts." Groesbeck *Journal*. December 9, 1909.
Cairo *News*, April 16, 1864.
Carney, Court. "The Contested Image of Nathan Bedford Forrest." *The Journal of Southern History*. August, 2001.
Christi *Caller Times*. October 6, 1940.

Castel, Albert. "The Fort Pillow Massacre: A Fresh Examination of the Evidence." *CWH*. 4/1958.
Chalmers, "Lieutenant General Nathan Bedford Forrest And His Campaigns." *SHSP*, October, 1879.
Chapin, L.W. Letter. *CV*. October, 1895.
Charleston *Mercury*. March 22, April 7, May 2 and 23, June 12-13, August 4 and 18, November 7 and 13, 1862; August 4, 1864.
Chicago *Tribune* in *The Anglo African*, May 7, 1864.
Cimprich, John and Mainfort, Robert C. Jr. "The Fort Pillow Massacre: A Statistical Note." *Journal of American History*. 1989 76(3).
Cimprich, John and Robert C. Mainfort, "Dr. Fitch's Report on the Fort Pillow Massacre." *THQ*, 44(1), Spring 1985.
Cimprich, John and Robert C. Mainfort, Jr. "Fort Pillow Revisited: New Evidence About an Old Controversy." *CWH*. 28(4): 293-306, 1982.
Cole, C.M. "Vivid War Experiences at Ripley, Miss." *CV*. June, 1905.
Columbus (Kentucky) *War Eagle*, December 12th, 1863. Courtesy of Derek Frisby.
Cook, V.Y. "Forrest's Capture of Col. R.G. Ingersoll." *CV*. February, 1907.
Covington *Leader*, August 20, 1889.
Croffutt, ___ "Bourbon ballads" in New York *Tribune* Extra No. 52.
Cupples, Douglas W. "Memphis' Confederate Civil War Refugees." *WTHSP*. 1995.
Deupree, J.E. "Capt. T.J. Kennedy." *CV*. June, 1909.
Donhardt, Gary L. "On the Road to Memphis with General Ulysses S. Grant." *WTHSP*. 1997.
Flanders, Edwin P. Papers. Michigan Historical Collections, Bentley Historical Library, University of Michigan at Ann Arbor.
Forrest, Nathan Bedford, "General Forrest's Report of Operations in December, 1863." *SHSP*. 8: 40-41, 1880.
Franklin (VA) *Repository*, April 27, 1864
Freemon, Frank R. "The Medical Challenge of Military Operations in the Mississippi Valley during the American Civil War." *Military Medicine*. 1992.
Pioneer Times, January 1985.
Hollis, Elisha Tompkin [William W. Chester, ed.] "The Diary of Elisha Tompkin Hollis." *WTHSP*. 1985.
Huch, Ronald K. "The Fort Pillow Massacre: The Aftermath of Paducah." *Journal of the Illinois State Historical Society*. Spring, 1973.
Hunter, J.N. "Forrest's Cavalry." *CV*, July, 1913.
"J.C.C." *Jewish Messenger*. April 10, May 6, June 2, July 16, September 4, and November 19, 1862; May 6 and July 16, 1863.
Lee, Stephen D. "Tribute to Gen. Bedford Forrest." *CV*. June, 1903.
Lockett, James D. "The Lynching Massacre of Black and White Soldiers at Fort Pillow, Tennessee, April 12, 1864." *Western Journal of Black Studies*. Summer, 1998.
Lockhart, Margaret Morphis. "Memories of the Civil War." *The South Reporter*. January 8, 1942.
Logan, S.H. "No Massacre by Forrest at Fort Pillow Says One Who Rode with Him: Interview with Robert Bufferd [Clarksville, Arkansas]." Nashville *Commercial Appeal*, September 2, 1934.

Lovett, Bobby L. "The West Tennessee Colored Troops in Civil War Combat." *WTHSP*. 1980.
Lowell [Massachusetts] *Daily Courier*. April 30, 1864.
Lufkin, Charles L. "Not Heard From Since April 12, 1864" The Thirteenth Tennessee Cavalry, U.S.A." *THQ*. 1986.
Lufkin, Charles L. "West Tennessee Unionists in the Civil War: A Hawkins Family Letter." *THQ*. Spring, 1987.
MacDonald, Ward. "Sensations in the Kentucky Backwoods." *CV*. May, 1895.
Mainfort, Robert C., Jr. "A Folk Art Map of Fort Pillow." *WTHSP*. 1986.
Mainfort, Robert C., Jr. and Coats, Patricia E., ed. "Soldiering at Fort Pillow, 1862-1864: an Excerpt from the Civil War Memoirs of Addison Sleeth." *WTHSP*. 1982.
Mainfort, Robert. Memphis *Commercial Appeal*, September 14, 1979.
Maness, Lonnie E. "A Ruse That Worked: The Capture of Union City in 1864." *WTHSP*. 1976.
Maness, Lonnie E. "Fort Pillow under Confederate and Union Control." *WTHSP*. 1984.
Maness, Lonnie E. "The Fort Pillow Massacre: Fact or Fiction." *THQ*. 1986.
Maness, Lonnie. "The Civil War: an Historiographical Essay – The Importance of the West and Tennessee." *WTHSP*. 1990.
Mason City, *Cerro Gordo Republican*. December 24, 1862; January 23 and 27, May 25, June 22, 1863;
Memphis *Commercial Appeal*. August 23, 1851; June 19, 1879; May 17, 1905; January 16 and February 29, 1929; July 13, 1940; February 15, 1974; December 10, 1975.
Memphis *Daily Appeal* (Printed in Atlanta, GA). May 2, 1864
Memphis *Daily Appeal* (Printed in Memphis.) October 30, 1877
Memphis *News-Scimitar,* April 30 and May 17, 1905.
Miller, M.A. "Under Sentence of Death." *CV*. April, 1905.
Mitchell, Bobby J., ed., "Stirring Up the Yankees." *The Gray Ghost*. July-Aug. 1999.
Moore, Kenneth Bancroft. "Fort Pillow, Forrest, and the United States Colored Troops in 1864." *THQ*. Summer, 1995.
Morris, Roy Jr. "Fort Pillow: Massacre or Madness?" *America's Civil War*. November, 2000.
Morris, Roy Jr. "The Committee on the Conduct of the War was as much a foe of wayward Union Generals as it was of Confederates." *America's Civil War*. November, 2000.
New York *Herald*. June 11, 1862; January 12, 1863; October 5, 1863; January 6, April 14, 16-17, 19, 21, 24, and 26, and May 3, 1864; May 23, 1865.
New York *Journal of Commerce*, undated clipping.
New York *Times,* October 31, 1877.
Olsen, Sue. Memphis *Commercial Appeal*. February 4, 1983.
Otey, Mercer. "The Story of our Great War." *CV*. March, 1901.
Owensboro *Monitor*. April 20, August 31 and September 14, 1864.
Parker. Albert F. Lauderdale County *Enterprise*, March 8, 1978.
Philadelphia *Press*. undated clipping [1864].
Rogers and Patterson. "Concerning the Nathan Bedford Forrest Legend," *Tennessee Folklore Society Bulletin*. September, 1938.

Sandel, Matthew. "Tilting at Statues," *Southern Partisan*. Summer 1988.
Sessel, Edwin H. "Cousin": August 14, 1862 in "Our Evacuation of Fort Pillow." *CV*. January, 1898.
Stanchak, John E., "A Legacy of Controversy: Fort Pillow Still Stands." *Civil War Times Illustrated*. September-October 1993.
Stokes, David M. "Feared and Revered: Bedford Forrest, Fort Pillow, and the Western Theater of the Civil War: A Bibliography." *Bulletin of Bibliography*. 1998.
Stonesifer, Roy P. "Gideon J. Pillow: A Study in Egotism." *THQ*. 1966.
Story County *Herald & Roland Record*. Undated, 1922. iowa-counties.com.
Tap, Bruce, "These Devils Are Not Fit to Live on God's Earth: War Crimes and the Committee on the Conduct of the War." *CWH*. June, 1996.
Taylor, Jerome G. "Upper Class Violence in Nineteenth Century Tennessee." *WTHSP*. 1980.
Tilly, Bette B. "The Spirit of Improvement: Reformism and Slavery in West Tennessee." *WTHSP*. 1974.
Trudeau, Noah Andre. "Kill the Last Damn One of Them." *MHQ: The Quarterly of Military History*. 1996.
Tubbs, William B. "A Bibliography of Illinois Civil War Regimental Sources in the Illinois State Historical Library." *Illinois Historical Journal*. Autumn and Winter, 1994.
Turley, Thomas B. Letter. *CV*. July, 1899.
Washington *Republican*, undated clipping [1864].
West Central Missouri Genealogical Society and Library. "Lafayette County Confederate Cemetery." *The Prairie Gleaner*. March, 1975.
White, Cora. (Mitchell, Bobby J., ed.) "Stirring Up the Yankees." *The Gray Ghost*. July-Aug. 1999
Whitesell, Hunter B. "Military Operations in the Jackson Purchase area of Kentucky, 1862-1865." *Register of Kentucky Historical Society*. 1966.
Williams, Edward F. (III), "Early Memphis and its River Rivals: Fulton, Randolph, and Fort Pickering." *WTHSP*. 1968.
Williams, Harry. "Benjamin F. Wade and the Atrocity Propaganda of the Civil War." *The Ohio State Archaeological and Historical Quarterly*. January, 1939.
Willoughby, Earl. "Church Grove, Camp Bell and Civil War," "A Cold Blue Wind: Waring's Brigade sweeps through Dyer County in 1864," "Colonel Dawson & the Shadow War," "Gunboats & Gumbo: The first six months of 1862," "Rev. George Washington Harris: The Unordained Bishop of West Tennessee," "Under the Black Flag." Dyersburg Tennessee *State Gazette*.
Wilson, (Mrs.) Robert H. Letter. *Liberator*, June 10, 1864.
Wooster, Ralph A. "With the Confederate Cavalry in the West: The Civil War Experiences of Isaac Dunbar Affleck."

UNPUBLISHED SOURCES
Agnew, Samuel. *Diary*. Southern Historical Collection, UNC-CH.
Alley, John. *The Memoirs of John Marshall Alley*. United States Civil War Center.
Bailey, Robert. "The 'Bogus' Memphis *Union Appeal*: A Union Newspaper in Occupied Confederate Territory." *WTHSP*, 1978.

Bancroft, Frederic. Papers, Box 11, Columbia University Special Collections
Barber, William. Letters. Center for Archival Collections, Jerome Library, Bowling Green State University.
Whetstone, Rea. *History of Knoxville College*. Unpublished manuscript. Undated. Westminster College Archives (McGill Library).
Berndt, Jon S. "The Slagg Family of Wisconsin During the Civil War." hal-pc.org.
Betts, Vicki. *A Revelation of War: Civilians in Hardin County, Tennessee, Spring, 1862.* hardinhistory.com.
Black, Hugh. Letters. Robert Manning Strozier Library, Florida State University.
Blackburn, J.K.P. "Reminiscences." The Online Archive of Terry's Texas Rangers
Boardman, Charles. Letter. mikebrackin.com
Bogle, J.C.M. Letters. Crutchfield Papers. The Gordon Browning Museum of the Carroll County Historical Society.
Bohrer, Zene. Letter. Iowa in the Civil War (web)
Brayman, Mason. Papers. Chicago Historical Society.
Breckinridge, John Cabell. John Cabell Breckinridge Collection, Chicago Historical Society.
Brown, Tully. *Nathan Bedford Forrest: Lecture Delivered at Vendome Theatre, Nashville, Tennessee, January 26, 1905.* TSLA.
Buford, James. Letters. The Junaita Brown Collection, University of Mississippi.
Bull, Augustus F. Papers. Web Center for Archival Collections, Bowling Green State University
Burney, Thomas. "The Famous Terry Rangers." Groesbeck *Journal*, November 25, 1909.
Burt, Richard W. "Civil War Letters From The 76th Ohio Volunteer Infantry." Courtesy of Larry Stevens. my.ohio.voyager.net.
Campbell, Given. Papers. UNCCH.
Campbell, Given. Papers. Southern Historical Collection, University of North Carolina at Chapel Hill.
Cannon, Newton. Papers. TSLA.
Carter, Joe. Papers. TSLA.
Chatham, William L. Letter. McCain Library and Archives, The University of Southern Mississippi.
Chears, Nathaniel Francis. Papers. TSLA.
Chester, William W., "The Diary of Sergeant Benjamin T. Bondurant, CSA." *Journal of the Jackson Purchase Historical Society*. June, 1988.
Collins, James. R. (Ken Lee and Gene Shields, eds.) "James R. Collins Describes His Civil War Experiences." iowacounties.com
Copley, John M. "A Sketch of the Battle of Franklin, Tenn.; with Reminiscences of Camp Douglas." UNC/CH. docsouth.unc.edu
Crutchfield, John A. "Letters of Captain John A. Crutchfield, Company 'F': Russell's 20th Tennessee Cavalry Regiment." Gordon Browning Museum (McKenzie, Tennessee).

Davis, Abraham. "What About Fort Pillow?" Unpublished ms. Tucson, 1964. Memphis Public Library.
Densmore, Benjamin. Family Papers. Minnesota Historical Society.
Doak, Henry Melvill. Papers. TSLA.
Dyer, W.R. Pocket Diary: 1864. TSLA.
Edmondson, Belle. Diary. UNCCH.
Edwards, Joseph R. Letters. John Gillette Collection, Michigan Historical Collections, Bentley Historical Library, University of Michigan at Ann Arbor.
Eggleston, George Cary. *A Rebel's Recollections*. 1998 electronic edition of 1875 original. UNCCH.
Eldred, Wellington. Letter. University of Missouri Western Historical Manuscript Collection at Rolla.
Faulk, W.L. Diary. Vicksburg National Military Park.
Fedric, Francis. *Slave Life in Virginia and Kentucky; or, Fifty Years of Slavery in the Southern States of America*. 1998 electronic edition of London, 1863 edition. UNCCH.
Fitzhugh, Lester N. "Terry's Texas Rangers, 8th Texas Cavalry, CSA: An Address by Lester N. Fitzhugh Before The Houston Civil War Round Table March 21, 1958." Terry's Texas Rangers Homepage
Flanders, Edwin P. Papers. Michigan Historical Collections, Bentley Historical Library, University of Michigan at Ann Arbor.
Fort, Dewitt Clinton [transcribed by Greg Newby]. *Memoirs of Dewitt Clinton Fort*. Memphis Public Library.
Frisby, Derek. "'Remember me to everybody:' The Civil War Letters of Samuel Henry Eells, Twelfth Michigan Infantry." Unpublished ms. Courtesy of the author.
Fulk, Martin. Letter to John Sprankel: December (20?), 1864. genealogy.org.
Gatlin, Jeffrey. "James D. Rowland -- Galvanized Yankee." rootsweb.com.
Giles, L.B. "Terry's Texas Rangers." Online Archive of Terry's Texas Rangers.
Green, Samuel. "An Historical Sketch of Groton, Massachusetts 1655-1890. Groton, 1894." at genexchange.org
Guthrie, J. Letter. Hyacinth Laselle Papers, Indiana State Library.
Harrison, Absolom. Letter to Susan Allstun Harrison: August 12, 1862. Private Collection.
Hart, Patrick, ed. The Civil War Diaries of Capt. Noah H. Hart. Web page. Noah Hart was an officer in the 10th Michigan Regiment. triadic.com.
Harvey, Joseph E. Letter to "Mary": May 31, 1864, Minnesota Historical Society.
Henry, Robert Selph. Papers. Special Collections Department, University Libraries of Virginia Tech. Aaron Crawford, researcher.
Hill, Robert I. Diary: August 1861 to June 1862. rootsweb.com/~mscivilw/hilldiary.htm
Holladay, S.W. Letters. Crutchfield Papers. The Gordon Browning Museum of the Carroll County Historical Society.
Howard, William T. Letter. Lionel Baxter Collection, University of Mississippi.
Howell, Robert Phillip. Memoirs. UNCCH.

Howlett, R.E. *Dr. R.E. Howlett in the Civil War.* Western Historical Manuscript Collection at the University of Missouri at Columbia.
Johnston, John. "Civil War Recollection." TSLA.
Johnston, John. "Forrest's March out of West Tennessee, December 1863, Recollections of a Private." TSLA.
Johnston, John. Diaries and Memoirs: 1860-65. TSLA.
Kempshaw, John. Letter. TSLA.
Kryder, George Kryder. Papers. Center for Archival Collections. Bowling Green State University.
Lash, Jeffrey N. "Stephen Augustus Hurlbut: A Military and Diplomatic Politician: 1815-1882." Dissertation. December, 1980.
Love, Cyrus. Letters. Tennessee Christian University.
Lowry, Thomas. Index to Civil War Courtmartial Records at the National Archives and Records Administration. (Ongoing project.)
Lyman, C.P. Letters and Diary. Private Collection.
Lyons, Mark. Letters to Amelia Horsler, 1861 Feb. -- 1865 Apr. 10. Alabama Department of Archives and History
MacMillan, Isaac. Letter. Indiana State Library. RMC.
Macmurphy, G.L. Diary. Online Archive of Terry's Texas Rangers.
Main Beverly M. DuBose. Letter to Robert C. Mainfort, Jr.: September 15, 1978. RMC.
Matlock, Philip N. Letters. TSLA.
Metcalfe, Frederick Augustus. Papers. Archives and Library Division of the Mississippi Department of Archives and History.
Mills, Theodore A. "Fort Pillow." Ca. 1931. RMC.
Monroe, Mosby. Parsons Papers, 1861-1862. Duke University.
Morris, William. *The Tennessee River Voyages of U.S.S. Peosta.* hardinhistory.com
Moses, Jefferson. "The Memoirs, Diary, and Life of Private Jefferson Moses, Company G, 93rd Illinois Volunteers." ioweb.com
Nutt, Leroy. Papers. UNCCH.
O'Connor, (Mrs.) T.P., *My Beloved South.* 1998 electronic edition of New York, 1914 edition. UNCCH.
Oberlin College Alumni Files (OC).
Patterson, Delicia Ann. Letter. www.rootsweb.com
Peters, H.N. Letter to Margaret Treueworthy: April 23, 1862. Special Collections, University of Arkansas Libraries at Fayetteville.
Powers, Auburn. "Juno: AKA 'Pinch': Henderson County, Tennessee." Parker's Crossroads Battlefield Association (TN), 1930.
Rabb, J.W. "The Civil War Letters of J. W. Rabb." The Online Archive of Terry's Texas Rangers.
Rees, William. Civil War Letters From William Rees. Rees Genealogy Homepage.
Royster, Charles. "Slaver, General, Klansman." *Atlantic Monthly.* May, 1993.
Ryan, John. "Reminiscences: December 1, 1863-1866." Clarke Historical Library, University of Michigan.
Saunders, Hubert. *Papers, 1862-1865.* Special Collections, Duke University.
Sayers, Althea. "Fort Pillow: What the Federal Government Didn't Tell." civilwarweb.com.

Shiflit, Hillory. Letters. www.geocities
Sink, Elijah. *Memoirs*. Indiana State Library.
Stearns, Ezra. Papers. Schoff Civil War Collection, William L. Clements Library, University of Michigan.
Stewart, Charles S. Letters. Archival Reference Librarian at the Alabama Department of Archives and History. Courtesy of Norwood A. Kerr.
Terrell, Kate Scurry. "Terry's Texas Rangers." Onlive Archive of Terry's Texas Rangers.
Tilly, Belle Baird. *Aspects of Social and Economic Life in West Tennessee Before the Civil War*. Memphis State University Ph.D. dissertation, 1974.
Toney, Marcus Bearden. *Diaries*. (TSLA).
Turnure, F.P. Letter to Mrs. H. Green: Fulton Tenn Apr 9, [1863]. Orrin Elmore Stanley papers. University of Oregon Library. RMC.
Van Vlack, A.A. "Cahawba Prison, Ala.: A Glimpse of Life in A Rebel prison." Bentley Historical Library, University of Michigan at Ann Arbor.
Wallace, Frances. *A Trip to Dixie: Diary, March 19-August 25, 1864*. 1998 Electronic edition of contemporary manuscript. UNCCH.
Walthall, George. Letters. Lionel Baxter Collection. University of Mississippi.
Warner, Liberty. Papers. Web Center for Archival Collections, Bowling Green State University.
Weatherred, John. "Wartime Diary of John Weathered. jackmasters.net.
Wickliffe-Preston Family Papers. University of Kentucky Special Collections and Archives
Worley, William. *Diary*. Indiana State Library.
Worthing, John P. Letters. McCain Library and Archives of the University of Southern Mississippi.

NATIONAL ARCHIVES AND RECORDS ADMINISTRATION

Among the records I reviewed at the National Archives in Washington, DC were the following, in alphabetical order:
Adjutant General's Office: "Generals' Papers and Books: Stephen Augustus Hurlbut: 1861-1865." • Book Records of the 11th USCT Infantry • Bureau of Refugees, Freedmen and Abandoned Lands • Carded United States Army Medical Records • Chalmers Papers • Collections of the Adjutant General's Office: 1780's-1917; Bounty and Claims Division: 1862-1878 and Records of slave claims commissions: 1864-1868 for Tennessee • Department of the Cumberland and Division and Department of the Tennessee, 1862-1870: Organization of U.S. Colored Troops: Records of Capt. R.D. Mussey. 1863-1864• Records of the Department of the Tennessee • Final Report of the American Freedman's Inquiry Commission: June 22, 1864. • Fitch, [Charles]. "Monthly Report:" April 30, 1864 in Regimental Papers of the 11th USCI: Letters Received, RG94, Records of the Adjutant general's office, 1780's-1917. NARA. • General and Special Orders: Organization of Colored Troops • Generals' Papers (USA and CSA) • Letters Received, ser. 360, Colored Troops Division, Adjutant General's Office NARA • Inspection Report of Colored Troops, Department of the Cumberland • Letter Book of Brigadier General Lorenzo Thomas • Letter Books of Officers of the United States Navy at Sea, March 1778-July 1908 • Office of Inspector General, Department of Tennessee: Letters Sent and Received. • List of Prisoners Cap'd by Major

General Forrest at Fort Pillow, & in Tennessee – Deserters, Men of Bad Characters, Flags &c. &c. • List of Wounded received from the rebels at Fort Pillow. • *Fawn* Log • Medical Records of the 13th Tennessee Cavalry (USA). • Memphis Subdistrict of the Bureau of Refugees Military Departments, Letters sent, Brig. Gen. James R. Chalmers's Brigade –February 1862-March 1863 • Naval Records Collection of the Office of Naval Records and Library: Records of Citizens of the United States: March 1778-July 1908. • Office of the Adjutant General Volunteer Service Branch • Office of the Provost Marshal, District West Tennessee • Papers of General E.A. Paine, Records of the Adjutant General's office, 1780-1912 • Pension Files for the 1st Alabama Siege Artillery, the 2nd USCLA, the 6th USCHA, the 11th USCI, the 6th and 13th Tennessee Cavalry (USA). • Prisoners in Military Prison in Fort Pickering Probably Detained without Sufficient Cause. • Quartermaster General Claims • Ration Commutation Claims for the 2nd USCLA, 6th USCHA, 11th USCI and 13th Tennessee Cavalry. • Records of Captain Robert D. Mussey, 1863-1864, Department of Cumberland and Department of the Tennessee: 1862-1870, Organization of Colored troops. • Records of the 16th Army Corps • Records of the 1st Alabama Siege Artillery (Colored), the 2nd USCAL, the 6th USCHA, the 11th USCI, and the 13th (14th) Tennessee Cavalry • Records of the Adjutant General's office • Records of the District of Columbus • Records of the District of Nashville. • Records of the Office of Quartermaster General • Records of the Office of the Secretary of War • Regimental Papers of the 2nd USCAL, 6th USCAH, 11th USCI and 11th USCI (New), and the 13th (14th) Tennessee Cavalry • Register of Letters Received by the Commissioner for the Organization of Colored Troops • Report of an Inspection of the Fortifications on the Ohio & Mississippi River, April 20, 1864 • Report of Court of Inquiry [into Cotton Speculation at Helena, Arkansas] by Major General Irwin McDowell. • Report of the American Freedman's Inquiry Commission. • Reports of investigations of conditions at the Irving Block Military Prison in Memphis, Tennessee April-May, 1864. • Reports on Loyal Citizens **[Paducah, Kentucky]**. • Semi-Weekly Return of Effective Force at the Post of Cairo: April 25, 1864 • Union Provost Marshal's File of Papers Relating to Individual Civilians.

SOURCES ON CD
Some of my sources came from a CD compilation of 19th and 20th century sources: an historian's dream, especially when it comes to the Official Records of the Civil War. *Since both are searchable, I have not indicated an entry's location in the original and confusedly edited and indexed printed sources.*
Confederate Veteran. H-Bar Enterprises.
Naval Official Records and Army official Records Covering MS, TN & Gulf Coast Operations. H-Bar Enterprises.
Slave Narratives containing the full text of Rawick, George P., ed. The American Slave: A Composite Autobiography. *Forty-one volumes. Westport (Connecticut), 1972-1979.* Ancestry View.
Southern Historical Society Papers. Folio Infobase.
The Civil War CD-Rom: The War of the Rebellion containing the complete text of The War of the Rebellion: A Compilation of the Official Records of the Union and Confederate Armies. Washington, 1882. Guild press.

www.ingramcontent.com/pod-product-compliance
Lightning Source LLC
Chambersburg PA
CBHW032040090426
42744CB00004B/68